D0852957

Gossip, Letters, Phones

GOSSIP, LETTERS, PHONES

The Scandal of Female Networks in Film and Literature

Ned Schantz

OXFORD
UNIVERSITY PRESS
2008

PR
830
.W6
S36
2008

OXFORD
UNIVERSITY PRESS

Oxford University Press, Inc., publishes works that further
Oxford University's objective of excellence
in research, scholarship, and education.

Oxford   New York
Auckland   Bangkok   Bogotá   Buenos Aires   Cape Town   Chennai
Dar es Salaam   Delhi   Hong Kong   Istanbul   Karachi   Kolkata
Kuala Lumpur   Madrid   Melbourne   Mexico City   Mumbai   Nairobi
São Paulo   Shanghai   Singapore   Taipei   Tokyo   Toronto

With offices in
Argentina   Austria   Brazil   Chile   Czech Republic   France   Greece
Guatemala   Hungary   Italy   Japan   Poland   Portugal   Singapore
South Korea   Switzerland   Thailand   Turkey   Ukraine   Vietnam

Copyright © 2008 by Oxford University Press

Published by Oxford University Press, Inc.
198 Madison Avenue, New York, New York, 10016
www.oup.com

Oxford is a registered trademark of Oxford University Press

All rights reserved. No part of this publication may be reproduced,
stored in a retrieval system, or transmitted, in any form or by any means,
electronic, mechanical, photocopying, recording, or otherwise,
without the prior permission of Oxford University Press.

Library of Congress Cataloging-in-Publication Data
Schantz, Ned, 1969–
    Gossip, letters, phones : the scandal of female networks
in film and literature / by Ned Schantz.
        p.   cm.
    Includes bibliographical references.
    ISBN 978-0-19-533591-0
    1. English fiction—History and criticism.   2. Women—Social
networks.   3. Women—Communication.   4. Communication
and technology.   5. Technology and women.   6. Women in
literature.   7. Women in motion pictures.   I. Title.
    PR830.W6S36 2008
    823'.0093522   2007042813

9 8 7 6 5 4 3 2 1

Printed in the United States of America
on acid-free paper

For my parents, Sandy and Mark

University Libraries
Carnegie Mellon University
Pittsburgh, PA 15213-3890

Acknowledgments

I must first thank Tania Modleski, who plucked this topic from a long list of grim alternatives many years ago, and who has remained an inspiration and most loyal supporter throughout what can only be described as a very long process. I am also deeply indebted to the sure friendship and brilliant imagination of Hilary Schor, whose tireless labor is everywhere on these pages. Leo Braudy, Marsha Kinder, and Jim Kincaid deserve thanks for their sustained good advice and their keen comments on the manuscript at various stages. Individual chapters were read with great patience, skill, and generosity by Derek Nystrom, Jesse Molesworth, Lindsay Holmgren, Kai Mah, Victoria Nam, and Joanna Donehower, and the final version reflects their important contributions. Joanna and Rick Mele provided invaluable research assistance on the project, and Billi Rakov and Wes Folkerth some crucial technical support. Many thanks to John Jordan and The Dickens Project for extending true hospitality to an incorrigible interdisciplinarian. Thanks also to the friends and colleagues who have helped my thinking in less formal ways, in particular Mary Beth Tegan, Michael Blackie, Paul Saint-Amour, Monique Morgan, Jonathan Sterne, Gordon Bigelow, John Bruns, and Peter Stokes. I owe most to my family and Anne—their bottomless faith has endured well past the point of reasonable doubt.

A portion of chapter 1 appeared as the essay "Jamesian Gossip and the Seductive Politics of Interest" in *The Henry James Review* 22:1 (Winter 2001): 10–23, and a portion of chapter 3 appeared as the essay "Telephonic Film" in *Film Quarterly* 56:4 (Summer 2003): 23–35. This book has been supported by fellowships from Diana Meehan, the Marta Feuchtwanger Foundation, the Ahmanson Foundation, and the University of Southern California Department of English. At McGill University I have received financial support in the form of startup funds and an AUS employment fund. I want finally to thank Shannon McLachlan, Christina Gibson, Bob Milks, and Ilene McGrath at Oxford University Press for their support and faith in the project. Without so much generosity the completion of this book would not have been possible.

Contents

Gossip, Letters, Phones

Introduction

Picture an old girls' network. Picture women using whatever resources they have at their disposal to support and promote each other—not in any Utopia or sheltered enclave, but in the modern world as it has developed since the eighteenth century. Picture therefore female networks at once fragmented and technologically extended, operating around and against powerful men with all of their advantages, redirecting the flows of knowledge, money, and affect that maintain gender among so many other devastating social asymmetries. In your forming this vision, I doubt you will find that the dominant narrative culture of this era—call it the British Novel and Hollywood Film—is of any great help. This culture tends either to confirm the hostility among women we already regret (and call it, say, *An Essay on the Art of Ingeniously Tormenting* in 1753, or *Mean Girls* in 2004), or to take women singly or "between men."[1] But female networking has been occurring all along. Far from innocent or pure, it nonetheless escapes envy, cruelty, and petty selfishness, if only for a moment, and makes its way toward the surface of culture, where we can finally begin to see how wide it spreads.

This book retraces the dominant historical legacy of narrative film and the novel in terms of its representation of female networks. Imagined as transmitting sympathy and strategy to women beset by patriarchy, female networks threaten the gendered circulation of meaning and power in a masculine culture. This conception is not mine but rather emerges as a special function of gossip to protect women on the marriage market. It grows increasingly idealized as female networks employ letters and then phones as private filters; theoretically at least, epistolary and telephonic women do not have to send, say, their resentment along with their sympathy, just

3

as they do not have to please male ears and eyes in sheltered exchanges. Once it becomes possible to expect the secure transmission of carefully regulated messages (however foolishly), female networking appears in the strictest sense as a model of proto-feminist action. At the same time, we would do well to hold onto the much broader sense of a gossipy culture—broader in fact than the sum total of connections among women, since men gossip too—if strict female networking is to find its proper context. So much of our culture travels through precisely these channels.

To be sure, narrative interest since the novel has been above all an interest in the private lives of other people—the interest of gossip—and hence participates, despite sometimes lofty claims, in disreputable feminine discourse. If the novel is gossip with an impossibly well-informed friend, cinema is gossip backed magically by our own ears and eyes. To enjoy such scandalous intimacy safely, both narrative forms consistently disavow female networks and the technologies that support them. In this analysis, the modes of female networking—gossip, letters, the telephone—return not only as pressing thematic concerns, but as formally decisive elements regulating the place and manner of narrative interest. My emphasis is on long readings of works that explore crucial aspects of these dynamic modes, works that in most cases have famously captured our interest. And it happens that the problem of communication and trust between women sustains a persistent tension between the narrative of courtship and its gothic nightmare, a tension unrelieved by the hysteria of certain comic modes. The challenge has been to read as if in a female network, returning insistently to the forgotten interests of female characters to explode easy assumptions about plot (does Isabel Archer necessarily return to Gilbert Osmond at the end of *The Portrait of a Lady?*) and character (is *Emma's* Mrs. Elton unaccountably bad?). Such a practice has often required a certain extravagance or overimagination, a "frankly inventive approach" in keeping with the gothic that draws as well from a double-edged engagement with crucial neighboring genres: sorting detective fiction's epistemological prowess from its arrogance; divorcing science fiction's stake in home from its indispensable alternate futures.[2] It is within this broad generic field—a field whose stakes would disappear into realism and cultural prestige—that female networking takes hold as a scandalous reading practice.

The reader then, like her double, the film viewer, is a recurring character in this book, and not a flat one. Like many good fictional characters, this reader amalgamates sources fluidly—my own responses, the available responses of others (professional or not), and an analytical sense of textual solicitation and positioning.[3] It is a reader prone to seduction and distraction by various dubious interests, but also a reader enjoined to do better, to strengthen and extend female networks in the face of massive cultural resistance. Ultimately, though, I would prefer less to push a doubtful didacticism than to tap powerful latent energies. Unorthodox as my readings may sometimes be, I offer them in full sincerity as well as playfulness because I believe in their capacity to move more than a reader's sense of duty. As this book traverses the rich and embattled terrain of sympathy and identification, it therefore accepts the dangers of engaging such affect directly.[4] It is my argument that fiction is a doubly suspect sympathy machine, giving cause for worry about not only those it spits out, but also those it takes up and works over. My idea is that these two suffering parties might join forces and that any projection of our selves along such trajectories, crossing up the cultural machinery, is well worth the risk.[5]

If the organization of this book is also something of a scandal, jumping backwards and forwards in history, my hope is that the comparative perspective these moves generate outweighs any lingering vertigo. Certainly the historical range has put extra pressure on the selection of texts, but this pressure helps us think about cultural connection in ways not possible when we are nestled securely within conservative estimations of period or genre. And while no doubt I betray my gothic sensibilities further by arguing for a past that fitfully and uncannily obtrudes, the surprises of congruence need special recognition at an intellectual moment still broadly ruled by what Rita Felski has critiqued as "the doxa of difference."[6] The point then will be to develop female networks conceptually, charting a path of increasing sophistication wherever it leads in space and time. If therefore formal logic trumps chronology in this argument, it nonetheless opens up the old ahistorical formalism, for the emphasis is on form as technology, whether letters or telephones, novels or films, all of which are inventions with their own history. Understood in this way, form no longer opposes history but rather becomes, in its evolution, the very sign of history. It is of course when we consider technology also as an important participant in history that things get more complicated, since each new technology, if it succeeds, engenders a range of competing designs, exploratory practices, and contested interpretations that never entirely disappear. Similarly, while we need never lose sight of the fact that *Clarissa* came before *Emma*, or *Sorry, Wrong Number* before *Pillow Talk* (despite their inverted positions in this book), we should accept that the historical emergence of something as fragile and threatening as female networks could never grow in a straight line.

The historical line from novel to film is also hardly straight; if anything, though, film scholarship has long overcorrected the wayward English professors of a generation ago, repressing film's novelistic legacy in order to secure its own distinction and legitimacy.[7] Laura Mulvey tells the story so as to eliminate the novel entirely:

> The cinema is descended from two, contradictory, ancestral lines that combined to make it the first ever medium to fulfill the longstanding aspiration to show moving images of the real world. Its relation to reality is, of course, shared with photography, and comes from the tradition of the camera obscura, while its movement belongs to the tradition of optical illusions that exploit a peculiar ability of the human eye to deceive the mind. (Death 33)

This summary is surely correct if the point is to plot the emergence of film as a strictly technical possibility that develops into early nonnarrative forms. But the term "cinema" suggests something more ambitious and longstanding, something institutional and cultural that still struggles to come to terms with the novel. In its retreat from the novelistic, film studies has been at once too hopeful and too pessimistic, wishing our narrative heritage away as a kind of premature surrender to its dominant currents. And yet if the novel is dauntingly powerful, it is also inefficient, curious, contradictory. Indeed the female networks of the novel reveal oppositional possibilities that narrative film still struggles to take up.

Chapter 1 focuses on Jane Austen's *Emma* to anchor a discussion of gossip as baseline female networking. In joining the many similar discussions that swirl around this novel, I try not to compound the snobbery that holds criticism above gossip. Instead, I propose a critical approach that brings to light the covert tendency of both novelistic and critical discourse to reproduce the dynamics of gossip in their pleasures and exclusions. To read the novel through the lens of gossip is therefore to see novels as not only about scandals, but also as scandalous themselves. This point becomes clear when we juxtapose Ian Watt's naming of *Emma* as the pinnacle of realism with the analysis of Patricia Spacks, who emphasizes the reader's nosy speculation about *Emma*'s mystery plot. Unable to function without gossip, realism itself becomes the scandal, but not in a way that necessarily discredits it. Rather, a critical attention to gossip frees the reader from the habit of greeting scandal with broad moral condemnation, opening up possibilities of reading that include new ways of defining our interest in a heroine and new ways of imagining where her best interests could lie. The chapter concludes with a consideration of Henry James's *The Portrait of a Lady* as a decisive endpoint in the history of readerly consent to scandalous subject matter. James draws on all the resources of gossip to solicit our interest in Isabel Archer, a "new woman" of the late nineteenth century. But when her independence, mobility, and relationships with other women strain the courtship plot and tempt the reader into the worst habits of sadistic gossip, James can only resort at the end of the novel to silence about the heroine's fate.

In chapter 2, on the epistolary novel, the problems of female networks become problems of long distance as female mobility puts increasing pressure on the secure transmission of information and affection. Samuel Richardson's *Clarissa* and Frances Burney's *Evelina*, two major early novels, both make painfully clear that the control of the female subject lies in restricting—or flooding—the channels of information, so that all large-scale networks must remain in the hands of a limited class of men. Richardson sustains interest in his monumental novel precisely by staging a cat-and-mouse game between the heroine as potential free agent and the villain as manipulative censor, only to give way in the end to a novelistic sadism that sacrifices its heroine to an ideal of individual integrity. Burney responds by seizing the power of censorship from masculine culture, referring to a correspondence between women that she does not show the reader, thus saving her female network by taking it underground and recasting female modesty as an authorship of restraint. Pursuing a materialist analysis of letters, I attempt to unfold the enormous space for fantasy generated by the rhythm of the post, arguing that it is precisely as fantasy that threatened female networks survive for the next generation.

Chapter 3 develops a theory of telephonic film, considering what it means to compare a film such as *Pillow Talk*, with its endless staging of telephone calls, to the epistolary novel, so that telephones are not simply dismissed as props but can be seen to entail surprising formal implications for narrative. It is a perspective that reveals, moreover, the centrality of the phone to films in which its role is less obvious, from *The Big Sleep* and *Chinatown* to *It's a Wonderful Life*. The analysis begins with the Classical Hollywood Telephone, an idealized phone that serves genre by transmitting a singular meaning. In this fantasy the phone always works smoothly, allowing its human masters to forget their bodies, their surroundings—indeed the apparatus itself—to engage in communication with perfect control.[8] If the Classical Hollywood Telephone never quite manages to exist, its influence as an ideal can nonetheless be keenly felt when films move toward closure, triggering the narrow expectations of genre. The foreclosing power of this ideal, however, meets resistance when films allow for coincidence to interrupt the smooth flow of singular telephonic meaning. As the phone ceases to behave itself, instead of delivering messages devoutly wished for, it unearths a repressed sense of isolation and chaos. But out of these nightmares we get a glimpse of a more hopeful kind of telephonic film, a film that makes use of the phone's inherent potential to route interest along unpredictable lines.

At the limit of the telephonic imagination, the fantasy of an ideal telephone turns into the fantasy of telepathy. As the phone in an uncanny state of dematerialization, telepathy retains and intensifies all the ambivalence we see surrounding the telephone, its capacity at once to serve and to betray. It is this complex fantasy that I explore in chapter 4, considering the means of access to the thoughts of characters as an essential point of comparison between film and the novel. Indeed what is a fairly routine effect of novels becomes a vexed site of cinematic technique as films search for the proper degree and means of telepathic representation. Thus a film like *Shadow of a Doubt*, while following a young woman's investigations, spends a great deal of energy discrediting both her telepathic pretensions and those of readers in general, whereas *Sorry, Wrong Number*, unwilling to abandon the desire for telepathy as the ultimate sympathetic connection between women, goes to unprecedented lengths to sustain this fantasy through cinematic technology. What these films share is a powerful sense that the female desire for telepathy is a response to claustrophobic domestic conditions and that it is a desire all the more important when these conditions turn gothic, subjecting the heroines to a murderous intimacy with the very men on whom they most depend. Both films finally discredit female knowledge by purchasing it only at the price of stifling paralysis. When invasive telepathy creates an intense yearning to be elsewhere, the fantasy of speed emerges as a vital alternative to intimacy.

The last two chapters consider female networks more fully in terms of space and time, identifying the spatial and temporal deformations that prevent the full emergence of female networks. What I would suggest is that these deformations make their presence felt in direct proportion to the manifest range and intensity of female networking and therefore have everything to do with the cultural management of new technology. My portrait of this ongoing backlash may at times seem overly dire, since after all vast horizons have opened up recently for the representation of women's relations. But the point is simply that essential ground is still being conceded, often in rather subtle ways. Thus in chapter 5, on "The Space of Crime," I analyze the cultural response to such technologies as cell phones, the Internet, and even a looming artificial intelligence, in light of an apparent tendency to enforce gothic claustrophobia, to subject the hi-tech heroine to the conditions of a locked room. One bright spot is the film *Bound*, in which two women use their superior trust and savvy to take control of the space of crime. Full of telephonic tricks and lesbian love scenes, the film nonetheless mobilizes a gangster ethos that fails to feel fully contemporary. To provide that aspect, the chapter features an extended discussion of *You've Got Mail*, a strangely less promising vision for what is by far the most ambitious mainstream attempt to explore the narrative implications of the Internet. Here lightning-quick Internet communications serve above all as a flight from the self, as the erotics of the disappearing heroine. *You've Got Mail* is a comedy, I would argue, in which narcissistic e-mail fantasies fail to keep the gothic sufficiently at bay, since the heroine finds romance only by yielding her professional and imaginative life to a ruthless business competitor who becomes a no less manipulative suitor. Pursuing an insidious twin strategy of spatial annihilation and gothic displacement, this film has by the end deleted every aspect of the heroine's prior self, making painfully clear the need for a politics of interest that would reclaim the Internet—and the movies—as a space for less brutally conventional fantasies.

In chapter 6, "Time Stalkers," I have pursued a strange discovery: the tendency for stalking narratives, seemingly all about movement through space, to betray a special obsession with time. To be sure, if the locked room is one weapon against female networks, then stalking is its logical counterpart, setting the isolated heroine in motion all the better to disrupt her access to sympathy and support. And yet in case after case, narratives that stalk their heroines refuse to rest content with mere spatial domination. From *Vertigo* and *Klute* to *Blade Runner* and *The Terminator*, the ultimate project of stalking is to separate the targeted heroine from a past defined by her relationship to other women. It is a project, moreover, increasingly bound up in temporal media, as *Vertigo*'s quaint portrait of Carlotta becomes *Klute*'s state-of-the-art tape recorders and then *Blade Runner*'s impossible photographs. In *The Terminator*, Sarah Connor sends both her voice and her face into a post-apocalyptic future, and this grim future responds, has already responded, with its time-traveling tag-team of human lover and cyborg assassin. If the ensuing action undermines female networks in predictable fashion, with the Terminator killing Sarah's roommate and mother and revealing her ongoing telephonic vulnerability, it is finally the nuclear holocaust itself that is the covertly desired ticket to Sarah's re-inscription in patriarchal destiny. Here and elsewhere, the stalker knows no limits. Against such devastating male fantasy, criticism must intervene to illuminate the fear and possibilities of female networks.

The book ends with the epilogue "Radio-Free *Middlemarch*," a thought experiment that redescribes the stakes and possibilities of reading the Victorian novel across the gap of history. Radio is an apt figure for this gap, as a place where our own ambient technology meets frenzied Victorian speculation. Crackling with the resonance of female networks across space and time, George Eliot's *Middlemarch* seems to conjure the very media that began to emerge so near its publication. It is a would-be radio novel, a novel that would gather, redirect, and amplify the lost voices of isolated women. It is moreover the novel that clinches the intrinsic place of novelistic discourse throughout this study, binding the question of media to the questions of gossip and sympathy habitually gendered feminine. And while the management of temporality through media will again be at issue, unlike in the ensuing cinematic tradition, here Eliot preserves the vitality of female networks across time. Within this feminist fantasy, the narrative traditions of novel and film begin to open a little wider, revealing nascent female networks awaiting us for their extension.

CHAPTER I

Gossip and the Novel

"Gossip is charming! History is merely gossip. But scandal is gossip made tedious by morality."
                                    Oscar Wilde, Lady Windermere's Fan

Oscar Wilde would liberate gossip from scandal, from morality, in part because he cannot abide the moralism of his day, but also, we might suspect from his reputation, because scandal arrests the proliferation of charming gossipy performances. And yet there is something left out of the formula "gossip + morality = scandal," for gossip remains nonetheless a dirty word, a put-down; it is already a scandal with its reckless pleasures, its unaccountability, its status as the not-quite-domesticated discourse of women.[1] Indeed, Wilde cannot celebrate gossip without disparaging it in the next breath. If gossip is so charming, why should he say that history is *merely* gossip, invoking its power as a term of diminishment? But this statement represents no confusion on Wilde's part, for wanting it both ways seems essential to the culture of gossip, and indeed for this book I will want nothing less.

Wilde may not have had the concerns of feminism in mind, but his rhetoric shows how feminism might navigate the stigma of gossip for itself. Clearly a feminist account of gossip must expand Wilde's categories of charm and tediousness, though insofar as they hinge on the concept of *interest*, they may offer more of a starting point than first appears. What matters at this point is that Wilde's ambivalence anticipates the paradox of my own feminist approach: on one hand, I hope to soften the stigma of gossip, emphasizing the value of discredited female discourse; on the other, I would wield this stigma to turn male discourse against itself, discrediting it with its own smear tactics—and bringing the scandal of gossip home to roost. Thus, contrary to its status historically in the discourse of men, gossip remains as essential as it is inescapable.

We need not look too long at the history of the novel to see the importance of gossip for an emerging feminist consciousness. At a time when the marriage plot seems the only woman's plot worth mentioning, gossip appears accordingly as a means of women's regulating the marriage market and gaining leverage on a heavily prescribed destiny. It is a kind of archetypal model of women using their informal connections both to sustain themselves on a daily basis and to intervene in the machinations of men, and it is therefore the most basic mode of what I call female networking. Gossip garners enough notice, for instance, to serve as a crucial turning point in Jane Austen's last novel, *Persuasion*, in a scene in which Anne visits Mrs. Smith, a lonely widow fallen on hard times. Mrs. Smith has already made a case for the importance of gossip during an earlier visit, defending it on the grounds of the emotional support and self-improvement it affords lonely women:

> "Call it gossip if you will; but when nurse Rooke has half an hour's leisure to bestow on me, she is sure to have something to relate that is entertaining and profitable, something that makes one know one's species better. One likes to hear what is going on, to be *au fait* as to the newest modes of being trifling and silly. To me, who live so much alone, her conversation I assure you is a treat." (168)

This apology, of course, is only the prelude to the intervention Mrs. Smith will make in Anne's life by relating the predatory history of her most visible suitor, Mr. Elliot. It is a heartening case of the power of gossip to counter the abuses of unscrupulous men. But we shouldn't begin the feminist celebration prematurely, for Mrs. Smith exposes Mr. Elliot only once she is convinced that Anne has no intention of marrying him; until that point, Mrs. Smith actually encourages the marriage because she thinks Anne could then use a wife's influence to have Mr. Elliot help Mrs. Smith recover some property. As we learn, moreover, Mr. Elliot led her late husband to ruin yet has been unwilling to help her, so in this context her decision finally to expose Mr. Elliot seems more about revenge than about any deep concern for Anne. The fact that Anne later admits to herself that she might in fact have succumbed to Mr. Elliot does little to redeem Mrs. Smith's act, for the saving force of gossip becomes in hindsight merely providential, exceeding the intentions of any individual. Since it is not a principled act, it remains gossip in its diminished state. And yet the fact remains that Providence in this case *takes the form of* a female network, thus showing the way for more assertive women who might want to make a little Providence of their own.

Less compromised female networking, then, would seem actually to require a certain distance between women, so that conflicts of interest do not intrude. A brief example here is Daniel Defoe's *Moll Flanders*, a novel whose form as the confessions of a sinner and criminal allows for the detailing of, among other things, a more scandalous version of gossip as a female network in action. The crucial difference in this case is that, unlike Mrs. Smith, Moll has no connection to the man she will gossip about. This episode begins when Moll discovers that the captain courting her neighbor has punished his intended bride for making use of her female network:

> and though she had near 2000£ to her fortune, [she] did but enquire of some
> of his Neighbours about his Character, his Morals, or Substance; and he
> took Occasion at the next Visit to let her know, truly, that he took it very ill,
> and that he should not give her the Trouble of his Visits any more. (113)

Moll perceives a dangerous precedent: if men believe they can extort women into accepting them on their word alone, then the power of female networks to regulate the marriage market will quickly disappear. Moll's advice, which she herself helps carry out, is that her friend avail herself of the power of malicious gossip:

> She should take care to have it well spread among the Women, which she
> could not fail of an Opportunity to do in a Neighbourhood, so addicted
> to Family News, as that she liv'd in was, that she had enquired into his
> Circumstances, and found he was not the Man as to Estate he pretended to
> be. (114)

As their revenge gathers steam, the rumors escalate: they claim he has a bad temper and shady morals and then, more concretely, that he had other wives and that his share of his ship was not paid for. Two things make this revenge rather scandalous: the heroine is the agent, not the beneficiary, of the gossip and is therefore more directly implicated in the decision to use gossip aggressively; and the gossip is almost entirely fabricated—the women consult only their imaginations in trumping up the charges that will thwart him in finding a wife. The effect of this episode is to offer a glimpse of the other side of slander, of gossip's potential as a pleasurable and powerful form of feminist storytelling. Of course since Defoe's sympathetic presentation of slander takes place under the umbrella of Moll's larger repentance, there is some question of how much Moll's behavior should be condoned on the novel's own terms. For the purposes of this example, however, I am less concerned with how we should resolve that question than I am with the fact that we can pose it, that what is at issue at such an early moment is the capacity of a novel to play traffic cop at this intersection, its fitness to contain and commodify the particularly volatile combination of a nascent feminism and a gossip that makes its own rules.

Catherine Gallagher argues that the novel emerges precisely as a shelter from the actionable exposure of gossip. In her account, fiction is "not only a story that claims *not* to be credited but also a story about nobody. Indeed, it is narrative that differentiates itself from lies and scandalous libels *by* being about nobody" ("Nobody's" 266–67). Fiction, then, lets you talk about people without talking about people. In this new discursive technology, the deployment of realistic detail preempts the epistemological claims of gossip: "The character came into *fictional*

existence . . . fully only when he or she was developed as nobody *in particular*. . . .
A generalized character would too easily take on allegorical or symbolic reference"
(269). The novelist's line of defense becomes clear: How can you say that Fred is
you, when Fred has brown eyes and you have blue? How successful this strategy
would ultimately be remains open to question—a certain brand of literary criticism has of course made much work for itself uncovering the hidden biographical
reference of various novels. More important, however, is the question of whether
fictionality protects the novel where it is most vulnerable. In other words, while
novels may, by obscuring biographical secrets, protect the public somewhat from
gossip, how do they protect it from gossiping?

In her extensive study of gossip and literature, Patricia Spacks probes this un-
purged affinity between gossip and the novel, placing due emphasis on gossip as an
activity, as opposed to mere information about the world. Thus while novels may
not offer the same kind of information about the world as gossip (they don't name
real people), they nonetheless involve readers in the same kind of experience: an intimate tête-à-tête with the narrator promising special voyeuristic access into characters' affairs. Indeed, the analogy goes deeper, as Spacks shows in a brief analysis
of Austen's *Emma*. She points out that *Emma* resembles a detective novel with its
central mystery of Jane Fairfax's engagement to Frank Churchill. The considerable
poverty of clues creates an atmosphere of wild, gossipy speculation that defines the
reading experience. Emma, you may recall, is at no loss for ideas about who sent
Jane's pianoforte, and our following her through the novel is largely a process of
entertaining and discarding such theories. Spacks concludes that "women or not,
we have been lured into acting like the women of moralistic stereotypes: lured into
the rewards and betrayals of speculative gossip" (169).

While Spacks's reading of *Emma* is therefore quite suggestive, a sense lingers
from her account that gossip is a kind of sideshow, adding interest and complexity
to the main attraction, the marriage plot, that eventually overtakes it. In generating
a fuller reading, I want to emphasize that gossip is in fact the business of this novel
in the deepest possible sense, as indeed it is with novels generally. In *Emma*, most of
the novel's "action" occurs at one remove from the saga of its primary couple, Emma
and Knightley, whose romance is strangely light on courtship—unless, that is, we
count all the times they get together to gossip about other people, whether Jane,
Frank, Harriet Smith, Miss Bates, or Mrs. Elton. In doing so they get to know each
other's minds, keep tabs on rivals, and stand close together. The only moment that is
romantic in a conventional sense is when Emma and Knightley dance, but this too
is a scene governed by gossip, for their physical coupling merely manifests the far
more crucial convergence of opinion that this scene represents.[2] Recall that Harriet
has been conspicuously snubbed by Mr. Elton, an act prompting Knightley to step
in gallantly and dance with her. These dramatic fireworks provide the occasion for
the first major reported agreement of Emma and Knightley's gossiping career, as
they form a consensus about the relative worth of Harriet and the Eltons. Then the

chapter ends, without showing us Knightley and Emma's much anticipated dance. But Austen has shown us what is important; she has shown us the gossip. Lest there be any doubt about what matters, Austen begins the next chapter with Emma's fond memories of the evening, showing what she took away from it:

> This little explanation with Mr. Knightley gave Emma considerable
> pleasure. It was one of the agreeable recollections of the ball, which she
> walked about the lawn the next morning to enjoy. She was extremely
> glad that they had come to so good an understanding respecting the Eltons,
> and that their opinions of both husband and wife were so much alike;
> and his praise of Harriet, his concession in her favour, was particularly
> gratifying. (260)

Finally, in case we are still not sure about the romantic implications, we learn a page later that Frank, Knightley's most serious rival, would not see her that day but that Emma "did not regret it" (261).

And yet, after all gossip does for him, Knightley betrays it in the end in allegiance to his gender. Giddy with his new engagement to the heroine, and carrying the news that Harriet will marry the worthy Robert Martin, Knightley makes a joke at the expense of gossip: "[Harriet] will give you all the minute particulars, which only woman's language can make interesting.—In our communications we deal only in the great" (371). It is worth noting that this need to play the man occurs so late, as if closure requires a shift in discursive registers that must occur precisely along the axis of gender. This shift may serve to compensate for the loss of the novel itself—the loss of reading—by disguising it as relief that gossip has been reined in, that after all we care most for the great. To be sure, Austen has her doubts about closure, as she indicates in *Northanger Abbey* when she refers sardonically to the readers "who will see in the tell-tale compression of the pages before them, that we are all hastening together to perfect felicity" (246). Like Knightley, Austen can explain the dynamic and make us laugh at it, but she can't make it go away. His throwaway remark figures ironically what continues in all earnestness. It is the masculine disavowal of gossip, the move by which the novel, passing off its sins on its older sister, asks to be taken seriously.

Disavowing Gossip

Thus gossip provides the contrast, in a male culture, by which to measure whatever "greatness" the novel would achieve in the hands of men. This was certainly the move made by an anonymous Marian Evans as she established the masculine terms for her career as George Eliot in "Silly Novels by Lady Novelists," an essay which twice invokes gossip pejoratively as it sorts the serious from the silly. But the dynamic becomes clearest, perhaps, not in works of the highest reputation, but in works that navigate the border between art and popular culture with some aspirations to the former. Thus we have the striking case of Wilkie Collins's "sensation" novel *The Woman in White*, which to this day suffers the odd perfunctory dismissal despite its elaborate attempts to suppress gossip.[3] Tamar Heller has read this novel as a "tale of the male artist in the marketplace," who establishes his professional credentials by differentiating his writing from its female gothic influences (111). Two specific points should be added. First, the novel is addressed to men, asserting its status as male discourse by appealing to a perspective and set of experiences that gentlemen would be assumed to share. Second, and more important, Collins adopts a narrative strategy whereby characters relate only that portion of the story of which they have firsthand knowledge. His first narrator explains this decision at the beginning, promising that "No circumstance of importance, from the beginning to the end of the disclosure, shall be related on hearsay evidence" (5). And what is hearsay after all but a legal word for gossip? Thus Collins's narrative strategy suggests that the novel's credibility is dependent upon a kind of courtroom environment in which gossip is inadmissible. But, as D. A. Miller points out in *The Novel and the Police*, this suggestion paints a highly disingenuous portrait of what the novel is about: "Nothing, however, could be less judicial, or judicious, than the actual hermeneutic practice of the reader of this novel, whose technology of nervous stimulation—in many ways still the state of the art—has him repeatedly jumping to unproven conclusions" (158). We might add that sustaining a sensational plot also means sustaining the gradual revelation of personal secrets. Thus, despite its opening disavowal, the narrative reverts to the status of gossip in substance as well as form, in the type of dirty laundry that gets aired as well as in how little evidence we may require to believe it.

So it seems the novel's effort to sanitize a male discourse against female contamination doesn't really work on this level. Failing to establish itself on this level, we might say, it punishes female discourse on another. Indeed, one of the novel's most dramatic moments, when we read Count Fosco's intrusive postscript to Marian's diary, is achieved by a violent shift from female to male discourse. Miller offers a pointed reading of this moment: "The Count's postscript only puts him in the position we already occupy. Having just finished reading Marian's diary ourselves, we are thus implicated in the sadism of his act, which even as it violates our readerly intimacy with Marian reveals that 'intimacy' to be itself a violation" (164). Indeed, in Spacks's terms our relationship with Marian is not real intimacy, but voyeurism; it is our relationship with Collins that is intimate, and this relationship is forged as reassuringly masculine upon the spectacle of feminine abjection.

It is a similar spectacle that Eve Sedgwick observes at the heart of Austen criticism, as if criticism too can qualify itself through the ritualized disavowal of gossip: "Austen criticism is notable mostly, not just for its timidity and banality, but for its unresting exaction of the spectacle of a Girl Being Taught a Lesson—for the vengefulness it vents on the heroines whom it purports to love, and whom, perhaps, it does" (*Tendencies* 225). Nowhere does this impulse seem so irresistible as in the critical response to the notorious humiliation of Miss Bates by Emma at Box Hill. For instance, Claudia Johnson, who has herself called Emma "the heroine critics love to scold" (122), nevertheless calls the episode "shameful" and can defend Emma only with the observation that she is not as bad as her foil, the "pert" upstart Mrs. Elton. Even the dependably iconoclastic D. A. Miller chimes right in with "We rightly protest when Emma shuts [Miss Bates] up at Box Hill" (*Narrative* 38). Recall the passage that elicits this response: the flirtatious Frank Churchill has just demanded that each member of the group entertain Emma with verbal performances, one if clever, two if so-so, three if dull. Miss Bates exclaims that she will have no trouble saying three dull things, whereupon Emma suggests mockingly that her difficulty will be not in producing three things, but in *limiting* herself to that number (291). I'm not going to pretend that I have never found myself disapproving of Emma's comment, but it is one thing to have a reaction and another to insist on its rightness. Why does it feel like an obligatory critical gesture to assume Knightley's position and obediently repeat the verdict "badly done"? (295). Is Emma wrong to tease Miss Bates? Once that question is posed, it seems impossible to say no. But perhaps we should ask something else when we read this scene.

One critic's reading deserves special attention as a rare effort to displace the question of the heroine's guilt. Adena Rosmarin's article proceeds from a distinction between "mimetic" and "affective" readings, by which mimetic readings treat characters as people (to be praised or scolded) while affective readings seek rather to describe the reader's experience of the novel (333). Not content to reproduce the limitations of prior mimetic readings, Rosmarin offers a dissenting view on the episode at Box Hill:

> The insult is so well prepared by our growing irritation, so irresistibly invited by Miss Bates's own remark, and so well camouflaged by its brevity and the surrounding pages of verbal play that we are distracted from both Miss Bates's pain and the implications of our distraction. All but the most meritorious of readers become Emma's ready accomplices and, thus, her fellow penitents. (332–33)

As we look back at the scene, Rosmarin's description seems entirely accurate. Indeed, the narrator records only Miss Bates's immediate reaction to the insult, whereas not until a page later, and with little fanfare, does Knightley register disapproval by speaking "gravely" (292). To what, then, do we attribute the overwhelming consensus that this is such a shocking, traumatic moment in the novel? And why do few critics come forward and admit how Emma satisfies their own aggression toward Miss Bates?[4] Rosmarin comes close to an overt charge of bad faith, to suggesting that, through a ritual of scapegoating the heroine, critics camouflage their own guilty reading (the term "perfidies" in the title of her article underscores this implicit charge). And no doubt there is always a risk of bad faith in the conversion of private affect into public discourse.

To sort this out, I would like to step back for a moment and analyze the context of this scene step by step, because by the time we consider this present discussion, the layers of gossip about gossip will attain a rather daunting thickness. For the purpose of this analysis, let's reduce gossip to its essential dynamic of forming a bond through talking about others not present. In the dynamics at Box Hill, then, the first level is simple: Miss Bates is a gossip. She is not called the "talking aunt" for nothing.[5] The second level is Emma's mean remark, which we might describe as Emma attempting to form a bond with the others in the party at Miss Bates's expense, an attempt that founders of course on the fact that Miss Bates is present, not on the fact that the remark is mean. The third level, though, is the most crucial, and at the same time perhaps the most covert. It is Knightley's private discussion with Emma after the episode, and its salient features tend to get overshadowed by the spectacle of Emma's shame. First, we must notice that Miss Bates remains more or less abject. In the process of defending her, Knightley not only adopts a rather condescending position, but also agrees with Emma that Miss Bates blends the good with the ridiculous. Furthermore, Emma's mistake, as always, is an occasion for intimacy with Knightley. In fact, Emma realizes her love for Knightley only twenty-five pages after their conversation, so we might want to go so far as to call the moment a seduction, though of course the crucial plot development in which Harriet Smith fixes on Knightley occurs in the meantime.[6] But without putting the weight of their whole relationship on this moment, we can still say that Knightley and Emma cement their bond at the expense of Miss Bates—it is the last step in the only dance they really know.[7]

Taking the Box Hill episode as a whole, we can now consider what work it accomplishes for the narrative. First, it punishes the gossip, with Knightley's correction only partly mitigating this effect.[8] Second, it propels Emma and Knightley together once and for all. Are these effects related? I would argue that the same reading is available as for *The Woman in White*, that a certain readerly coherence acquires definition through the abjection of the female gossip. Again we see a novel working in the mode of gossip, and again this mode must be disavowed, for if the clear consensus is that Miss Bates is half ridiculous, then the novel cannot risk too much open attachment to such a figure. But if Miss Bates falls victim to some show of sacrifice, she also enjoys a crucial covert status, as Austen buries many of the best clues to the Fairfax affair at the end of Miss Bates's monologues.[9] She is even granted a brief moment to shine, her volubility put to good purpose in that one glorious entrance where she outtalks Mrs. Elton as only she could (252).

What remains unanswered is why Austen criticism has become so invested in punishing Emma, a collective reaction we could characterize as the fourth level of gossip about the Box Hill affair, in that the critics are indeed bonding at Emma's expense. Moreover, the bond this consensus forms is much the same as the bond between novelist and reader, forged on the reassurance that *this* discourse will not be gossipy and ridiculous.[10] But here is where the real scandal lies, not in the ephemeral idiosyncrasies of a moment's reading (how *did* we respond to the episode at Box Hill?), but in the possible hypocrisy of published response. And we critics would seem to learn our hypocrisy from Mr. Knightley, for the episode becomes an alibi for what, if we believe Sedgwick, has likely been a sadistic desire to "correct" Emma all along. Moreover, Emma complains about Miss Bates precisely from the rhetoric of a judgmental male discourse in which women talk too much, so that we castigate Emma at the exact moment that she comes into her own as this sort of critic. It is like bringing Emma into the fold of masculinity through gang initiation.

But of course, however much Knightley and other critics capitalize on Emma's remark, their doing so can hardly be her reason for making it. It is only through apprehending this distinctly female reason that we can begin to recast the terms of this crime. Emma lashes out at Miss Bates not as some patriarchal police agent, but simply as a woman who is sick of her, and for reasons stemming from her own female difficulties. Indeed most of the hostility Emma displays, whether toward Miss Bates, Jane Fairfax, or Mrs. Elton, can be traced to the basic, and widely understood, frustration of her situation: Emma doesn't know enough people![11] As a small-town girl who has never seen the sea, Emma's isolation entails a significant shortfall of friends, acquaintances, and love interests—a significant shortfall of people to gossip with and about. Above all, I would suggest, Emma lacks a female network, and indeed this lack makes itself felt from the very first page, as she mourns the loss of her governess, Miss Taylor, to marriage. In this scenario Miss Bates holds the position of a special tormentor, for she is a major source of news but she makes her listener work so very hard to get it. Miss Bates's only crime is that she is not a good sorter; Emma's is that she lashes out at the voice that unwittingly mocks her profound boredom, a boredom the reader has had only a taste of. In this way the Box Hill debacle tells us less about Emma's need for correction than her need for relief, a need that Knightley, with his trips to London, cannot fully share.

A New Critical Gossip?

> *We must be aware of the dangers which lie in our most generous*
> *wishes. Some paradox of our nature leads us, when once we*
> *have made our fellow [people] the objects of our enlightened*
> *interest, to go on to make them the objects of our pity, then of*
> *our wisdom, ultimately of our coercion.*
>   Lionel Trilling, *"Manners, Morals, and the Novel"*

To reconcile female and critical discourse must mean in part to gossip openly, to embrace its rewards while carefully assuming its risks. Indeed, in my own commentary thus far, we could surely detect a fifth level of gossip about Box Hill in my attempt to bond with my readers at the critics' expense. That the critics as a body do not cohere as an abject female figure may be one thing in my favor. And yet such a figure is lurking in my argument, offering herself in sacrifice to any consensus we may be building. This figure is Mrs. Elton, the character we *really* love to hate, who, in a little noticed twist, happens to be the novel's most outspoken champion of female discourse. As a provocative combination of unpleasantness and representativeness, she is exactly the sort of figure whom feminist critical methodology must come to terms with. Of course such a critical practice is already much in evidence, for what I propose extrapolates from the fundamental feminist strategy of restaging narrative in ways that highlight the roles of female characters, or retelling history to emphasize women authors.[12] It is also in sympathy with Alex Woloch's study of character-systems in *The One vs. the Many*, which analyzes the social and formal means by which a protagonist emerges from a field of minor characters. But I want to suggest that a healthy feminist culture should be understood in terms of connections *between* women, rather than the success or failure of any single female character. Indeed, in this book we will see time and again that the attention showered on a heroine may be double-edged precisely in its isolating effects. At issue are not only questions of distribution (in whom are we asked to take an interest?) but of quality (is that interest sympathetic? condescending? sadistic?) and timing. Critically effective gossip therefore requires more than being fair and kind, it means developing a generous and *linking* attention where it is most needed. It is quite simply a cultural politics of interest, of its value and its violence, and it is as much as anything what *Emma* is all about.

Consider the basic structure of the novel. As the plot unfolds, Emma has two main chances for female friendship: Harriet Smith and Jane Fairfax, but until the end she botches both. The first she jeopardizes through meddling; the second through misunderstanding. Taken together, Emma's clumsy interactions offer a veritable case study on the problem of taking an interest in other people, and the questions they allow us to ask are politically (and morally) fundamental: in whom should we take an interest, and how should we show that interest? What is the difference between kind attention and cruel interference? Between mercy and neglect? What are the limits of human empathy, identification, or generosity? All of this is complicated, of course, by the fact that our field of interest cannot be cultivated systematically, like a garden. Other people have a tendency to move about, to develop their own interests. Accordingly, Harriet and Jane bear some share of responsibility for the fizzling friendships—Harriet for being tractable and lovesick, Jane for being standoffish and secretive. Neither grows according to Emma's interests.

It is perhaps only in fiction, or possibly history, that the people we imagine hold still long enough to reward our interest dependably. And there, at least, we can do them less harm. For these reasons a novel can be a good place to practice sympathetic attention, to refine our interest and consider its implications.[13] On the other hand, there is the danger that we will forget the difference between characters and people, demanding of real people an unfair level of interest and predictability. It is along these lines that Emma falls into a version of the standard trap, most fully elaborated by Austen in *Northanger Abbey*, of reading the world as a novel. For instead of friendship, we might say, Emma chooses readership.[14] Instead of having Harriet Smith or Jane Fairfax, she has *Harriet* (with its comedy of errors and Family Romance of Harriet's unknown parentage), and the much darker *Mystery of Jane Fairfax*.

Onto this scene of reading charges Mrs. Elton. She is at first an object of curiosity herself, with the foremost question for the local gossip to settle being "whether she were very pretty indeed, or only rather pretty, or not pretty at all" (211). Her strain to sustain this interest, as a married woman with few possible plots, is painfully apparent as she attempts the impossible task of spurring gossip about herself with such ill-conceived lines as "my friends say I am not entirely devoid of taste" (216). But what will ensure Mrs. Elton a prominent place in her new community is to attend to the plots of others around her, to give up being a heroine to become a reader—indeed, to become an author, launching heroines on their careers. It is of course Emma herself whom she first wants to sweep up in a "coming out" trip to Bath, sounding a note that resonates all too deeply with Emma's situation: "It could be a charming introduction for you, who have lived so secluded a life" (215). Not about to give herself up to someone else's design, however, Emma ignores all overtures, and the two instead become rival readers.

What is particularly striking about this rivalry is how it temporarily aligns Mrs. Elton with Knightley in her tendency to place less value on Harriet and more on Jane. It is an alignment that grates on Emma all the more in light of the familiar tone Mrs. Elton takes with Knightley (218). In this context, it becomes crucial that Emma recruit Knightley to her ill opinion of Mrs. Elton, and he does not disappoint, finding Harriet "an unpretending, single-minded, artless girl—infinitely to be preferred by any man of sense and taste to such a woman as Mrs. Elton" (260). And while the consensus of Emma and Knightley would seem to generate an almost overwhelming narrative authority, it is worth noting how hard it is to pin the narrator down on this point. For instance, an earlier chapter ends with the narrator reporting with lacerating wit that "Mr. Knightley seemed to be trying not to smile; and succeeded without difficulty, upon Mrs. Elton's beginning to talk to him" (245). In many ways nothing could be more devastating than this remark. But in the absence of direct instructions from the narrator, there is just enough space to gain the clearance we need from Knightley's point of view to see it as *his*, with no necessary extension to the narrator or us. It is just possible to see in this moment, instead of the irony of his suffering on cue, the pathetic spectacle of a woman, without friends nearby or the skills to acquire them, talking valiantly to the most important man in town, who doesn't like her. This is not to say that we don't see enough of Mrs. Elton's behavior to judge for ourselves; her cruelty to Harriet and her bullying of Jane are especially hard to accept. I do want to insist, though, that we extend enough sympathy in her direction to recognize how much her actions are attempts, however misguided, to compensate for the trauma of being uprooted by marriage, a trauma that she notes "is quite one of the evils of matrimony" (213).

When we first meet Mrs. Elton, she has just left her friends and family behind to follow a husband she has known just four weeks and start a new social life from scratch.[15] At first she copes with this trauma through a display of self-sufficiency, telling Emma: "*the world* I could give up—parties, balls, plays—for I have no fear of retirement. Blessed with so many resources within myself, the world was not necessary to *me*" (216). Our embarrassment at such boasting should not obscure for us the seriousness of Mrs. Elton's rhetorical dilemma, a dilemma that stems from her need to do two things at once. On one hand, she needs to complain; she has real grievances that deserve attention, as she catalogues further: "Certainly, I had been accustomed to every luxury at Maple Grove; but I did assure him that two carriages were not necessary to my happiness, nor were spacious apartments" (216). On the other hand, she needs to advertise; her happiness depends on how much her "resources" can attract others, especially Emma, for we soon learn that this monologue has been the buildup to a proposal: "I think, Miss Woodhouse, you and I must establish a musical club" (217). Seen in this light, the conversation becomes an interview, an audition. Applying to Emma for a social position, Mrs. Elton attempts simultaneously to prove her need and her qualifications. As we know, she doesn't get the job—in part because she is not up to the demands of the rhetorical situation, in part because Emma is predisposed to reject her. If Mrs. Elton will later insist too emphatically on the privileges of a new bride (standing first at the dance, taking her coach first, etc.), it is because they are the only things that give her any semblance of a place in the community, as if the only answer left to her question "Where do I come in?" is "first."

If anything makes her situation bearable, it is a female network of her own, her correspondence with her friend Selina, who serves not only as a contact with her past, but also as an audience for her gossip as she comes to (largely hostile) terms with her new community. In such a situation the importance of the postal system for female networking cannot be overstated (an issue that will be pursued at length in chapter 2). Indeed, Jane Fairfax, living at the mercy of Frank's comings and goings, expresses her own deep appreciation for the postal system: "The post-office is a wonderful establishment! . . . So seldom that a letter, among the thousands that are constantly passing about the kingdom, is even carried wrong. . . . And when one considers the variety of hands, and of bad hands too, that are to be deciphered, it increases the wonder" (232). But it is Mrs. Elton who raises the issue of gender when she protests Mr. Weston's opening of a letter addressed to his wife, declaring: "I always take the part of my own sex; I do indeed. . . . I always stand up for women." (240). While Mr. Weston's action is innocuous enough in the context of *Emma*, anyone who has read some of the prior century's epistolary fiction (especially *Clarissa*) can imagine how much is ultimately at stake in women's having uninterrupted access to the outside world. Indeed, until the invention of the telephone, letter-writing would be gossip's crucial supplement in maintaining a vital female discourse over distance. When the privacy of this network is compromised (and this vulnerability is inherent), female narrative slides quickly into the gothic.

So if Mrs. Elton is a figure, and occasionally a spokeswoman, for important women's issues, why hasn't she received more nuanced critical attention? What I've felt during the course of my own writing, at least, was a tension between my loyalty to Austen and my feminist theories, insofar as part of being loyal to Austen meant, as it seemed to, hating Mrs. Elton.[16] Indeed, if there is a greater critical consensus than the belief that Emma does badly at Box Hill, it is surely that Mrs. Elton does badly throughout the novel; it has come to be the meaning of her character. But I have already suggested that this meaning is a function of our allegiance to the converging perspectives of Emma and Knightley and should not necessarily be seen as coextensive with the novel's meaning in its full range of possibilities for understanding Mrs. Elton. Perhaps, then, we should feel freer to occupy the slight breathing room Austen has left for her. What makes doing this so hard, however, is that Mrs. Elton is too familiar in both senses of the word. Not only does she insinuate herself into others' lives, but she reminds us too much of ourselves, is indeed a kind of secret figure for the reader. After all, is the reader not an outsider, a latecomer with pretensions to familiarity, prone particularly to getting too close to Knightley? Is hating her part of how we disavow our own tenuous position? If we see Mrs. Elton through this novel, we find she does not go quietly, but kicking and screaming, stealing the novel's penultimate line:

> The wedding was very much like other weddings, where the parties
> have no taste for finery or parade; and Mrs. Elton, from the particulars
> detailed by her husband, thought it all extremely shabby, and very inferior
> to her own.—"Very little white satin, very few lace veils; a most pitiful
> business!—Selina would stare when she heard of it."—But, in spite of
> these deficiencies, the wishes, the hopes, the confidence, the predictions
> of the small band of true friends who witnessed the ceremony, were fully
> answered in the perfect happiness of the union. (381)

In some ways Mrs. Elton coincides here with the familiar comic villain who must be expelled for the community to come together at the end.[17] But her position, if a kind of exile, is not fully isolated, as again she invokes Selina's sympathetic ears (and eyes, in this case) to challenge the orthodoxy of Highbury. And if we make too much of her absence from the wedding, we must remember that it mirrors our own—our own vital report comes only at a distance. To compensate, we turn to our own female networks, professional or not, and gossip about the novel.

Jamesian Gossip

There are several reasons I want to turn to Henry James to advance this discussion. Here, for instance, we can begin to see the pressure that modern intercontinental travel and communication bring to bear on female networks. Gossip as a resource strains to remain informative even as it grows increasingly interesting, for what is striking about the wide world of James is how it nonetheless feels more claustrophobic than a place like Highbury, its social circles, its marriage market, at once more intimate and more opaque. If James and Austen share a deep preoccupation with the risks and rewards of placing female characters at the center of attention, then in James the usual mode of this concern comes into historical jeopardy, as we wonder how long the courtship plot can continue to be the main business of the novel (indeed as early as 1893 George Gissing would divert the courtship plot into the question of female vocation in *The Odd Women*). Moreover, James represents an unusual opportunity for refining the study of gossip and the novel in the way he blurs the roles of author and critic, particularly in his prefaces to the New York Edition of his works. Thus it is only with these historical and professional contexts in mind that we can continue to develop what I see as James's most important legacy, a sustained commitment to what I am calling a cultural politics of interest.

Despite this commitment, it might be a mistake to imagine James as too much of a feminist prophet. Clearly, problems of interest proved so generative in his work precisely because he could not resolve them. Consider the unease James articulates in the preface to *The Portrait of a Lady*:

> By what process of logical accretion was this slight "personality," the mere slim shade of an intelligent but presumptuous girl, to find itself endowed with the high attributes of a Subject?—and indeed by what thinness, at the best, would such a subject not be vitiated? Millions of presumptuous girls, intelligent or not intelligent, daily affront their destiny, and what is it open to their destiny to *be*, at the most, that we should make an ado about it? The novel is of its very nature an "ado," an ado about something, and the larger the form it takes the greater of course the ado. (10)

Lingering over this passage, we catch a whiff of circular logic: that she is a subject because she is presumptuous seems clear—it is why James finds her interesting. But is she not also presumptuous because she is a subject? James calls his heroine presumptuous for "affronting her destiny," when both the presumption and the destiny are of his own design, then he worries about why this should interest us.

His anxiety, I would suggest, turns on the definition of the novel as a great ado, as implicitly something that must rise above trivial gossip. Indeed, to trace the word "gossip" through *The Portrait of a Lady* is to find a consistently pejorative usage.[18] Moreover, it is precisely the gender of his subject that produces the anxiety: he asks of young women "what is it open to their destiny to *be*?" as if a fully adequate answer to that question were self-evident for young men.

Of course James does not balk at the question—he did go on to write the book. As it turns out, what is open to Isabel Archer to be is a sensitive and expansive consciousness. James relocates the scene of interest to the inside of her head, as in the section he calls "obviously the best thing in the book," where Isabel stays late by the fire, meditating on what has happened to her: "It is a representation simply of her motionless *seeing*, and an attempt withal to make the mere still lucidity of her act as 'interesting' as the surprise of a caravan or the identification of a pirate" (17). Regarding this statement, Peter Brooks points out that "The terms of reference in the adventure story are mocked; yet they remain the terms of reference: moral consciousness must be an adventure, its recognition must be the stuff of a heightened drama" (6). Moreover, how are Gilbert Osmond and Madame Merle *not* pirates, given their financial and emotional plundering of Isabel? It is after all Isabel's contemplation of the novel's criminal element that makes her consciousness such an adventure—that and James's marked reserve about this very criminality, a reserve that makes the plot of consciousness an exotic plot indeed, and which bears a special relationship to gossip.

What feels most forbidden in Jamesian discourse is that basic dimension of gossip whereby acts are named (however euphemistically) and relationships spelled out. In its place is a tantalizing discretion that extends to the most unlikely characters, so that even a "vulgar" woman like Osmond's sister, the Countess, waits a long time to make Isabel aware of Osmond and Merle's prior relationship, and then only through a minor triumph of indirection, announcing, "My first sister-in-law had no children" (576). In this light, Brooks's designation of James as a special example of what he famously calls "the melodramatic imagination" seems odd at first (as Brooks admits), for his definition of melodrama seems to belie such discretion:

> The desire to express all seems a fundamental characteristic of the
> melodramatic mode. Nothing is spared because nothing is left unsaid; the
> characters stand on stage and utter the unspeakable, give voice to their
> deepest feelings, dramatize through their heightened and polarized words
> and gestures the whole lesson of their relationship. (4)

By conventional standards, of course, there is an enormous amount left unsaid in James. But perhaps only by resisting certain kinds of utterances can James avoid obstructing what he is really after, a "metaphorical approach to what cannot be said" (Peter Brooks 11). Obstruction is a concern because gossip forces its subject into a narrative mold that smooths out particularity, into what Gillian Beer calls its "repetitive formulaic stories . . . which can only ever imagine simple motives and simple outcomes to stories" ("Circulatory" 60). The classic gossip's line, which the Countess avoids, would be something like "Merle slept with Osmond," a statement that disguises its violence in the apparent simplicity of its "truth" and that invokes a story as powerful as it is old. But *The Portrait of a Lady* makes it clear how violent such a statement would be, both in its traumatic impact on Isabel as a listener, and in its distorting simplification of the Merle/Osmond relation—indeed, it risks shutting off that relation forever behind a hard wall of fact. In James, gossip is crude not because it is intrusive (who is a more intrusive writer than James?), but because it is a blunt, disfiguring instrument that offends singularity.

In its stead James develops a kind of supergossip, a discourse at once to heighten gossip's potential and diminish its violence.[19] Foregrounding gossip's double aspect as an engine of both exclusion and intimacy, a novel such as *The Portrait of a Lady* draws us in with the threat of scandal even as its monumental restraint promises something finer.[20] But as a critical endpoint in the long history of gossip and the novel, the exquisite Jamesian rendering of female singularity confounds female networks. My concern then is to articulate what is at stake in *our* seduction as readers into a novelistic narrative contract that requires our interest, and to assess what resources remain for reading differently. Of use here is René Girard's theory of mimetic desire, in which the object of desire is always identified through the interest of another. I am calling this process "seduction" to call attention to how the structure of gossip generates interest, raising the issue of the reader's consent as a way of gauging what violence we are submitting to, or inflicting, when we read this or other novels. Such violence is a question not only of excluding characters like Mrs. Elton, but, again, of the very ways we tend to love our heroines. Ultimately, James arrests the slide of narrative desire into violence, releasing our attention toward new ways of understanding the heroine's best interests.

Seduction, Sadism, and The Portrait of a Lady

Often lost among the major surprises and disappointments of *The Portrait of A Lady*—in particular the common frustration at Isabel's decisions to marry Osmond and, as it's assumed, return to him at the end—is a sense of the strangeness of the process that launches the heroine's career as an interesting woman in the first place, as indeed a woman who is particularly worth writing or gossiping about. Once Isabel leaves the novel's opening scenes at Gardencourt, of course, the basic question of interest has already been established and taken for granted: Isabel is interesting, we understand, because she has refused Lord Warburton's excellent offer of marriage. Thus, as her cousin Ralph puts it, we will "have the thrill of seeing what a young lady does who won't marry Lord Warburton," a thrill in which Ralph literally, and tragically, invests by ensuring that Isabel inherits a large chunk of his fortune (170).[21] In choosing to begin his novel at a place called Gardencourt, James of course alludes to Paradise and The Fall, and perhaps also to Grandcourt, the villain of George Eliot's *Daniel Deronda* and Osmond's clear predecessor in marital sadism. But we might also consider the term "garden" in its mundane sense. A garden, we might say, is a systematically cultivated field of interest, and Ralph's problem is that he cannot plant Isabel in a garden. Like Harriet Smith or Jane Fairfax, she will move about, develop her own interests. His "seed money" will not bring him the return he expects. But for the novel, this investment indeed yields compound interest, multiplying Isabel's attractions. By the time she succumbs to her fatal attraction to the reptilian Osmond, mimetic desire will in fact have produced a crippling inflation. Working backward through the plot: Osmond becomes interested in Isabel because Madame Merle gossips about her, saying quite directly: "I admire her. You'll do the same" (262). Madame Merle is interested in her because Ralph fueled his interest with money, which Madame Merle wants for her daughter Pansy, and Ralph is interested in Isabel, again, because she refused Lord Warburton. Osmond ultimately thinks he has a triply interesting bride: someone to admire, someone with money, and, to get back to the apparent source of interest, "a young lady who had qualified herself to figure in his collection of choice objects by declining so noble a hand" as Lord Warburton (328).

But why is everyone, including, presumably, the reader, content to accept Lord Warburton as the source of interest in Isabel? What does he find so attractive in this young American that he proposes to her after spending "about twenty-six hours in her company?" (123). Looking over the scenes at Gardencourt, all we can really say is that he finds Isabel interesting because he has been prepared to find her interesting—that is, his desire is mimetic as well; he is not the source after all. James gives us the finishing touches of Warburton's preparation for love in such suggestive remarks as Mr. Touchett's that "The ladies will save us. . . . Make up to a good one and marry her, and your life will become much more interesting" (26). But the implication is that Lord Warburton's education began long before, in his experience as a reader of novels. When he proposes to Isabel, he fails to recognize the role novels have played in his falling in love with her "at first sight" (124). Instead of considering their possible role as a *source* of these feelings, he accepts their counsel as merely the wise echo of a desire he imagines was born within himself. As a symptom of this misrecognition, he reserves a special triple emphasis for precisely that aspect of his belief that is most unknowable: "I don't go off easily, but when I'm touched, it's for life. It's for life, Miss Archer, it's for life" (125). Knowing this about himself in advance can only mean that it's written elsewhere, that Lord Warburton recognizes himself, though only half-consciously, among the historic cast of characters who love properly—that is, at first sight and for life.

As readers, we thrive on the consumption of interest and are likely as eager as Lord Warburton to believe we have found it, despite its unaccountable source.

Indeed, any assent to his proposal, any tendency to find his love for Isabel credible, testifies loudly to our own training in novelistic discourse. We may in fact experience the opening of the novel as a sort of flattering allegory of reading:

> Under certain circumstances there are few hours in life more agreeable than the hour dedicated to the ceremony known as afternoon tea. There are circumstances in which, whether you partake of the tea or not—some people of course never do,—the situation is in itself delightful. Those that I have in mind in beginning to unfold this simple history offered an admirable setting to an innocent pastime. The implements of the little feast had been disposed upon the lawn of an old English country-house in what I should call the perfect middle of a splendid summer afternoon. (19)

It seems quite natural to associate the "little feast" with the novel, and the "innocent pastime" with reading. The scene is remarkably cozy, launching the reader straight into the comfort zone, the "perfect middle," of novelistic subjectivity—a position all the more precious because it obtains only, we agree, "under certain circumstances." Indeed, glancing through the rest of the first paragraph, we see the key terms of reading take their cue: leisure, pleasure, privilege—especially privilege, since we are making a side door entrance to the show: "The front of the house overlooking that portion of lawn with which we are concerned was not the entrance-front; this was in quite another quarter. Privacy here reigned supreme, and the wide carpet of turf that covered the level hill-top seemed but the extension of a luxurious interior" (20–21). What we are looking at here is the scene of a seduction—ours, as James dangles a fantasy of luxurious interiority before us, the quintessential novelistic fantasy. All that is missing is the mood music, furnished later by Madame Merle on the piano.

What is the promise of this seduction? Most simply that James is going to tell us the right story, the story we want to read. My argument is that he does not do so, indeed, that he cannot. Like many seductions, there is a bait and switch: what is received is not exactly what is promised. For me, though, it remains an awfully good seduction, and one whose mechanics are well worth attending to as we think about why we come to care so much about the private affairs of such a "slight" personage. With respect to mimetic desire, we would do well not to neglect our own position as the final link of the mimetic chain, accumulating interest with every cue to regard Isabel. Indeed, the problem of committing blindly to this position is captured in the fact that, upon her entrance to the novel at Gardencourt, Isabel is noticed first not by any of the characters loitering on the lawn, but by the dog, emblem both of the potential idiocy of desire and of our need to believe it is something natural, something like instinct—and our best friend.

Our seduction, however, is actually well underway before Isabel appears on the scene. The first mention of her existence takes the form of a predictably stimulating

prohibition: her uncle tells Lord Warburton: "[Y]ou may fall in love with whom-
soever you please; but you mustn't fall in love with my niece" (27). James couples
this alluring taboo with the attractions of novelty (we've never heard of her) and
absence (she is not in the scene) to amplify our curiosity. Underscoring the sense of
absence are the telegrams by which, as we learn momentarily, her uncle has learned
of her imminent arrival from America. Ralph explains to Warburton:

> "We hardly know more about her than you; my mother has not gone into
> details. She chiefly communicates with us by means of telegrams, and
> her telegrams are rather inscrutable. They say women don't know how
> to write them, but my mother has thoroughly mastered the art of con-
> densation. 'Tired America, hot weather awful, return England with niece,
> first steamer decent cabin.' That's the sort of message we get from her—that
> was the last that came. But there had been another before, which I think
> contained the first mention of the niece. 'Changed hotel, very bad, impudent
> clerk, address here. Taken sister's girl, died last year, go to Europe, two
> sisters, quite independent.' Over that my father and I have scarcely stopped
> puzzling; it seems to admit of so many interpretations." (27)[22]

As figured here, the telegram is the mortal enemy of the novel, opposing novelistic expansion with a technology of such "condensation," as Ralph says, that
it achieves syntax without subjects. Accordingly, Isabel's "first mention" hardly
forecasts the vaunted self-possession of a heroine who would come to "find itself
endowed with the high attributes of a Subject" (10); instead we glimpse her doubly possessed, a "sister's" girl now "taken." But poised between telegraphic and
novelistic discourse is gossip, which combines the crudeness of the former with
the loquaciousness of the latter. And it is gossip that guides both Isabel and the
reader back to the novel's warm embrace as Ralph shows us how to domesticate
the telegram, generating a hermeneutic problem that will govern our pursuit of
Isabel throughout the novel:

> "But who's 'quite independent,' and in what sense is the term used?—that
> point's not yet settled. Does the expression apply more particularly to the
> young lady my mother has adopted, or does it characterize her sisters
> equally?—and is it used in a moral or in a financial sense? Does it mean
> that they've been left well off, or that they wish to be under no obligations?
> or does it simply mean that they're fond of their own way?" (28)

The table is set for a very interesting arrival.

As the novel unfolds, however, our interest in Isabel requires less stimulation
than regulation, as our seduction gets cut to the measure of the exact plot James has
in mind. And as we will see, what gets most regulated in this novel are its female

networks, which are never granted the interest that they nonetheless do so much to generate. Where everything is at stake, then, is in moments where James says, in effect, "but I digress," cutting short our pursuit of interests deemed irrelevant. One largely irrelevant detour would seem to be the middle section of Isabel's travels, situated between Osmond's declaration of love and their eventual engagement. James moves through this chapter extremely quickly, claiming "it is not, however, during this interval that we are closely concerned with her" (345). But the fact that Isabel's travels include an extended tour with Madame Merle makes this a striking suppression of interest, particularly in light of Melissa Solomon's claim that Merle is the novel's not-so-secret erotic center—the original "interesting woman." By denying our close concern, James seems to want us to believe that nothing relevant is happening between Isabel and Merle, that in her travels all Isabel really does is orbit around Osmond.

Indeed, it is just this sense of Osmond's almost hypnotic control that Jane Campion develops in her film adaptation. Despite its stylistic extravagance, Campion's treatment of Isabel's tour with Merle seems quite faithful—perhaps too faithful—to a conviction that the tour must be mere delay or detour, since during Isabel's travels we hear Osmond's voice repeating his declaration of love and see his disembodied lips surrealistically multiplied on a plate. If there is a difference, it seems mainly that Campion's revolting "little feast" brings the underbelly of seductive offerings to light and prepares us more for the coming sadism (though of course we're already more prepared, most likely, because *The Portrait of a Lady* is such a famous story and because John Malkovich usually plays libertines and villains). As striking as Campion's sequence is, we might wonder if she missed an opportunity for something better, for I think that when James denies the importance of this section, we have to register the denial as defensive, as betraying a certain doubt about what Merle and Isabel are doing together, and a certain anxiety that the doubled interest of their combination could steal the whole show.

There are of course hints of what we miss in the hasty summary of their travels, which upon reconstruction begin to look like a great tragic romance. In the first place they include nothing less than the "consummation" of Merle relating her own history (with, we know, key omissions) as well as a significantly heightened mood: "the girl had in these days a thousand uses for her sense of the romantic, which was more active than it had ever been" (350, 351). But they also contain the final touches of the novel's central crime—Merle's transfer of Isabel's affections from herself to Osmond, and here James's reticent treatment of criminality becomes a serious issue, reduced as it is to a host of dark insinuations, such as that Merle exhibits "a different morality," "an occasional flash of cruelty," and a "conception of human motives [that] might, in certain lights, have been acquired at the court of some kingdom in decadence" (351). We should recall also that James presents the beginnings of this process, as Merle prepares Isabel to meet Osmond, in summary form: "Madame Merle . . . it must be observed parenthetically, did not deliver herself all at once of these reflections, which are presented in a cluster for the convenience of the reader" (219). Given this representational strategy, it is no wonder that Merle seems such a shadowy figure operating behind the scenes. But whatever effect is achieved by this enforced exile, belatedly literalized in Merle's banishment to America, must be weighed against its cost. Indeed, wherever characters stray into the category of the irrelevant is a potential site of violence—sadistic violence to the extent that it underwrites any further enjoyment of the novel. We might say that in this section the novel turns doubly sadistic, not only because it submits its heroine to the force of the villain's gravitational field, but because it does so by sacrificing in large part what may be its own most interesting relationship. Instead we could trust Solomon's reading, which declines to follow the mimetic chain as Isabel is handed off from Merle to Osmond. As I see it, the novel never fully recovers from this unexplored detour. No matter how many scenes of revelation James stages in the second half of the novel, Isabel remains firmly lodged in Osmond's orbit.

Or does she? *The Portrait of a Lady* features what has been called "arguably the most delicately understated ending in all Victorian fiction" (Sutherland 176). Realizing the awful truth about her relationship with Osmond, Isabel has defied him by going to see the dying Ralph in England. After Ralph's death she is approached by her original American suitor, the relentless Caspar Goodwood, who demands that she turn to him at last. Isabel flees his embrace, and then James gets subtle. The scene ends with the following description of her mental state: "She had not known where to turn; but she knew now. There was a very straight path" (628). The novel ends as Henrietta informs a bewildered Caspar that Isabel has left for Rome, supposedly to return to Osmond. In its extreme restraint, James's conclusion short-circuits the flow of gossipy narrative information, questioning the reader's straightforward "right to know."

Historically, this ending has both confused and troubled some readers—that is, some readers did not understand what happened, while others thought they understood but didn't like it. Over time, though, and with a little help from James himself in a revision, both of these concerns have waned in favor of a general consensus not only that Isabel is certainly going back to Osmond but also that she must, or should, do so. In other words, most readers now seem to agree both about what happens at the end and that this conclusion is appropriate, if not happy.[23] The revision to the text that promotes this consensus came as a response to a contemporary reviewer, R. H. Hutton, who read Isabel's "straight path" at the end as leading to adultery with Caspar (Sutherland 176–83). Here is the new end of the novel, with the revised portion italicized:

> Henrietta had come out, closing the door behind her, and now she put out her hand and grasped his arm. "Look here, Mr Goodwood," she said; "*just you wait!*"

On which he looked up at her—but only to guess, from her face, with a
revulsion, that she simply meant he was young. She stood shining at him with
that cheap comfort, and it added, on the spot, thirty years to his life. She walked
him away with her, however, as if she had given him now the key to patience.
(628)

All that is indicated by the few lines that James adds is that Caspar is, at least for now, out of luck. Yet it is an odd leap of logic to take this revision as clear evidence that Isabel is returning to Osmond, as if eliminating one commitment implies another. J. Hillis Miller, for instance, takes this leap on the strength of James's intimations in his notebooks, thus confusing intention with achievement (737). But if James wanted readers to know that Isabel goes back to Osmond, he wanted far more to avoid the gossipy vulgarity of spelling this out.

I submit that the real effect of the ending is to keep Isabel away from us, and criticism should accept and even take advantage of that. It is fitting that we finish the novel in the position of Caspar, chasing an Isabel who won't be caught. In fact, whether we like Caspar or not, whether we side with him or hope he wins Isabel, the conclusion remains a disappointment, because structurally we are out of the loop.[24] To find ourselves thus excluded is to find ourselves flung out of our armchairs into the vast loneliness outside of gossip. From this perspective, the critical consensus around the ending looks like compensation, enabling readings that convert disappointment into satisfaction as they convert narrative silence into critical knowledge. But in restoring the comfort of gossip, the intimacy that consensus produces, we bear some complicity with the sadistic turn the novel takes. Leaping to a clear understanding of Isabel's "straight path," we succumb to the final seduction of the novelistic, the promise of full intelligibility and the completion of linear progress at the expense of other interesting possibilities.

Before sketching one of these possibilities, I want to consider J. Hillis Miller's analysis more fully, for he makes an important move, considering how Isabel's return to Osmond might be understood as being in her own best interests. And while he ultimately remains agnostic on Isabel's motives, some of his speculations are rather seductive. His richest vein circles a central meditation on kissing as a kind of speech act that delivers the self as much or more than the other (729). Following this vein back to the most important speech acts of the novel, Isabel's marital vows, it would seem appropriate to call Isabel's stake in returning an erotics, or auto-erotics, of the promise. As a performance, the promise achieves at least three things: it binds the speaker, it tests the auditor (in this way becoming an invaluable tool for discovering the world), and it excludes third parties. Thus the promise produces a self with enduring capacities for intimacy and knowledge. I would not deprive Isabel of these capacities, for they seem to me the strongest justification for imagining the nonexistent ending with Osmond. But this seems a propitious moment to remember that Isabel is a fictional character. The question is really *who is the reader who would demand this for her?* My fear is that this reader is precisely the reader whose seduction and betrayal I have outlined, a reader who would thereby redeem the novel's own erotic promise at Isabel's expense. Married, as it were, to the novel, such a reader is in danger of accepting any and all violence as the price of sustaining novelistic intimacy and knowledge. It is in the face of this risk that Miller is agnostic in all the wrong places. Insistent on the what but not the why of the novel's ending, Miller eschews the textual resources that might redirect the tremendous sexual energy that pins Isabel to Osmond in the cultural imagination.[25] And yet he concludes with a concession: a committed reading of the novel may not be "completely verifiable," but as a "performative intervention" it is nonetheless the fullest response to the demand of the text (746). In a formulation that remains vaguely erotic, others are finally permitted to take the passionate "leaps in the dark" that Miller would not venture (746).

I would like to offer one such leap for the conclusion of *The Portrait of a Lady.* This would be a leap, not onto any straight path, but onto a perpetual detour, one that is also located, not coincidentally, in a connection between women. My fantasy of this detour is based on the unfounded guess that Henrietta could be *lying* at the end to Caspar. What if she has finally realized that Caspar is also wrong for Isabel, and she actually has our heroine stowed away somewhere, preparing for a daring break from *all* the possessive men in her life? Such sympathetic speculation is not just our right but our job as critical readers. James would seem almost to agree when he writes that Isabel "would be an easy victim of scientific criticism if she were not intended to awaken on the reader's part an impulse more tender and more purely expectant" (69).

This alternate ending returns us to a tension in James's preface, where he classes Henrietta among the characters that are "but wheels to the coach" (15). Such insistence on her insignificance, however, cannot but make us wonder what the difference is, what it would mean to think of Henrietta as more than a mere reporter. Moreover, James's very need to explain her, and the awkwardness of his attempt to do so, betrays a telling anxiety about her place in the novel: "I have suffered Henrietta (of whom we have indubitably too much) so officiously, so strangely, so almost inexplicably, to pervade" (16). After a long detour into other issues, the only explanation James can provide for this supposed excess is that Henrietta was there to amuse the reader, that she corresponded to his "wonderful notion of the lively" (18). But why should a character that can provide amusement not also generate real interest and become a source of plot? Indeed, James's thinking about Henrietta seems betrayed by his initial metaphor of the coach: wheels drive, and so speculation about an indispensable Henrietta seems positively invited.[26] I would suggest that, at a deep level, James senses that Henrietta *is* somehow essential, but beyond his imaginative reach. All he can do is gesture toward this plot beyond the plot, this unimaginable horizon, as when Ralph, perhaps the novel's most authoritative character, says that "Henrietta, however, does smell of the Future—it almost knocks one down!" (113).

Isabel's readiness for this future is suggested in her final encounter with Pansy, at the convent where Osmond has placed her. In this scene, Isabel proposes with breathtaking boldness that Pansy come away with her, and while the possibility is quickly shut down by Pansy's hopeless subjection to her father, it is worth noting that this other plot, the plot James can't or won't let happen, is again a plot between women. At the same time, the loss of this plot means that any fantasy of a future with Henrietta will likely feel incomplete if it leaves Pansy to her plight. But is this not the most insidious patriarchal ploy, to trap women in personal commitments, in the very emotional ties they have come to depend on? After all, one thing Osmond makes sure of is Isabel's interest in Pansy. In fact, this interest figures as the final touch of Isabel's seduction when, after their initial weeks together, Osmond has her visit Pansy on her way out of town. Thus, however sympathetic Pansy is, she is also the final iron link in Isabel's chains of mimetic desire. There is no easy way out of this dilemma, but the best advice James can provide may come from Osmond's sister, the Countess, who tells Isabel not to worry too much about Pansy: "Don't try to be too good. Be a little easy and natural and nasty; feel a little wicked, for the comfort of it, once in your life!" (582). Strangely, to resist a sadistic reading may be to license a little ruthlessness in others, particularly in female characters, the regular victims of masculine sadism. While Isabel, Emma, and Mrs. Elton certainly present a range of female behavior, judging them can no longer be our most pressing task. Feminism might insist instead that future readers of the British Novel become better gossips, learning to take a greater interest in a female character's comfort—and freedom—than in some image of the crude or the refined, the bad or the good, or simply "the way things were" that she is made to represent, one that somehow always seems to require her massive suffering.

CHAPTER 2

Letters to *Clarissa*: The Fantasy of a Female Network

At a distance, female networks are at once more important and more vulnerable than face-to-face gossip. No text could make this case more persuasively than Samuel Richardson's enormous epistolary novel *Clarissa*, which sustains interest for the bulk of its 1,500 dense pages by representing the vitality of a single female correspondence against a series of threats. Stuck between a horrible family who would sell her to the highest bidder and a charismatic suitor who cannot be trusted, Clarissa Harlowe's only links to the world outside this tug of war are her letters to her friend Anna Howe, and no one in the novel fails to understand the importance of these letters. Her family attempts to censor their content and eventually to stop their production altogether, and the ultimate threat eventually comes from Lovelace, the notorious rake who will make Clarissa his prisoner. Forging a letter in Anna's handwriting, Lovelace has "Anna" tell Clarissa that she thinks Lovelace will finally behave honorably and marry her, thus threatening the network from within by simulating the essential function of screening suitors that we saw in my discussion of *Moll Flanders* and *Persuasion* in chapter 1.[1] In the face of all this opposition, Clarissa is by no means passive; her countermeasures include a full range of tactics as well, from stashing spare writing materials to employing secret messengers. Thus a great deal of the plot of *Clarissa* is simply about the struggle to write in hostile territory, with each letter taking on the status of military intelligence.

But for a writer as prolific as Clarissa, letters must be understood as going well beyond tactical considerations. They are indeed the space of her life, insofar as she is able to sustain it in any positive sense, where her fantasies can escape circumstances that so painfully contradict them. Lovelace is a tremendously prolific writer himself, and his fantasies, which include a famous metamorphic dream and an elaborate conceit about murdering his conscience, certainly flourish under the

34

conditions of epistolarity as well, conditions defined first by the expectation of privacy and second by the experience of waiting at a distance.[2] In Bernhard Siegert's materialist analysis of letters, the invention of the fold leads to the invention of privacy, which in turn leads to the invention of the soul. The soul comes about, in other words, as the hallucination of interiority, as the essential figure of a postal ideology custom fit to justify the material conditions of privacy. But what does the soul do while it waits for the next letter? In the long gaps between letters the materiality of writing (pens, ink, paper) and sending (envelopes, seals, messengers) disappears for the lonely epistolary subject. Indeed many writers, Clarissa Harlowe among them, fill this void by getting out their supplies and writing some more. Reading the novel, of course, we can't do this. Our curse as readers of epistolary fiction is that we can't write back. And yet, as the critical record shows, we try. It is the law—or perhaps the anarchy—of letters that we fill the gaps in space and time with fantasies that go well beyond the compulsory rediscovery of the soul.

I would like to offer a reading of *Clarissa* that is more faithful to the fantasy space of epistolary suspension, and indeed to the formidable length of this novel itself, which necessarily dramatizes the speculative richness of the unfinished condition for a sizeable chunk of the reader's life. Following Dorothy Van Ghent's eminent lead, *Clarissa*'s critics have been preoccupied with the conclusion, focusing most attention on the bitter circumstances of the heroine's demise as if that were all Richardson's remarkable novel had to offer. Van Ghent opens her account by drawing a contrast between *Clarissa* and *Moll Flanders*, noting that *Clarissa* seems to proceed with far less action and "very little subplot." (45–47). Van Ghent is surely right to see great differences between these two early novels, but her description obscures a key feature of *Clarissa*: the fact that this is a novel that devotes enormous (perhaps unequaled) space to considering different plots, to speculation. The actual plot seems so meager not because *Clarissa* isn't about plotting, but because most of the plots in the novel remain unrealized, as indeed we should expect from the epistolary form. Unlike the typical narrator of later novels, a letter-writing character looks forward with as much ease as she looks back, and indeed a difference along these lines has not gone unnoted.[3] Picking up on Lovelace's famous claims of writing "lively, present-tense" (882) accounts "to the moment" (721), critics have focused on the immediacy of writing in the letters and the lack of secure reflection available to the characters as they narrate events.[4] But less attention has been focused on how heavily *Clarissa* is invested in the future tense. Representative is Anna's much-quoted daydream: "How charmingly might you and I live together and despite them all" (133). As the characters look to the future, so doubtless does the reader, producing a reading experience that has as much to do with speculation as it does with attending to the words on the page.

In its structure as a "double yet separate correspondence" (35), the novel's three principal fantasists are Clarissa, Anna, and Lovelace, though indeed there are others. Belford, Lovelace's correspondent, is a conspicuously reluctant fantasist, and indeed his continual failure to act can be seen as a rather damning indictment of passive, nonspeculative reading, of just waiting to see what happens. Among the other characters, first and foremost is Clarissa's brother, James, whose greed sets the plot in motion as Clarissa seeks an escape from marriage to the repulsive Solmes. In James's "happy ending" Clarissa marries Solmes, adding wealth to the family estates and confirming James's status as the *de facto* head of that family. This inaugural fantasy of Clarissa's future generates a plot that is precisely a fight for that future, as she so clearly sees: "I should not give up to my brother's ambition the happiness of my future life" (105). Early on, though, Clarissa's own tendency is to resist fantasizing altogether, for her epic struggle with her family has less to do with realizing any specific alternate future than with a simple refusal, the right to her "negative" (307). Not unlike Isabel Archer, to whom she is sometimes compared, she seems to find fantasy oppressive in part for its concreteness, the way in which it forecloses other possibilities.[5]

But fantasy is never really absent from Clarissa's life as she reports it. Rather, it is distorted into a death wish that would seem to be a kind of anti-fantasy, representing the desire for absence above all else. Already in her first letter Clarissa is contemplating death: "I have sometimes wished that it had pleased God to have taken me in my last fever, when I had everybody's love and good opinion" (41). Consider, however, the progression of Clarissa's fantasy life as her family besieges her:

> About Solmes: "I had rather be buried alive, indeed I had, than have that man!" 101
>
> To Solmes: "I will even consent to enter into the awful vault of my ancestors, and to have that bricked up upon me, than consent to be miserable for life." 305
>
> Clarissa's dream: "[Lovelace] stabbed me to the heart, and then tumbled me into a deep grave ready dug, among two or three half-dissolved carcasses; throwing in the dirt and earth upon me with his hands, and trampling it down with his feet" 342–43

The language grows steadily more specific and detailed, suggesting that her death wish has more content than a simple desire for absence. In fact it offers a clear psychic economy, allowing her to avoid imagining her "future life" without giving up imagination, to assert her social negative while reveling in the force of her prose. And indeed this economy may serve a more directed psychic function. Tania Modleski has pointed out that "death can be a very powerful means of wreaking vengeance on others who do not properly 'appreciate' us" (*Loving* 18), and several critics echo her in attributing revenge fantasies to Clarissa. Moreover, when communicated to her oppressors, these fantasies become threats—rhetorical acts in a strategy of resistance. If Clarissa is going down, she lets the world know, she is taking others with her.

It is Anna who dares to entertain more positive fantasies: "If you allow of it, I protest I will go off privately with you, and we will live and die together. . . . London, I am told, is the best hiding-place in the world" (331). When Clarissa rejects this idea and falls under Lovelace's power, Anna steps up her efforts to imagine a way out. Her most ambitious plan summons the figure of Mrs. Townsend, a great smuggler who, Anna promises, can whisk Clarissa away with "a whole ship's crew at your devotion" (622). Much like Clarissa's fantasies, this one grows over time, so that when Anna again presses the issue she writes: "[Mrs. Townsend] is sure she can engage them, in so good a cause and (if there be occasion) *both their ships' crews*, in your service" (860). Here is an early and prime example of a female network imagined as a response to patriarchal oppression. In this fantasy of multiplying sailors, men of course play a part, but only as a sort of vague mass—a malleable supply of power and pleasure. It is the women who recognize the problem, find the solution, and mobilize the resources. Beyond the level of plot and character, though, this fantasy points to Anna's role as Clarissa's main correspondent, her main reader, and reveals the way she shares that role with the reader of the novel. As I have argued in chapter 1, reading itself is a crucial site of female networking. To read *Clarissa* as if in a female network is to fill letters—and the gaps between them—with wildly generous fantasies.

Many critics have cautioned against this practice. Hilary Schor, for instance, argues that in fact "we can't think (any more than can Anna) of ways to save her—or at the least, of any she would accept as liberation . . . her vigilance over her virtue acts as a control even on readerly imaginations. Our desire to see her escape becomes a threat, a dismissal of her desire to become 'a Clarissa'" ("Notes" 104–5).[6] I have my doubts, though, about whether what Clarissa becomes—the singularity forged by Lovelace's savage and protracted tests—can be said to be what she set out to be. To be sure, what is so attractive about Schor's reading is the way the novel becomes a kind of double experiment, so that the endless testing of Clarissa by her acquaintances is equally Clarissa testing them, testing moreover the common sense of her entire society. Such an active Clarissa is my kind of Clarissa. And I can't help but agree that we tend to fail her with our imaginary female networks, though surely the problem is too little rather than too much imagination. Indeed, Clarissa the experimenter may wear the same hat as Clarissa the fantasist after all. If we describe what Clarissa tests as "expectations," these must be derived not only, as Schor observes, from dead maxims and proverbs, but from a vibrant inner life that makes them matter. No science without fantasy. And what is crucial finally to recognize is that, while the gothic plot that confronts Clarissa as so much unwelcome data is not an experiment of her design, it does interrupt one—Clarissa's ongoing experiment in female friendship with Anna Howe. It is there that she explores a condition of "permeable" selfhood that Schor locates with the reader but not with the later Clarissa of tested singular integrity ("Notes" 112).

Female friendship announces itself loudly in this novel—so loudly, in fact, that there might be a tendency to mistake it for a form of politeness or wishful thinking. Lillian Faderman's scholarship, however, persuasively situates this type of rhetoric within an important tradition of what was called "romantic friendship."[7] Her point is that claims of intimacy should be taken at their word—that is, to dismiss them as the showy language of a sentimental culture is to miss the profound bonds women often formed with female friends. Taking this rhetoric seriously, then, we can go beyond affirming these relationships to inquiring about their cultural status. I want particularly to consider how their metaphors reveal a certain fantasy of subjectivity—one at odds with the emerging individualism of the eighteenth century that Ian Watt has described with reference to this same novel. He in fact sees Clarissa as "The heroic representative of all that is free and positive in the new individualism," though we should emphasize that, as with Isabel Archer, these qualities are something of a lightning rod (222). Beginning with her inheritance from her grandfather, who singles her out in his will, Clarissa's distinguishing traits attract the predators who cause all her problems. And the danger is that we could become one of these predators ourselves if we take her character as nothing but the place to stake our claim on female virtue.

But Watt's claim for Clarissa's individuality comes in the same breath in which he declares her "without allies," strangely ignoring the one great alliance that draws so much attention in the novel. He seems interested in letters mainly as a formal problem for Richardson, and therefore less in terms of how they define Clarissa as an epistolary subject. But it is precisely our sense of Clarissa in alliance with Anna Howe that complicates Watt's theory of individualism. Anna is the novel's most committed anti-individualist, as a short list of quotations should make clear:

> "When your concerns are my concerns? when your honour is my honour?" (40)
>> "We have but one mind between us." (131)
>> "If it be possible, *more* than *myself* I love you!" (356)
>> "Let your Anna Howe obey the call of that friendship which has united us as one soul and endeavor to give you consolation." (577)
>> "[Clarissa] is my soul!—for I now have none!—only a miserable one, however!—for she was the joy, the stay, the prop of my life! Never has woman loved woman as we love one another!" (1045)

The feeling, moreover, is clearly mutual, as in these lines from Clarissa:

> "You, my dear, who are *myself*, as it were." (236)
>> "That sweet familiarity, which is one of the indispensables of the sacred tie by which your heart and mine are bound in one." (359)

"The more than sisterly love which has for years uninterruptedly bound
us together as one mind." (1163)

"[Anna,] whose love to me *has passed the love of women*." (1338)

The language of these friends is saturated with terms of sharing and merging on almost every rhetorical level imaginable, whether social ("honour"), bodily ("heart,"),
or spiritual ("soul"). Moreover, such language may be contagious, infecting critical discourse as in Terry Eagleton's description of Anna as "part of Clarissa's own
unconscious," or Christina Marsden Gillis's idea that the correspondents are "two
sides of a split personality: one soul" (78; 121). Lovelace himself fears this merging
phenomenon, though with his usual resisting irony: "And why should it be thought
strange that I, who love them so dearly, and study them so much, should catch the
infection of them?" (790). Perhaps as the rhetoric spreads, we see an antidote to
individualism. In the case of Clarissa and Anna, we become unable to think of one
without the other.

But this is not to say that their friendship is altogether glamorous. It is not insignificant that Clarissa's first words to appear in the novel are "How you oppress
me, my dearest friend" (41) (nor are Lovelace's first words inappropriate: "in vain").
Both characters place tremendous burdens on each other. Anna, for instance, insists on total divulgence from a friend whose exhaustion from relentless writing
will hasten her own death: "Pray inform me of everything that passes between
you and him" (407). Clarissa is at times no less intrusive or demanding: "Had you
married on your mother's last birthday, as she would have had you, I should not,
I dare say, have wanted a refuge that would have saved me so many mortifica-
tions, and so much disgrace" (524). It is no wonder that a relationship carrying such
emotional weight can sometimes feel claustrophobic.[8] Moreover, critics have been
quick to observe how the relationship eventually wanes: "After literally hundreds
of pages, Clarissa and Anna virtually cease to correspond. The friendship seems to
have written itself out—and off. . . . An explanation of this breakdown is an explanation of the novel itself" (Ostovich 158). While we should acknowledge the limits
of their friendship, then, I want to be careful not to collapse hundreds of pages of
heroic struggle against destiny into its eventual failure. We should consider more
closely the conditions of epistolary suspense that mitigate this collapse, the temporal
and spatial tricks that hold the dreaded future at a distance.

At least three moments in time are invoked simultaneously as we read a letter
in an epistolary novel: the time of the events narrated, the time of narrating, and
the always invisible but always implicit time of reading by the recipient. As a result
there is no stable "here and now" in epistolary fiction, but rather "the letter . . . may
lead its addressee freely through frames of time and space because its only context
is the state of mind that creates it" (Gillis 113). In long stretches of narration, the
effect of this instability on our reading can be somewhat muted, but self-reflexive
moments can be disruptive, as in Clarissa's frequent references to the writing and

sending of her letters. For example, when she wants to entreat her parents in full humility, she writes, "on my knees I write this letter," hoping, of course, that they will picture her in this posture when they read it (1180). A similar logic governs the way she closes a letter to Anna: "If I am prevented depositing this and the enclosed, as I intend to try to do, late as it is, I will add to it, as occasion shall offer. Meantime, believe me to be—Your ever affectionate and grateful Clarissa Harlowe" (312). Her "meantime" of course creates a paradox: Anna cannot know what she is supposed to believe in the meantime until the letter arrives, but once the letter arrives the meantime has passed. It would seem there are two ways of explaining why Clarissa writes this passage: the first is that it is written strictly for herself, for her own fantasy of an audience; the second is that it is written for Anna as a special and sophisticated kind of reader, one capable of undoing the paradox by engaging in a retrospective fantasy of being with Clarissa as she wrote the letter. In an important sense, though, these explanations dovetail in a fantasy of intimacy that each correspondent has of the other, an intimacy that envelops the reader and retards the relentless march forward.

The question of space in *Clarissa* is perhaps still more vexed, and not only because the three moments of letter writing tend to correspond to three different spaces. Leo Braudy has described this novel's diegetic space as an "almost nonvisual world" ("Penetration" 194).[9] Indeed, what has become the customary novelistic descriptions of the characters' surrounding environment is strikingly absent from the novel. Margaret Anne Doody attributes the sparseness of description in *Clarissa* to a principle of economy: "There is never any detail to distract us from the main effect. . . . The major impression here is one of enclosure" (*Natural* 193). But the deep claustrophobia of this novel produces correspondingly far-flung fantasies—fantasies of hiding in London or settling in America—that appeal in part because they invoke a vastness beyond description. What we find in *Clarissa,* then, is not simply a sense of tight spaces, but a sense that description can create a claustrophobic effect by the mere fact that it confines the mind to a specified image. To ignore this distinction is to conflate the effect of what is not described with the effect of what is. While in a given scene minimal description may indeed create a focused effect, the reader's cumulative disorientation in the face of undescribed space does not so much eliminate distraction as invite it.

We might say that virtually no space is described in *Clarissa* but that this blank space has a kind of positive value and is in fact a well-functioning nowhere, supporting the intimate fantasies of characters and readers with a narrative space as flexible and yielding as the novel's narrative time. If it is Clarissa's singularity that gets her in trouble, we should note that her correspondence creates a counterforce that makes her difficult to pin down. The stakes may increase further if we take the reader's experience as similarly elastic, for perhaps "the new individualism" has carried the means of its own undoing all along. In political terms, this sort of fantasy life may be the lifeblood of female networks. Anna's aforementioned sailor fantasies do seem to pass the tests of vagueness and fluidity, even as they focus on a clear strategic goal. Moreover, as a reader, Anna is figured as an interventionist, not detached (as Belford is for much of the novel) but involved, heavily invested in speculation about the future. Anna's reading is indeed a kind of writing, one that recalls some of Richardson's first readers and special beneficiaries of the unfinished condition, his "female coterie" who read the novel in progress, arguing all the while for an ending that would suit their fantasies.[10]

Nor is this wishful thinking necessarily so different from our work as critics. The case of Leslie Fiedler provides an interesting example, for he once made the rather imaginative assertion that "Lovelace is killed in a duel by his closest friend" (63).[11] Most attentive readers who have gotten to the end of the book will think this just plain wrong. It is wrong, to be sure, but maybe not so plainly. Perhaps Fiedler never read *Clarissa* at all. But I would prefer to imagine him less the irresponsible big shot and more like one of us, a reader who has grown a little tired by the end of what still seems the longest book in the English language and drifted off a bit. Maybe one of his daydreams seemed awfully vivid as he went to write his book, perhaps years later, and found its way into his plot summary as fact. This makes sense to me because part of me felt that Lovelace's best friend, Belford, *ought* to have killed him in a duel. It was one of my own speculations about how things might go, and in some ways I still prefer it. Instead of Cousin Morden, the largely unknown (if prophetically named) avenger, swooping in from Italy, why not Belford, a reader of Clarissa's story just like us? It would be nice to think that the ties of narrative sympathy were stronger than the novel's generally oppressive ties of blood, that Clarissa was really on to something when she argued that "the world is but one great family" and the "narrow selfishness" of familial obligation is "but relationship remembered against relationship forgot" (62). Belief in the possibility that Belford would be stirred to action on her behalf helps sustain the belief that we might have been heroic ourselves.

Such liberties with the facts can make for a good fantasy. The unkind term for this condition is, of course, *delusion*, but it is harder to be dismissive when fact and fantasy seem less distinguishable. If Clarissa's rape, as many critics claim, is at the center of both the novel and the scholarship about the novel, then this center is marked by an odd confusion, one that stems from the question of consciousness—that of both Clarissa and the critics.[12] Is Clarissa unconscious or not during the rape? Watt claims that the rape occurs "when Clarissa is unconscious from opiates," and many have followed him in this belief (227).[13] But Mark Kinkead-Weekes has countered that "The drug makes her alternately drunken and numb, but not unconscious" (230). Clarissa's description of the scene seems closer to his version:

> Let me cut short the rest. I grew worse and worse in my head; now stupid, now raving, now senseless. The vilest of vile women was brought to

frighten me. Never was there so horrible a creature as she appeared to me
at the time.

I remember, I pleaded for mercy—I remember that I said *I would be
his*—indeed *I would be his*—to obtain his mercy—But no mercy found I!
My strength, my intellects, failed me!—And then such scenes followed—
Oh my dear, such dreadful scenes!—fits upon fits (faintly indeed, and
imperfectly remembered) procuring me no compassion—but death was
withheld from me. That would have been too great a mercy!

THUS was I tricked and deluded back by blacker hearts of my own sex,
than I thought there were in the world; who appeared to me to be persons
of honour: and, when in his power, thus barbarously was I treated by this
villainous man!

I was so senseless that I dare not aver that the horrid creatures of
the house were personally aiding and abetting: but some visionary
remembrances I have of female figures flitting, as I may say, before my
sight; the wretched woman's particularly. But as these confused ideas might
be owing to the terror I had conceived of the worse than masculine violence
she had been permitted to assume to me, for expressing my abhorrence
of her house; and as what I suffered from his barbarity wants not that
aggravation; I will say no more on a subject so shocking as this must ever be
to my remembrance. (1011)

It might be reasonable to believe that Clarissa had moments ("fits") of unconsciousness, but clearly this account derives from some state of awareness, and clearly there
is more that she withholds. She has memory, but it is imperfect; she has ideas, but
they are "confused." This state of semiconsciousness is actually a tidy solution for
Richardson, letting him have things two ways: Clarissa is unconscious enough to
avoid the charge of complicity and consent, but conscious enough to remember and
narrate. In this way her status as the heroine remains intact, for, as Tania Modleski
has succinctly put it: if you are a heroine, "to be alive and conscious is to be suspect"
(*Loving* 52). Indeed the account's very vagueness is something Modleski identifies as a recurrent technique in romance novels: "More specific language would
destroy the reader's complex relationship with the heroine—causing us either to
identify with her too closely or to become too detached" (42). Clarissa's memory
may be necessary too, for it motivates her decisive withdrawal from Lovelace and
the world at large, allowing the novel to get on with the business of her death, of
turning her not only into an example for "the youthful reader" (34) but also a ringing indictment of her society.

Her memory has another effect as well. After the rape is first reported, Clarissa is lost to us. It is not until 128 pages after Lovelace tells Belford "the affair is
over" that we get Clarissa's account, a structure that demands a protracted and
excruciating readerly unconsciousness.[14] Elizabeth Ermarth has remarked that

"The experience of reading *Pamela* or *Clarissa*, as compared with the continuous past-tense narrations of the nineteenth century, closely resembles the heroines' own struggles to maintain consciousness and memory against overwhelming odds" (101). Indeed, it is Clarissa who fares better in this part of the struggle. Her reemergence is impressive in many ways, but her reticence about the rape effectively separates her from the reader, shattering our epistolary intimacy. The resulting distance, moreover, should not be seen as any gain for the reader. Critics inclined to bash the romance tradition have linked this distance to Richardson's well-known pedagogical impulses, describing the movement of the novel as a readerly education away from the seductive plots and rhetoric of the romance novel toward this supposedly sophisticated new detachment.[15] But the reader's detachment at the end of the novel is more an emotional liferaft than a pedagogical achievement. If, following Anna's cue, readers tend to withdraw from Clarissa to a certain extent, they do so not because they have now graduated and learned to resist romantic fantasies, but because they have lost hope for her and must now, after what have likely been exhausting trials, resignedly invest their interest elsewhere.[16] This may ultimately be the reason for all the critical talk about Clarissa's unconsciousness: imagining her conscious is simply too horrible. Thus critics are rewriting the novel, not only in a way that matches their missing experience but in a way they can bear.

To read on to the grim conclusion of this novel is to kill the fantasy of a female network in both its aspects: we must give up plotting to save Clarissa just as we give up our readerly intimacy. Female correspondence wanes in favor of letters between men. Thus if we resist a reading that would fixate on the novel's conclusion at the expense of other interests, we must nonetheless concede that such fixation is exactly what Richardson comes to ask of us, that *Clarissa* disavows the female network that has sustained it. In Lovelace's words, we are "all *Belforded* over" (823), left to witness the spectacle of Clarissa's death and its aftershocks largely through Belford's passive, worshipful eyes. As Raymond F. Hilliard suggests in his provocative article "*Clarissa* and Ritual Cannibalism," Belford's role is "prophylactic," shielding us with talk of personal reform from the recognition that the novel may be "itself a ritualized cultural institution, [with] each novelist supplying at least one avatar of the female sacrificial victim and inviting readers to assume the stance of spectators, at once deploring and relishing the 'fate,' often the rape and death, of a persecuted woman" (1093, 1083). Hilliard understands this ritual as a bridge between the psychological and the social, substituting a cannibalistic spectacle for "the original desire to devour the mother" (1094). This conception leads him to portray the female characters of *Clarissa* as a gallery of cruel, persecuting mothers, gnashing their teeth at the daughter who would demand their sympathy. Seen in this light, the saving potential of female networks would seem slight indeed, for the older women who might offer support to Clarissa must instead sacrifice her to sublimate their own aggression. But there is a strange inversion at work in this account of the ritual, because if it is the older women who come to occupy the position of the aggressive child in the sadistic oral phase, then it must be that Clarissa is in the position of the "guilty" mother, blamed by the child for her withdrawal. Thus what Hilliard fails to make entirely clear is that, for the ritual to make sense in these terms, Clarissa must be misread as a mother.[17] The question, then, is how much this misreading is indeed the work of the novel and how much it is Hilliard's.

There is no doubt that the novel devotes considerable space to imagining Clarissa as a mother, whether in Lovelace's grotesquely vivid fantasies ("a twin Lovelace at each charming breast" [706]) or in the widespread speculation about her pregnancy toward the end of the novel. What remains doubtful is whether this fantasy is a primary one for the reader, for even if the process of sublimation obscures the role of the mother to the point where Clarissa need not (or must not) be consciously recognized as one, we must ask if Clarissa does in fact suffice, does in fact succeed in galvanizing readerly aggression. Hilliard's claim implicitly turns on this process: "The writing and reading of a narrative about a woman broken in pieces by more or less unanimous blame . . . might . . . be construed as a further communal sublimation of the primary ritual action" (1094). Does the reader blame Clarissa? Certainly some have, though only rarely to any great extent.[18] By no means, however, has there been such a consensus, and what is the status of ritual without consensus?

Perhaps the best statement of Hilliard's case would introduce something like René Girard's notion of sacrificial crisis: *Clarissa* indeed sets something like ritual cannibalism in motion, but the ritual doesn't work; "The mechanism of substitution has gone astray, and those whom the sacrifice was designed to protect became its victims" (40). Hilliard comes close to such a formulation: "Far from halting the impetus toward projective violence in the world of *Clarissa*, the heroine's sacrificial death incites a frenzied hunt for a new scapegoat, a 'chorus' of mutual recrimination" (1093). But there is a difficulty in locating the reader's stake in this ritual in that many readers have likely sung in this chorus since the beginning of the novel. It is a small one, to be sure, led mainly by Anna and Clarissa's nurse Mrs. Norton, but one that loudly deflects blame from Clarissa. Moreover, part of what characterizes the voice of protest is its insistence that Clarissa be a daughter, not a mother, as in Anna's wistful daydream: "Were I ever to marry, and to be the mother of a CLARISSA" (860). Mrs. Norton in particular is firmly established as the "mamma" in the rhetoric she shares with Clarissa, to the point where Clarissa calls her nurse her "more natural mother" (1405). Conspicuously absent from the group, however, is Clarissa's birth mother, Mrs. Harlowe, and it is her role that must ultimately illuminate the status of the mother in this novel.

Terry Castle has described Mrs. Harlowe as the novel's "original non-mothering mother," and unfortunately there is much to fuel this hostility (*Clarissa's* 98). Overcoming the sympathy she feels for her daughter, Mrs. Harlowe maintains the policy throughout the novel, as she says, to "sail with the tide" (1154), enforcing the family's hard-line position for Solmes and against Lovelace. The high emotional cost of this policy is clearest early in the novel in a series of agonizing confrontations with her daughter. On Clarissa's side, resisting her mother's pleas involves a double rejection, for she must reject not only what her mother says, but the conditions that make her mother say it; she must reject, ultimately, her mother's destiny as one acceptable for herself: "Would anybody, my dear Miss Howe, wish to marry, when one sees a necessity for such a sweet temper as my mamma's either to be ruined or deprived of all power?" (92). It is not surprising, then, that Clarissa repeatedly proposes to her family that she remain single, hoping that doing this will at least satisfy their hatred for Lovelace. Their rejection of this proposal is equally predictable. For them, a single woman represents an unfinished story, as her mother explains: "While you remain single, Mr. Lovelace will have hopes—and you, in the opinion of others, inclinations" (111). To a certain extent Clarissa exhibits what Nancy K. Miller calls the "danger of singularity," in that her efforts to negotiate seek out "a language, an idiolect, that . . . break[s] with the coded rules of communication" (43).[19] There is no way for her to mean what she wants to mean with marriage plots lurking in the wings, threatening to devour any alternatives she can devise. On the other hand, the "coded rules of communication" are exactly what is in crisis in the novel, so drastic measures are needed to prevent her enormous narrative efforts from irrupting into full meaning. Thus, as Castle points out, these early dialogues are also characterized by Clarissa's violent interruption—Clarissa's words are perceived as such a threat that they are best not heard at all (63–66).

But there may be more to be said about these conversations, particularly in those in which the interruption is a bit less one-sided:

> Let me not have cause to regret that noble firmness of mind in so young a creature, which I thought your glory, and which was my boast in your character. In this instance it would be obstinacy, and want of duty—Have you not made objections to several—
>
> That was to their *minds*, their *principles*, madam—But this man—
>
> Is an honest man, Clary Harlowe. He has a good mind—He is a virtuous man.
>
> *He* an honest man! *His* a good mind, madam! *He* a virtuous man!—Nobody denies him these qualities.
>
> Can *he* be an honest man who offers terms that will rob all his own relations of their just expectations?—Can *his* mind be good—
>
> You, Clary Harlowe, for whose sake he offers so much are the last person that should make this observation.
>
> Give me leave to say, madam, that a person preferring happiness to fortune, as I do; that want not even what I *have*, and can give up the use of *that* as an instance of duty—

No more, no more of your merits!—You know you will be a gainer by
that cheerful instance of duty, not a loser . . . For it is not understood as
a merit by everybody, I assure you, though I think it a high one; and so did
your papa and uncles at the time—

At the time, madam!—How unworthily do my brother and sister, who
are afraid that the favour I was so lately in—

I hear nothing against your brother and sister—What family feuds have
I in prospect, at a time when I hoped most comfort from you all! (92)

Of course Castle's point holds for this exchange, since on balance Clarissa is still
the one being bullied. But recognizing a pattern of *mutual* interruption allows
us to see this relationship in a different light. It is important to remember that
Mrs. Harlowe insists on her own suffering, no matter how selfish or unmotherly it
seems that she does so, because this insistence is a sign of the fundamental opposition between a mother and daughter in the social structure they inhabit. As Doody
observes, Mrs. Harlowe's "sphere of activity has narrowed to a constant attempt to
keep the peace and placate her husband," so that to her "[t]he good . . . means the
serene" (102). Married to a thick-headed man, Mrs. Harlowe has found life most
tolerable by not opposing him, and her happiness, to the extent it can be called that,
depends upon Clarissa's quiet capitulation to his will. In a way Mrs. Harlowe does
assume the position of a needy child, demanding that Clarissa sacrifice her superior independence (which is an independence not only of mind but, thanks to her
grandfather's will, of fortune) to take care of her. What becomes clear is that nobody wants to play the mother in this relationship, and with good reason. Thus we
might say that Clarissa and her mother disrupt any full articulation of the other's
point of view because this state of interruption actually suspends, if only for the
briefest moment, the greater violence that seeks to define *both* of them as mothers.
Indeed, to listen to each other's full stories would be to endure a mutual erasure—
if one finishes, the other is finished.

What the novel never succeeds in imagining is the rescue of Mrs. Harlowe—or,
for that matter, any of its suffering women not named Clarissa. *Clarissa*, we might
say, is a novel that loves only one of its daughters, finally singling out its heroine
for a destiny, and attention, that no one else can deserve. Indeed, coupled with
the Christian issue of how to transcend a bad life with a good death, such focused
interest leaves little room as the novel nears the end for exploring the social conditions of epistolarity.[20] Richardson in fact explicitly disavows these interesting conditions in the postscript, describing the plot merely as "a variety of incidents sufficient
to excite attention . . . so conducted as to keep the reader always awake," and not
to be confused with matters of higher purpose: "The story was to be looked upon
as the vehicle only to the instruction" (1499). Feminist critics have nonetheless read
Clarissa's death in a way that makes her more than saint or scapegoat. Hilary Schor,

for instance, claims that by choosing "writing and death," Clarissa "fights for a fuller version of subjectivity" ("Notes" 105, 110), while Elisabeth Bronfen argues similarly that the "aesthetically staged performance of death" provides "control and power" (*Over* 141). Death affords access to new genres (the will, the epitaph, the eulogy) and new media (the coffin, the gravestone, and, as Bronfen points out, the corpse itself), many of which Clarissa makes use of. Such resources indeed allow Clarissa's monumental experiment to continue beyond the grave. My concern, though, which both Schor and Bronfen acknowledge, is that we take care not to continue blindly with *Richardson's* experiment, for if he has succeeded in turning Clarissa into a shining example, it is nonetheless an example that is literally and obviously unlivable.

The conclusion "supposed to be written by Mr. Belford," which reports on the fates of most of the characters, reveals nothing of an emerging feminist consciousness. Mrs. Harlowe dies a perfunctory death about two and a half years after Clarissa, while Anna tamely marries Hickman, a suitor who, despite his canine loyalty, is no intellectual match, and whose erotic credentials would never pass muster in an Austen novel. The conclusion ends oddly with Mrs. Lovick, a character so minor as not to merit an entry in the list of forty-one "principal characters" at the beginning, and whom we have had little opportunity to care about for her own sake. It seems her value lies in the kind attentions she pays to the dying Clarissa, and, as the conclusion has it, in her ability to persevere in a motherly role: "the worthy Widow LOVICK continues to live with Mr. Belford; and by her prudent behaviour, piety, and usefulness, has endeared herself to her lady, and to the whole family" (1494). Thus this novel so deeply restless about female destiny finally settles on the most banal of characters, as if all we have to wish for is a society that would produce more mothers like her.

And yet there is a way in which ending with Lovick points to other possibilities for women, affording a glimpse of novels that Richardson did not write but that he helped make imaginable. As a widow, Lovick represents her culture's most accepted model of female independence. She has gone through the narrative dead end of marriage and come out the other side, and there is a latent implication that new stories could await her, however little energy goes here to pursuing them.[21] It is, moreover, Richardson's own apparent need to recuperate motherhood that brings *Clarissa* to this threshold and holds it back. Indeed Norton, the novel's other favorite mother, is also a widow, as if women must actually be freed from marriage for healthy mothering—though not yet other things—to take place.[22] Their example brings Mrs. Harlowe's abjection into sharp relief, since family relationships may actually be the first enemies of female networks insofar as they generate conflicts of interest among women's closest contacts. When it is finally time to stop reading *Clarissa*, therefore, and pursue a female network in another novel, the next version of the heroine will frequently be an orphan.

In the Shadow of Clarissa

To read Frances Burney's *Evelina* after *Clarissa* is uncanny in that the later novel could be taken for a strange continuation of *Clarissa*, a projection into an alternate fictional future (*Clarissa: The Next Generation*) defined largely by the same issues and roles but with an urgent sense that things must turn out differently. We could indeed mount an impressive case that *Evelina* was, in fact, an explicit continuation and revision of *Clarissa*. The form, of course, remains epistolary, and the basic outline of the story is the same: a heroine entering the marriage market must struggle for virtue (and with a desire she cannot admit) in the face of a relentlessly hostile—and relentlessly seductive—world. The backstory of *Evelina* carries the resemblance further: facing the prospect of a forced marriage, Evelina's mother (Caroline Evelyn) eloped with the libertine Sir John Belmont, married him privately, and became pregnant, only to have him deny their marriage when it brought less financial gain than he expected. Bitterly disappointed, Caroline grows weak and dies giving birth to Evelina, whom Belmont never acknowledges. The similarity between Caroline's and Clarissa's story is unmistakable until Evelina comes into the picture. Evelina, in other words, is very much the daughter that Clarissa would have had if all the rumors of her pregnancy had proved true.

The two novels are, moreover, clearly written in the same idiom, as *Evelina* frequently echoes *Clarissa*'s concerns in nearly identical language. For instance, I challenge readers to guess the source of the following quotations:[23]

1. "My wish is to remain quiet and unnoticed."
2. "She sat like a cypher."
3. "Sir, vouchsafe but once to bless your daughter."
4. "Yet in what terms,—oh most cruel of men!—can the lost [heroine] address you, and not address you in vain?"
5. "In this last farewell, which thou wilt not read till every stormy passion is extinct,—and the kind grave has embosomed all my sorrows."

Indeed the similarity of language extends to the names, as Belford becomes Belmont (suggesting that there is not much difference between the rake and the rake's friend?) and Lovelace becomes Lovel. (Lovelace in fact abbreviates his name Lovel. in a letter he writes to Belford about an encounter with Morden on page 1279.) And the names Clarissa and Caroline start with C. Whether this case is ultimately convincing, however, is less important to me than that we accept the case for comparison. Regardless of whether Burney was absolutely thinking of *Clarissa* as she wrote her novel, she was responding to issues best captured by that novel—what we might call the "Clarissa problem," the problem of women writing in a world where men control the official circuits of discourse, of whether it is safer for a woman inside or outside, and finally of the status of epistolary female networks.

On the surface then, *Evelina* seems, if anything, a step backward from *Clarissa*'s unfinished fantasy of a female network: the mother is not weak, she's dead; the widow is not unrealized, she is ridiculed in harsh detail; and the main correspondence is not between the heroine and a female friend, but between the heroine and Villars, her male guardian. And certainly as a work of speculation, *Evelina* falls far short of *Clarissa*, shying away from the latter's numerous detailed fantasies in favor of vague and foreboding references to the future such as "There is to be no end to the troubles of last night" (34). Perhaps this is an inevitable pressure of casting a story as a romantic comedy—what it loses in diverse speculative energies it makes up for in the concentrated realization of its main fantasy, in this case the marriage of Evelina and Lord Orville. Of course their disparate social standing requires a detour through Family Romance, and it is here that the novel's speculative impulses enter most strongly, as when Evelina learns that someone else occupies her place as the daughter and heiress of Sir Belmont: "What a field of conjecture to open!" (315). Even then, Evelina does not spend much time investigating this field—she is, we should stress, no detective. Indeed, much of *Evelina* smells of a cover-up, from the whitewashing of Belmont's crimes to the mysterious accusations against Villars to all the letters we never see, and more is at stake in this cover-up than the feminine decorum Evelina upholds when, for instance, she writes that Orville inspires "sensations—which I dare not mention!" (334).

It seems that pulling off a marriage plot requires a policy of careful forgetfulness that governs even the most obsessive acts of memory. Consider the strategy adopted by Evelina and Lord Orville to consolidate their love:

> We have had, this afternoon, a most interesting conversation, in which we have traced our sentiments of each other from our first acquaintance. I have made him confess how ill he thought of me, upon my foolish giddiness at Mrs. Stanley's ball; but he flatters me with assurances, that every succeeding time he saw me, I appeared to something less and less disadvantage. (389)

Love—or a certain harmony of narratives—secures itself through a ritual of retrospection that subdues the errant past.[24] Evelina's appearance "to something less and less disadvantage" corresponds to her progress through the narrative of education many critics have observed, a narrative that makes the past bearable by making it necessary.[25] Once Orville did not love Evelina, but his delicate blend of confession and assurance soothes the sting of that fact by implying essentially that the unloved Evelina was not the same (educated) Evelina he now loves. All the suffering she endured as she made her way through the plot is retroactively transformed into the lessons she needed to become worthy of him.

What is also forgotten, but never accounted for, is the waywardness of her own desire. Evelina's relationship with Maria Mirvan is much like the "romantic friendship" of Clarissa and Anna Howe, with the same rhetoric of intimacy. For instance, at one point Evelina declares: "As to Miss Mirvan, she is my second self, and neither hopes nor fears but as I do" (122), and later she describes her as "the friend of my heart" (159). This intimacy could become a threat to the marriage plot if it were ever allowed enough narrative space, but there are no sailor fantasies here, because the one who would articulate them is kept silent.[26] Indeed, despite the fact that Evelina corresponds with Maria more or less continuously, we never read a letter Maria writes. As Julia Epstein observes, "There is a second novel here, over which *Evelina* rests like a palimpsest: the novel that Evelina's letters and conversations with a peer, another young woman, would comprise" (102). Thus the contrast between Evelina's letters to Maria and her letters to Villars underscores the limited view of events from his position. Indeed anything Evelina writes to Villars, Epstein reminds us, must be taken in light of her dependence and consequent need to please him.

Does a female network then lurk beneath the palimpsest? Epstein seems to think so, arguing for instance that Evelina "divulges her real thoughts and feelings only to Maria" (101). But as appealing as this fantasy of an underground network may be, we should stress that the reader never benefits much from it—on the contrary, our knowledge of Maria creates not a sense of intimacy but one of loss, of being left out. References to Maria's unseen replies, such as "You accuse me of mystery, and charge me with reserve" (255) and "I MUST own myself somewhat distressed how to answer your raillery," (259) emphasize how much goes on that we're not privy to. More important, the correspondence itself is not described as the privileged site Richardson imagined. In contrast to the fantasies of intimacy Clarissa and Anna share, Evelina stresses the distance a letter signifies: "My sweet Maria will be much surprised, and, I am willing to flatter myself, concerned, when instead of her friend, she receives this letter;—this cold, this inanimate letter, which will but ill express the feelings of the heart which indites it" (253).[27] Thus even what little we do see of this buried correspondence serves to shut us out.

In this way *Evelina* seeks to repress *Clarissa*, to resist what the older "mother novel" represents and what it leaves for its heirs.[28] In doing so, it buries much of *Clarissa*'s fantasy of a female network, but this fact does not mean that the repression of *Clarissa* can be reduced to that effect, as if to make Richardson the better feminist.[29] As we will see, Burney emphasizes epistolary distance because she places a very different value on the conditions of epistolarity and so is far less interested in solving the problem of waiting than in guarding the expectation of privacy. Thus it is worth considering what exactly Burney resists in Richardson's proto-feminism, and how this resistance forms a critique of the earlier novel.

Such a critique gets articulated with considerable directness in the preface when Burney describes what it means to follow her literary predecessors: "I presume not to attempt pursuing the same ground which they have tracked; whence, though they have cleared the weeds, they have also culled the flowers, and though they have rendered the path plain, they have left it barren" (9). The resounding weight of "barren" as the last word specifically calls to mind the childless

Clarissa, particularly in light of Burney's statement that her heroine will be "no faultless Monster, that the World ne'er saw" (8). Hardly a source of inspiration, Clarissa seems rather for Burney a specter of impossible and destructive virtue. The bar—and the price—have been set completely out of reach. If Burney cannot find a literary model that her heroine would want to emulate, then, as Margaret Anne Doody puts it, "the inheritance of woman is . . . no inheritance at all" (51).[30] Richardson's conclusion is so apocalyptic that it fails to transmit a strong sense of how to carry on. Far more than Richardson, Burney is concerned with the fate of women past the age of eighteen. A crucial example is the infamous "old lady race" that a group of Evelina's male acquaintances stage to settle a bet. This scene has been widely discussed as Burney's indictment of a cruel and misogynistic culture, though a closer look at the preface suggests that the metaphor of the race has still further resonance for Burney:[31]

> While in the annals of those few of our predecessors, to whom this species
> of writing is indebted for being saved from contempt, and rescued from
> depravity, we can trace such names as Rousseau, Johnson, Marivaux,
> Fielding, Richardson, and Smollet, no man need blush at starting from the
> same post, though many, nay, most men, may sigh at finding themselves
> distanced. (7)

If writing is a race (and a futile one at that), then perhaps the spectacle of the old lady race represents Burney's most haunting image of her own efforts—it is not hard to picture Burney as a young author imagining the mockery of her audience (indeed, this is very much the anxiety of the novel's dedication "to the authors of the monthly and critical reviews"), or even feeling that this audience, like gamblers organizing a race, entirely dictates the terms of her performance. With this idea in mind, we might read with a different emphasis: no *man* need blush at starting at the same post, but the exposure of publication may indeed prove embarrassing for a woman.

Nevertheless, Burney does, of course, enter the race, writing a novel that to most readers fits snugly enough into its tradition.[32] On the other hand, to use her other metaphor for writing, she also breaks new ground, not in any flamboyant, immodest way that could only exacerbate her exposure, but through a strategy of reserve. This strategy is most striking if we consider her early career, in which she burned her first novel, *The History of Caroline Evelyn*, without seeking publication. While the motives for this act were no doubt complex, it raises an intriguing perspective on novel writing as a solipsistic activity, one that Burney herself suggests when she claims that she wrote the first novel only "for her private recreation."[33] In this context the later decision to publish *Evelina* anonymously suggests a similar, if less extreme, withholding, setting up a game quite different from Richardson's collaborative writing process, one in which Burney knows more than her readers.

The contrast seems fundamental: Richardson imagines the reader as female and draws her in; Burney imagines the reader as male and shuts him out. Moreover, as I suggested earlier, this process does not end with the revelation of Burney's authorship, since *Evelina*'s epistolary structure and rhetoric subtly circumscribe the reader's participation in the story. Thus in an important sense Burney did not publish *Evelina*—not, that is, the intimate, uncensored *Evelina* that a gossipy novelistic culture had come to expect. And why should she, when her image of audience is a cruel man screaming at an injured old woman to get up and finish the race? Returning to this particular scene of the crime, we see that Burney also places a different kind of spectator on the scene, and this is Evelina herself—no passive Belford, but a bold, critical interventionist. When the old lady falls down, Evelina reports, "I sprung forward to assist her" (312).[34] As both the best reader and the main writer of the novel, Evelina represents an implosive narrative tendency in which writing loses its communicative dimension and becomes private, a way of talking to one's self. Like Mrs. Elton, Villars—and the reader he stands in for—remain out of the loop, even as the ending promises closure and reunion. As the readers of the final letter, we cannot be at the wedding. Indeed, whatever else a letter says, it always includes the message "You are not here." The closing sentence of the novel can only compensate for an intimacy that remains out of reach: "I have time for no more; the chaise now waits which is to conduct me to dear Berry Hill, and to the arms of the best of men" (406).

Obviously the reader's exclusion is not the only thing to be said about a novel that offers romantic pleasure of the first order. After all, as Julia Epstein points out, many readers have seemed fully convinced that they get the whole story. My point, however, is that here the whole story is finally a representation of the danger that produces reserve in women. In episode after episode of female "trials," Burney dramatizes her own frustration and terror, makes it the experience of the reader, insists, moreover, that *this* is the experience with which readers must come to terms. Most important, this experience inverts *Clarissa* in a crucial sense, as the earlier novel's claustrophobia gives way to a more pervasive agoraphobia.[35] Thus while in *Clarissa* carefully guarded interiors are the space of female fear and humiliation, in *Evelina* this space is the garden, the park, or the ditch. If *Clarissa* tells us that the scapegoat's place at the center of culture is no place to be, then *Evelina* insists it can't be worse than being outside and exposed, where the degradation, if less concentrated, is more regular. Burney briefly turns the tables in the novel's final dramatic scene, taking the principle of humiliation, as embodied by Captain Mirvan and his stylish monkey, and applying it to Lovel, the first thoughtless suitor to embarrass Evelina. As I have already suggested, revenge against Lovel sounds a lot like revenge against Lovelace, and indeed against Richardson, who in the final analysis has altogether too much Lovelace still in him, remaining committed to a narrative that reduces woman to virtue and puts her to the test. Evelina's tests, on the other hand, tell us not about the nature of woman, but about the male-dominated world—and the results are not happy. Indeed, Orville's vague benevolence remains the exception that proves the rule of masculine ruthlessness. What Burney must have wanted is something like a female post office, an underground network for women's writing free from the sadistic eyes of men. And so to picture *Evelina* in the shadow of *Clarissa* is finally to capture the frustration of a woman trying to participate in masculine culture—a culture to this day so powerfully defined by a man who, despite an enormous interest in the potential of woman, cannot finally bring himself to believe she is not a witch, until she drowns.

CHAPTER 3

Telephonic Film

The movement from letter to phone and novel to film is abrupt and demanding, both culturally (or so I've gathered) for those who experienced it and conceptually for those who now try to understand it. But it is this double shift that puts female networks to the test of keeping pace with modernity. Narrative film loves the telephone—and not just the usual suspects like *Dial M for Murder*, *Pillow Talk*, or *When a Stranger Calls*, but films that may not advertise their phones: *The Big Sleep*, *It's a Wonderful Life*, *Chinatown*. As our favorite way into the homes and offices of fictional characters, the telephone serves novelistic interest as it moves into the twentieth century, affirming that individuals are still worth watching. Our gossipy desire to know becomes a desire for the phone to ring, or to place a call ourselves, and Richardson's epistolary dream of "to the moment" narration of personal affairs is no longer laughable when the phone provides instantaneous communication.[1] We might indeed ask if the phone is not to the cinema what the letter is to the novel: the vehicle for the incorporation of multiple positions from which to narrate—the somewhat wobbly vehicle that, in its inherent vulnerability to interception, delay, misunderstanding, or disguise, dependably delivers the conditions of instability that make narrative possible.[2]

As if in exchange, film gives the phone eyes, transporting our vision to the other end of the line.[3] Consider how rarely in film we share the strictly limited vision of a character on the phone, and how often we see what that character cannot. But this visual supplement ultimately does the phone no favors, for it subjects the claims of the voice to a visual verification that could at any moment decide that the phone is not to be trusted, while reserving for the camera the authority to verify. In this respect telephonic film is less like the fully epistolary novel of the eighteenth century (for which the exact analogy might be a telephonic radioplay such as Lucille Fletcher's *Sorry, Wrong Number*, where all narrative information comes through the phone) and more like the nineteenth-century novel, with its occasional letters embedded in a larger narration capable of supervision and correction.[4]

It remains useful nonetheless to remember the letter's literary importance if we are not simply to take the presence of phones in the movies for granted as the modish furniture of the modern world, as simply one object among many in the careful composition of mise-en-scène. Of course the filmic phone has not gone unnoticed, but critics have perhaps been too quick to assimilate it into larger theories of the cinema. Two studies in particular deserve mention: Michel Chion's *The Voice in Cinema* and Tom Gunning's "Heard Over the Phone: *The Lonely Villa* and the de Lorde Tradition of the Terrors of Technology." Gunning perceptively contrasts D. W. Griffith's film about the rescue of a besieged family with its darker antecedents in French theater, unfolding a rich spectrum of narrative effects as the telephone either tortures the absent father with the dying voices of his family, or summons him home in the nick of time. By the end of the essay, however, Gunning has swept up these telephonic issues in a more general field: the phone serves as an emblem for all modern technology, while the viewer of early narrative film becomes "a switchboard operator of narrative messages" (195).[5] Chion, meanwhile, begins what he calls "a typology of telephonic figures in film," considering the various possibilities of what the viewer can see and hear of a filmed phone conversation, only to abandon the analysis as merely amusing (65). What really interests him is the "relationship between the vocal connection, umbilical cords, and telephone cords," and so the complexity of his typology collapses into a model of regressive telephony (62). All of these ideas are highly suggestive. After all, to be a switchboard operator is, against the expectations of much film theory, to be a woman, and we are reminded of the force that binds the telephone to the maternal every time our culture exhorts us to call our mothers.[6] But in letting the phone itself drift into metaphoric status, both studies allow it to recede from view just as it was getting interesting.[7] To explore the full importance of the telephone for film, we may then wish to recast the formulation of Bernhard Siegert, who has gone so far as to proclaim literature "an epoch of the postal system" that occurs "in the (self)-restraint and prolongation of the mail" (13). If the telephone replaced the letter and became the ubiquitous modern instrument for pursuing business or pleasure at a distance, and if film replaced literature as the dominant narrative form, what would it mean to think of cinema as an epoch of the telephone system?

I will argue that this question has particular urgency for feminism, for "Ma Bell's" phone system has from almost the beginning been a heavily female domain. Not only are the stereotypical gossiping housewife and teenage girl among its most avid users (perhaps most memorably captured in *The Women* (1939) and *Bye-Bye Birdie* (1963), respectively), but the twin female occupations of operator and secretary install an anonymous female network at the very heart of male telephone traffic.[8] That these positions hold considerable power and trust, moreover, can be confirmed in films such as *The Blue Gardenia* (1953) and *Bells Are Ringing* (1960), which show the female phone worker drawn into the lives of the callers she serves. Indeed, Friedrich Kittler's epic media analysis would locate the female office worker in general at the center of modern discourse. For him, though, what is most noteworthy is how the rhythm of modernity bounces its female subject back and forth between the typewriter and the cinema: "Every night the movie-continuum has to treat the wounds that a discrete machine inflicts upon secretaries during the day" (*Gramophone* 175). As striking as this pairing of film and typewriter is, in omitting the telephone it surprisingly ignores half the insight of Kittler's fellow prophet (and acknowledged influence) Marshall McLuhan: "The typewriter and the telephone are most unidentical twins that have taken over the revamping of the American girl with technological ruthlessness and thoroughness" (266). Indeed, what story of the American girl and the movies would be complete without the telephone by which she waits, and on which she makes plans, compares notes, confides her desires?[9]

The telephone and the cinema share a parallel history: born in the late nineteenth century, each achieved a certain kind of stability in the first half of the twentieth century, and each has now entered a period of mutation and complex interconnection with other technologies. For the purposes of this chapter I am interested in the middle period of relative stability, when (supposedly) movies were movies, and phones were phones. This confidence reflects nothing more than the predominance of certain uses over others, and the growth of institutions that support those uses. As we shall see, it is a confidence easily shaken. The normative model of telephone use became, of course, the private dialogue, banishing to the margins of culture such alternatives as telephonic concerts or party wires.[10] The corresponding stability in the cinema came in retrospect to be called Classical Hollywood Cinema, defined above all by the systematic effacement of the technology of production in the service of ideological interests.[11] If such critical terminology has come under fire in recent film theory, I would suggest it is nonetheless worth bearing in mind long enough to discover the Classical Hollywood Telephone, even if this theoretical object should give way in its turn. Such a conception will help us evaluate what cultural resources remain for female networking under history's most dominant cinematic regime. The task, then, will be to consider what our fantasies of the phone and our fantasies of the movies have to do with each other.

The Classical Hollywood Telephone

> *Few Americans found the telephone dramatic beyond about*
> *1910.*
>
>   *Claude S. Fischer*

The closer the telephone comes to perfection, the more we forget about it.[12] Understood as communications technology, the ideal telephone disappears into the content of the message it transmits. Moreover, it always reaches the person you want, when you want, without exposing you to unwelcome interruption. Its sound is clear. And it represents us as well as—or better than—we could represent ourselves in person, conferring advantages not unlike those of correspondence by letter, which the shy Samuel Richardson notoriously preferred to face-to-face conversation. Much like letters, telephone conversations seem more subject to control, and more capable of perfection, than exchanges that depend on our whole bodies. As a critic of the great epistolary novelist has put it, "anything too inert and physical, anything that is resistant to the subject is filtered out" (Warner, *Clarissa* 101). Such analysis lies in close parallel to the rhetoric of one telephone enthusiast: "The telephone was the first device to allow the spirit of a person expressed in his own voice to carry its message directly without transporting his body" (Boettinger 205). What quickly becomes apparent is how the fantasy of limitless self-extension through technology calls forth an equally idealized self to be extended.

But if phones are every bit the means of self-creation that letters were, there remains a crucial difference. To be sure, the general conditions of epistolarity still obtain, for phone users still expect privacy (however foolishly) and still wait at a distance. But the difference lies in the nature of this waiting, which can no longer be attributed to the slowness of the post. It is much more difficult to fill the time of telephonic waiting with generous fantasies when it always signifies our neglect. Fantastic excuses for the nonringing phone will still appear from time to time—and we will see examples in the discussion of *You've Got Mail* in chapter 5—but such excuses rarely seem less than desperate. Deprived of the "meantime" of epistolary correspondence, the telephone can only offer attention in the strictest binary mode. Indeed, these high stakes may account for the considerable affective charge, both positive and negative, that the telephone is capable of carrying, and that allows it to erupt out of quotidian dormancy into dramatic significance.[13] Corresponding to the poles of affect, the ideal phones of Classical Hollywood Cinema speak endless messages of love and death. When a character picks up a phone, entranced viewers are prone to feel that entire worlds are "on the line," without taking particular note of the apparatus itself. This feeling suits genres that deliver love and death as a matter of course.

In fact the problem of genre builds on the problem of the heroine's singularity that we saw in the previous chapters (and will return to in chapter 6), as the phone preempts the heroine in the struggle for what she will be made to represent. The Classical Hollywood Telephone speaks singular messages, denying the forking claims of female networks in favor of generic destinies. This phone appears in full force in *The Big Sleep*, and my analysis will begin there, going on to chart a path of increasing deviation from this ideal in other films, moving from the tidy disavowal of the ideal in *It's a Wonderful Life* to the generically messy disavowals of *I Saw What You Did* and *Pillow Talk*, and finally to the utter negation of the ideal telephone in *Lady in a Cage* and *Chinatown*. Together they fill out a spectrum of telephonic culture that, in its seeming diversity, forecloses all the more forcefully on female networks, and this spectrum needs to be understood in some detail before we can appreciate the two ways out (telepathy and speed) I will show in chapter 4. As I hope will become clear, the ideal telephone is a powerful fantasy that lures women and men alike, but only men find this fantasy reliably sustained for them in the movies.

Perhaps no film deploys a more classical telephone than the notorious hybrid of romance and detective film: Howard Hawks's *The Big Sleep* (1946), in which Humphrey Bogart's Phillip Marlowe, that most idealized of male selves, dispenses love, death, and other ostensibly just desserts through his consummate mastery of the telephone. It is a well-known story that the film deviates from Raymond Chandler's novel to serve as a star vehicle for the team of Bogart and Lauren Bacall, but what remains unappreciated is the role the phone plays in promoting this fantasy.[14] The main changes from novel to film were a plot more flattering to the couple of destiny, and more scenes for Bacall, two of which involve important phone calls. In the first, Bacall's character (Vivian Rutledge, née Sternwood), blackmailed over a compromising photograph of her sister, comes to Marlowe's office to discuss what to do. When he asks why she didn't go to the police, she calls his bluff and picks up the phone. As she is about to identify herself to a cop, Marlowe grabs the phone and begins talking a game of nonsense, passing the phone to his "mother"—Vivian— who now willingly carries on the game (see fig. 3.1) To be sure, this game calls more attention to the phone than we might expect from my definition of the classical ideal, flirting with the radical telephonic possibility of fluid identity. But it is

Figure 3.1 Humphrey Bogart controls the telephone in *The Big Sleep*.

important to keep in mind that the game's nonsense in no way competes with the sense of the scene, which remains singular and entirely in Marlowe's control. To clarify that meaning, the scene continues with Marlowe's announcement to Vivian that, as a reward for her participation, he is "beginning to like another one of the Sternwoods." Thus the telephone ushers in the love plot, though not in the equal way many have claimed for the film, as Marlowe entirely sets the terms of the game he initiates and concludes.[15] If anything, Vivian's romantic eligibility lies in her capacity to appreciate his abilities and follow his lead.

This point is confirmed by the other important phone call that Hawks adds, by which Marlowe arranges the final encounter with the gangster Eddie Mars, deceiving him about his location to set up a deadly ambush. Here Vivian's role is reduced to that of redundant commentator, reflecting back to Marlowe—and the viewer—the obvious fact that he is "taking an awful chance." Indeed, for Marlowe and other classical heroes, using the telephone is a high stakes game. But a critical look at *The Big Sleep* can show us precisely what disappears into the intimacy of the classical phone: any sense of what might be at stake outside that intimacy. Not only will Eddie Mars join the long list of casualties at the film's end for reasons that look a lot like personal revenge, but the film also achieves its final coupling at the expense of the bad half of the Sternwood sisters, since Vivian's loyalty must be pried from her sister, who will be institutionalized.

Gerald Mast has called the telephone the "perpetual means of telling lies and spinning strategies in the film," but I should again stress that this fact makes the representation of the telephone no less idealized, for its potential threats to the narrative's double generic program are always diffused (294). When Vivian twice attempts to deceive Marlowe over the phone, for instance, he is not fooled. Never jeopardizing his control of either the romance or detective plots, the phone is Marlowe's friend. And so this happy partnership is one of mutual cover. As an audience, we can forget that Marlowe needs the phone to be master of his situation, and we can forget that our fantasy of an ideal phone needs the marvelous Marlowe as a front. Leaving us to our fantasies of mastery, the telephone goes quietly about its business.[16]

We might say that with the Classical Hollywood Telephone there is a very powerful way in which the medium is indeed the message, in that when we see a character grab a phone in a movie, the fact that she has picked up the phone potentially tells us more, without any thought on our part, than whatever she has to say. It tells us that the scene is receptive to the singular messages of genre, signifying in turn a character's availability, or her vulnerability. In other words, when the phone disappears from notice, it returns as the repressed to exercise a far more powerful and economical narrative function. My claim is that the economy achieved by forgetting the telephone, seductive though it may be, is therefore achieved at high cost, and that necessary critical gains can be made by calling attention to the phone and breaking the spell.

Indeed, as we will see more fully in chapter 4, some films tell us a different story about the telephone if we know how to listen, reminding us above all that the phone traffics in *coincidence*. I don't mean by this just the common telepathic sensation of calling someone only to have her say something like "I was just about to call you." Even if we routinely plan calls, subjecting them to all the rationalized coordination of clocks and time zones, we must understand each call as being ripe for the occurrence of multiple, contingent events. We could dial a wrong number, or pick up a neighbor's call, or simply get disconnected. And when everything goes right with the phone itself, there is still the question of controlling our immediate environment, for despite our breathless concentration, enhanced by phone booths and cued in the movies by the close-up, we are not just a mouth and an ear when we talk on the phone.[17] Our whole body remains open to an unpredictable world, to noise, interruption, assault. Nor is our participation in physical space merely passive. Indeed, to describe phone conversations as only "point-to-point" communications belies the very nature of sound, for of course we cannot easily confine our voice to the mouthpiece. It will tend to bounce around the room, subjecting us simultaneously to the hazards of disturbing others and to eavesdroppers—an enormous issue even before we consider the extension, the party line, or the wiretap. But while this openness might seem scary—will indeed be strenuously made to seem scary by some films—it presents much-needed alternatives to the closed circuits of masculine meaning. Indeed when films notice coincidence, they risk giving away the secret tryst between male-dominated cinema and the ideal telephone. But as we shall see, sadly, this risk can be assumed if a film is prepared to disavow its own telephonic sophistication. Such is the case in a film with which any discussion of Classical Hollywood Cinema must come to terms, Frank Capra's *It's a Wonderful Life* (1946).

In *It's a Wonderful Life* destiny arrives through the telephone. Famously torn between desire and duty, adventure and community, George Bailey has his fate sealed by a remarkable phone call that interrupts a stormy visit to Mary, the woman he loves but so desperately does not want to marry. As romantic phone calls go, it is hardly typical. Instead of protecting the privacy of the romantic dyad, this telephone call opens up to no fewer than four major parties—George and Mary sharing an old-fashioned phone, her boyfriend Sam in New York, and her mother eavesdropping on and off the extension upstairs—all talking at cross-purposes.[18] Mary wants to marry George, but her mother wants her to marry Sam. Sam wants George to invest in soybean plastics, while George wants nothing to do with any of it. If anything, of course, this cacophony is far more erotic than the typical telephonic duet: for George mimetically because of the confrontation with his rival, for Mary because of the dependably stimulating effects of maternal disapproval. And of course it is above all the old phone technology, with its separate transmitter and receiver, that allows them to share the conversation and thus stand so close together. As the scene's erotic intensity overwhelms the couple, the phone literally drops out—we hear it bang on the floor and then George launches into his passionate denial turned embrace. In fact the scene represents a triple rejection of audio technology in all its voices, beginning when Mary smashes a record before answering the phone, and ending with George's refusal of Sam's offer, "the biggest thing since radio."

Thus the telephone both puts George in contact with what might have been and represents the alternative that must be rejected. That is to say, George not only hears the voice of the big city over the phone, the phone becomes the emblem of that voice, particularly as we notice that Sam speaks on a more modern phone (the one we have come to know, with receiver and transmitter in one unit) and has two telephones to spare on his desk.[19] In case we miss this detail in the short and single appearance of Sam's office on screen, the pattern repeats: the phone George uses in the Bailey Bros. Building and Loan is also old-fashioned, while the evil banker Potter issues his threats and directives from a modern phone. And yet some sleight-of-hand is at work in establishing this low-tech bias. After all, the only character to demonstrate more than a naive awareness of the telephone is Mary, with her keen sense of how to manipulate the positions of multiple listeners. But this female agency is dangerous to a story bent on proving only the vital importance of George, as is the mere fact that Mary also has choices to make over the phone. A full recognition of George's debt to the powerful alliance of the telephone and female agency is intolerable because that alliance itself is intolerable, for if in *It's a Wonderful Life* the telephone represents the siren call of the great modern world, then Mary must be the opposite, standing for the redeeming hearth and home of a bygone age. It finally takes nothing less than the film's Dickensian magic to convert Mary from a trap into a reward, for it is only in the vision of her as a spinster in a world without George Bailey that she is the dependent he needs to imagine her to be.[20] Unthinkable in this film is a female network that would rescue her, because that would require her to have interests beyond George. George's disavowed debt will nonetheless continue to accrue, for it will be Mary's quiet rallying of support, beginning with a phone call to her uncle, that achieves George's financial rescue behind the scenes while Clarence the wingless angel rescues him spiritually.

At the end the film does acknowledge communications technology, but only in the form of Sam's telegram from London: a generous loan offer reduced by the town's outpouring of support to a kind of redundant homage to the "richest man in town". This putting of technology in its place prepares us for the ultimate fantasy of a perfectly idealized—and archaic—telephone that speaks only one message. As George comes to learn, "Every time a bell rings, an angel gets his wings." In such intimate contact with a divine elsewhere, George can finally lay down his travel brochures. Thus the film concludes, like its great television rival, *The Wizard of Oz*, that there is no place like home, and we don't need E.T. to tell us that this message comes not from heaven but from science fiction and the telephone system.

Dial in Generic Confusion

If *It's a Wonderful Life* is science fiction cleverly disguised as melodrama, then the telephone, we might say, is the giveaway, the telltale object that must be hidden for generic satisfaction. Indeed whatever temporary alliance the cinema may achieve with the phone is always apt to be undermined by the phone's versatility. The vast channels of female networking opened up by the telephone put enormous pressure on romance in particular, the genre whose function historically is to regulate the necessary but risky business of setting a woman in motion, so as to transfer her from her father's to her husband's house.[21] Many cultural fear tactics go to making sure that a woman's one fully sanctioned journey is speedy and straight, lest she never find her way to her proper place. So perhaps it is not surprising to find a cinema that regulates telephonic romance with a "healthy" dose of telephonic terror, and to find that the intensity of this regulation increases in direct proportion historically to gains in women's mobility. I want to single out two films on the cusp of the social upheaval of the late 1960s for their strange mixings of comic romance with much darker elements: William Castle's *I Saw What You Did* (1965) and Michael Gordon's *Pillow Talk* (1959). Generally speaking, of course, generic alchemy can produce a great deal of narrative energy and critical perspective. What concerns me about these films, however, is that their wild energies give way to abrupt closure, foreclosing the space of telephonic coincidence in which feminism can take hold. The critical value of whatever generic parody we might discern in this abruptness must be weighed against the cost of these narrative resolutions—in both cases the phone, as the agent of generic contamination, gets repressed, and with it any sense of the female characters' independence and well-being. We should not applaud a hybrid genre when the point of the hybridity is at once to menace women and to deny that it is doing so.

I Saw What You Did (1965) is obsessed with the phone, and one of the most wonderfully tone-deaf films I can remember seeing. Its off-key effect comes from a seeming inability to decide if it is a light teen-comedy or a vicious horror flick, an indecision betrayed by a rapid oscillation between the two moods, as cued especially by some very obtrusive music. To be sure, the combination of horror and comedy is hardly unusual, but here the confusion can be seen to achieve some disturbing cultural work. In this film Libby, a teenage girl, invites her friend Kit to spend an evening with her and her little sister Tess at their house outside of town, during which the girls amuse themselves by making crank calls. Most of the calls do little beyond possibly stirring up some marital discord, until they begin saying to their unknown victims: "I saw what you did. I know who you are." As it happens, one man they call has just brutally murdered his girlfriend and buried her body. Exposing male criminality as if through magical surveillance, the film gives a startling flash of female networking at its most uncanny. What is complicated, though, is not just the fact of this remarkable coincidence, but how the girls' response to the killer's barely contained panic resists any rapid assimilation of coincidental events into a single meaning. When the killer says he wants to meet her, Libby describes him with glee as both a "swinger" and a "sex maniac," though of course his sole purpose is to eliminate the apparent witness to his crime. Thus, in her generic confusion, Libby hears sex when the killer means murder.

This misreading sets off a chain of events that confronts Libby and Tess with the killer at the end, only to have them saved by Kit's father and a policeman in the nick of time. With the killer apprehended, *I Saw What You Did* wastes no time in reverting back to a comic tone. When Tess seems unduly upset by the consequences of this terrifying attack, Libby responds with a strange speech of reassurance: "They can fix the window. But we're not going to be using the phone for a long, long time." By the time she speaks the word "phone," a smile has spread over her face and her tone is again that of innocent teenage mischief. As soon as she delivers the line, the two immediately prance off to the return of the comic music. Neither adult intervenes to correct their attitude or otherwise insist on the seriousness of what has transpired. Why is Libby so happy and shameless? Is being stalked by a killer not enough to give a teenage girl pause? Moreover, without the use of a phone, and living in a remote house, is there any reason to assume she can enjoy a successful social life? If horror vanishes with the telephone, doesn't romance as well? The film is not prepared to tell us.

A trailer for the film can perhaps shed some light on this resolution by giving us a clearer idea of what the film is selling us. In this trailer, we first see a phone book and are told with alarm that "Your name is in this book! It could happen to you!" It is strange that the phone book is made to represent the vulnerability of us all, even though in the movie it is only the *killer* who suffers, via the crank call, for having his name in the phone book. You could presumably avoid the problem of "it" happening to you by not killing anyone. Thus it would seem that this trailer is a bad fit, an advertisement for the wrong film, but in fact the very looseness of its logic closely mirrors the film's own complex representation of the telephone. For indeed if we take the phone book in a more general way as an emblem of the telephone as a rationalized system, then clearly the film as much as the trailer wants to show the dark side of this system, a network of fearful proximity to unpleasant coincidence, *and to represent that nightmare as a female network*. Thus in another sense the trailer is amazingly forthcoming about its audience. What "could happen to you" is that your crimes against women could be exposed by uncanny female networks.

The trailer ends with a series of ringing phones, then another, more fundamental displacement: "Don't answer it—see it!" As revolving pronouns continue to proliferate, the telephone becomes identified with the film at the same time as we

are prepared for the correct choice of movies over phones. The telephone then becomes the scapegoat of the film, its banishment at the end in Libby's speech meant
to restore a happier teenage world, one in which girls can safely leave their homes
to spend disposable income on horror flicks (though how will they make plans?).
In this sacrificial economy, two things remain sacred: happy-go-lucky, movie-going
teenage sensibility, and the movies themselves. The trailer sells in advance a story
in which the phone will become responsible for the film's own excesses. But the
unredeemed gothic side of the story cannot be banished so easily. What we saw on
the other end of the line is a story that should continue to haunt any alert teenage
girl: two women savagely stabbed in the belly—acts of raging misogyny. Moreover,
both murders are presented as triggered, if not caused, by the girls' crank calls.
Tormented by technological female reproduction, the furious man strikes back at
the site of biological female reproduction. It is as if he finds he must counteract
the displacing effects of technology—in particular his inability to maintain a desired distance from women—by marking the "place" of women as primitively as
possible. His brutality, though, merely echoes the cultural policy of a film that cuts
the girls' phone cords at the end to keep them safe from men—a severance that
I am arguing is actually, and fantastically, about keeping men safe from them. Thus
the girls' game of crank calls gives way to the boys' game of moviemaking, for one
rule of the boys' game is to cut off any unruly female communication that disrupts
the profitable recycling of meaning that we call genre. With the girls off the phone,
the lines are free to transmit genre again, though as the cinema of this era grows
increasingly alert to telephonic coincidence, it will be a struggle for films to understand their phone calls as single events with single meanings.

This struggle absolutely defines the plot and mise-en-scène of *Pillow Talk*, one
of the most popular phone films of all time, and yet a film that abandons the telephone as surely, if not nearly as cleanly, as *It's a Wonderful Life* does. The first phone
call of Gordon's film is an unfortunate coincidence to the heroine, Jan Morrow, an
interior decorator and single woman forced to share a party line with playboy song-
writer Brad Allen. Jan picks up the phone in the morning to call her office, only to
find Brad already on the line with a young woman. For him the call is seduction;
for Jan it is a provocation that offends her morals and prevents her from conducting business on the line. The call is presented in a rare triangular split screen, with
Jan's wedge dividing Brad and his prey—a strategy that emphasizes not only that
she comes between them but also the multiplication of spaces and events that com-
pete over a party line. But as the film unfolds and the phone calls add up, this
complexity is ground through the mill of romantic convergence. Jan becomes the
target of Brad's seduction and the calls are between them alone. Moreover, the now
traditional split screen reveals a closely matched mise-en-scène, suggesting a com-
patibility that sharply narrows what the phone calls can mean. It is almost as if the
phone is no longer overcoming distance, because the apartments it connects are the
same place. In any case, there are no apparent coincidences, nothing else happening

but the flirtation on the phone. This tendency culminates in the famous bathtub scene, where Brad and Jan lie toe-to-toe in perfectly mirrored positions. There is in fact a moment where Brad moves his foot and Jan draws hers back as if in response to being tickled, for an instant dissolving the split entirely and seeming to achieve a playful fusion of space and event through telephonic fantasy.[22]

But the fantasy is Jan's and Jan's alone. Indeed, Jan's ticklish foot becomes the butt of a romantic joke, and a lesson about romantic fantasy and the telephone. We laugh, of course, because Jan and Brad are *not* in the same space, however "close" she might feel him to be over an idealized phone line. We laugh at Jan, moreover, because we know something that she does not, that she is talking to Brad, the guy she can't stand. Brad has after all been pretending to be someone else—a rube from Texas named Rex—to seduce her. How can their conversation mean only one thing when there are different versions of who is talking? Nothing spoils singularity like duplicity, though indeed women would do well to take their singularity as always already spoiled by an isolating narrative culture inherited from the novel.

In Brad's case, our introduction should have alerted us not to expect sexual or telephonic monogamy from him. When we meet him, he sings, "You are my inspiration, [your name here]" over the phone to a series of interchangeable young women. Since he is a writer of romantic songs, seduction is his business, as is his use of the party line if we take his victims to be a kind of unwitting focus group. Thus from the start his phone conversations have a kind of double meaning that the invention of Rex only elaborates. Jan's telephonic needs are hard to separate as well: her business, interior decorating, is also her pleasure, rehearsing her assumed goal of taming male space through the cohabitation of marriage. But this apparent symmetry between the characters' relationships to the phone grows increasingly asymmetrical as the film invokes the ideal of a coincidence-free telephone as a naive, feminine fantasy into which even the most resistant woman will dependably retreat. It is interesting in this light that the film retains the split-screen strategy for the phone calls as the romance plot moves forward, instead of resorting to the cross-cutting so many films use to represent the characters'—and demand our—undivided attention. Through this insistent visual strategy, we are never allowed to forget that Brad's double-dealing gives the lie to Jan's fantasy of romantic convergence, and that the distance she would dream away remains open to exploitation.

What semblance of acceptable romantic closure the film does achieve becomes possible, then, only by avoidance of the telephone. Brad never has a successful romantic call with Jan while playing himself, and he must eventually bridge the distance between their apartments rather violently, by marching into her apartment, picking her up against her will, and carrying her down the street to his place in her pajamas. There is much good criticism about how Rock Hudson's status as a partly closeted gay man strains the film's romantic closure.[23] I would add only that some such strain of cultural categories should be the expected result of a film that is actually less interested in heterosexual coupling than it is in the telephone, though it will pretend otherwise. To notice the telephone, I would argue, is to notice it splitting events and making coincidences, including the wonderful coincidence described by Richard Dyer as "Here is this gay man (Roy Scherer Junior, Rock's real name) pretending to be this straight man (Rock Hudson) pretending to be this straight man (the character in the film) pretending to be a gay man (for the sequence or gag in the film)" (31). Moreover, as vexed as Brad's participation in marriage may be, it is hardly more so than Jan's. For all the rhetoric of marriage as a man trap, there is little question whose autonomy is really on the line, as captured in the fact that Jan must forever give up her dream of having her own phone.[24]

Much as in *I Saw What You Did*, there is something wrong with the tone of *Pillow Talk*: it cannot come to terms with the sinister implications of its plot. What I want to suggest is that Jan is a gothic heroine trapped in a comedy, for there is something disturbingly familiar about her situation. As E. L. McCallum puts it, "what marks Jan's singleness and autonomy more than anything is the absence of parents or kin; she is the modern subject in the urban space, ostensibly free from traditional family networks and expectations" ("Mother" 77–78). With a mother in Milwaukee and no female peers in sight, Jan lives in radical isolation from supportive female networks. Indeed, in a movie full of phone calls, Jan never talks on the phone with a woman![25] Her only female friend is her older maid, Alma, whose considerable charm (she is, after all, played by Thelma Ritter) cannot mask her role as an agent of the marriage plot, as in her definitive pronouncement: "If there's anything worse than a woman living alone it's a woman saying she likes it." Of course when we meet Jan, she is doing just fine in spite of these conditions. Thanks largely to the poise and energy of Doris Day's performance, our consistent impression is that Jan is a woman who can handle herself. She has no trouble fending off the attempts of her rich friend Jonathan to buy her love, or the more aggressive advances of a "Harvard man." But once Brad puts on his Rex act, Jan is faced with the epistemological difficulties of a gothic heroine. Her situation bears a disturbing resemblance to the classic scenario of *Gaslight*, where the husband isolates the wife and systematically challenges her perceptions. What happens to the heroines of these films can be described in terms of a denial of triangulation, of reference to the perspective of a third party who could confirm the heroine's own perceptions, and hence her sanity. Brad can forgo this process because Jan has isolated herself twice over—first in moving to the city, second in talking on the phone with him. Though verification by phone remains a resource for Jan (she could, for instance, try to contact some of "Rex's" associates in Texas), her need to believe in a romantic phone fantasy seems far stronger than any appropriately paranoid caution she might summon. Brad manipulates this self-imposed isolation with insidious cleverness, providing the illusion of triangulation by pretending to "interrupt" her calls as himself to criticize Rex, thus allowing Jan to confirm her ideas about Rex through a kind of negative verification (i.e., Brad suspects Rex, so Rex must be all right). It is this trick that ensures Jan does not recognize the gothic character of her situation until it is too late and that keeps her moving toward romantic closure.

But since this trick is not played on the audience, something else must induce us to look the other way, to trade away Jan's autonomy for generic satisfaction, if we allow the film to proceed toward closure without protest. This other maneuver is very familiar and has much in common with the tried-and-true alibi of much sexist humor: it's just a joke. And so Brad's Rex routine is just a game. But feminism has little patience for games that women don't get to play. There is, however, one joke that Jan gets to play on Brad before she accepts his proposal, and that therefore bears a great deal of weight in the film's attempt to restore some sort of balance to their relationship. This joke takes the form of an outlandish makeover of Brad's apartment into a hideous parody of the seducer's lair. But as much as we may admire this blow she strikes against the predatory male, how can it be enough? Indeed the joke is in some sense also on herself, since Brad planned to have her move in with him. More important, there are still enormous obstacles to this marriage. Put most simply, Jan knows nothing about him, except that she cannot trust him. There is therefore no way to account for our instant acceptance of his proposal except to say that we remain trapped in a maxim that Samuel Richardson set out to disprove in *Clarissa* over 200 years earlier: "that a reformed rake makes the best husband."[26] According to the logic of this hard-dying maxim, the mere fact of a marriage proposal is proof of reform. Indeed, all *Pillow Talk* offers beyond Brad's proposal as proof of his reform is another gag, letting us witness the dismissal of his comically heartbroken girlfriends over the phone—an action, moreover, that Jan is not there to witness, so it cannot count as evidence for her.

Critics have been right, however, in emphasizing that something else is going on at the end of the film, a kind of hysterical displacement that troubles the serene singularity of romantic union. In the last scene the film returns us to one of its most vexed sites: Brad's body. The scene reprises a running gag in which, thanks to a string of coincidences, an obstetrician thinks Brad is pregnant and wants him corralled for observation. Brad had ducked into the doctor's office in the first place to avoid being seen by Jan and Jonathan, their only mutual friend and therefore the one person who could blow Brad's cover. Once inside, he claims vague symptoms to explain his presence. There is a clear sense here of multiplying duplicity, of the way that lies create the need for more lies. Brad's body, moreover, becomes vulnerable to identification and abduction by the medical staff because he has lapsed into play-acting without the protection of the telephone, thereby falling victim to his own telephonic habits. But such a rational explanation won't account for the anxiety here about the proper limits of science and technology (the doctor admonishes his skeptical nurse with the declaration that "medical science still has many unknown regions to explore"). It is as if the serial displacements of telephonic promiscuity call down a corresponding—and overcorrecting—fantasy of punishment: the impossibly overembodied space of the pregnant man.

Against this literal fantasy of male reproduction, the film continually opposes a different, but still fantastic, version of Brad's body in terms of its enormous size and strength. Indeed, in an analogy that he offers his friend he comes off with nothing less than the stature of a tree:

> Jonathan, before a man gets married, he's like a tree in the forest, he stands there independent, an entity unto himself, and then he's chopped down, his branches are cut off, he's stripped of his bark, and he's thrown into the river with the rest of the logs. Then this tree is taken to the mill. And when it comes out it's no longer a tree. It's a vanity table, a breakfast nook, baby crib, and the newspaper that lines the family garbage can.

This other version of Brad's body is of course hypermasculine, with conventional castration anxiety and fear of domesticity, but it is unclear from the rest of the film how such a body will fare in an urban environment, whether it will dominate or get its branches lopped off. We see, for instance, how the awkwardness of his squeezing his bulk into a foreign sports car becomes the ease with which he slings the "Harvard man" over his shoulder, or carries Jan down the street.[27] What kind of body is this that Jan finds so attractive (her word for it is "marvelous"), and what problems does it pose for an understanding of this attraction in generic terms?

While the humor in all of these scenes may preserve the confidence of an adoring public in the myth of Rock Hudson's All-American masculinity, an understanding of Jan's predicament requires that we substitute a gothic reading of Brad's body for a comic one and that we register the menace behind the film's smiling assurances.[28] Jan's own prior assessment should be our cue as we recall her reaction to the considerate attentions of Rex: "What a relief after a couple of monsters like Tony Walters and that Brad Allen!" If her other suitors are monsters, what then is left for Jan once Brad's exposure reveals Rex as a fantasy? We might say finally that the film can't decide if Brad is Frankenstein or Frankenstein's Monster. Is he a genius of male reproduction, not only in his many incarnations on the telephone but in his own body? Or is he a cruel brute of monstrous physical prowess? Thus the film covertly raises the classic question for the gothic heroine: man or monster?[29] Since the film does little work to resolve this question, we can only wonder if poor Jan, the gothic heroine in denial, finally *has* lost her mind to accept Brad in such incoherent fashion. This bad news is finally all that *Pillow Talk* has to say about the fate of the female subject on the telephone.

Telephonic Nightmares

By the time of *Lady in a Cage* five years later, this subject would be in full retreat, an exotic—and highly endangered—species exhibited for the amusement and curiosity of predators. Walter Grauman's horrific film places Olivia de Havilland alone with a broken hip in the large house she shares with her son Malcolm, leaving her entirely dependent on technology in the forms of a cane, an elevator, and the telephone. When the power shorts out, de Havilland's character, known only as Mrs. Hilliard, finds herself trapped in the elevator between floors. The elevator is equipped with an alarm that rings outside the house, but her calls are ignored and, in fact, draw attention to her vulnerability. (This is a film that likes to make a point, and one of its many heavy-handed points is that the world is a callous place.) She soon falls prey to a series of home invasions—first by an older generation of petty thieves, followed shortly by a far more vicious young gang, who are led by a thug named Randall—James Caan in a role that makes Sonny Corleone look tame. Mrs. Hilliard eventually escapes the gang, but not before she has been subjected to an extended ordeal of equal parts frustration, terror, assault, and blame. And while the film does finally turn its sadism against Randall, running over his head with a car, his death only makes a further spectacle of Mrs. Hilliard's abjection by drawing a crowd of onlookers. We last see her sitting outside under her air-conditioner, laughing as its dripping water tells her the power has finally been restored. But as the signal that communicates this ironic message, the drip looks an awful lot like Chinese water torture. Information in *Lady in a Cage* is indistinguishable from pain.

Brutal as this film is, I want to discuss the apocalyptic discourse it mobilizes around the figure of the technologized woman, a discourse that shows just how threatening that figure must be to the forces of reaction. Much of this discourse takes the form of a generalized ambience of hysteria: a voice on the radio shrieks, "Have we an anti-satan missile? While we've been conquering polio, and space, what have we done about the devil?"; a drunk shouts "graven images!" and "repent!"; and indeed the camera itself frames the narrative proper with a series of disturbing and disorienting images, from low-angle shots of traffic to a dead dog, each accompanied by discordant sound effects. But as the story moves forward, the terms of this vague unease become increasingly well defined. "I am a human being, a thinking, feeling creature," Mrs. Hilliard protests to the gang as they take over her house, and what becomes abundantly clear is that the category of the human is under siege in this film, caught between two alien forces, the animal and the machine.[30]

It is machines that allow Mrs. Hilliard to navigate and defend her home, but that also betray her when she needs them. Not only does she get trapped in her elevator, but it is her confidence in the phone that leads her to ignore the danger in her son's departure for a holiday weekend. "I'll call Nellie if I need her, you if I need you, [the] ice company if I need ice, the coal company if I need coal, and the happiness company if I need happiness," she tells her son before he leaves, and in so expressing her assumed telephonic omnipotence, she articulates the full promise of the telephone for women. Indeed most basic is the promise of the telephone to end gothic isolation.[31] We can imagine a world in which continuous sympathetic contact among women would eliminate domestic terror. Thus in a revisionist gothic story such as Angela Carter's "The Bloody Chamber," the heroine can call home so that her mother, who intuits that something is wrong, will ride to the rescue. But the long cinematic history of telephonic terror does indeed suggest a sustained interest in throwing this security into doubt. We might say it could only be a naive optimism that drives a character such as Vargas in *Touch of Evil* to leave his wife in a remote motel on the assumption that he can keep in touch over the phone. Of course the telephonic rescue of women has been frequently represented on film (most dramatically perhaps in *The Slender Thread* and *When a Stranger Calls*), but typically only after they are subjected to a torturous experience of the tenuousness—or invasiveness—of the link. Rescue is rarely so routine as to live up to the promise of the telephone.[32] Moreover, the dialectic of the phone is such that it encourages the isolation it ostensibly alleviates, thus generating scenarios in which disconnection spells doom.

So it goes for Mrs. Hilliard. As the petty thieves ransack her kitchen, the phone rings far below her cage, where she can't reach it. When she cleverly throws a bar from the elevator to knock the phone off the hook and shout for help, the thieves simply cut the cord, greatly diminishing the possibility of rescue. Not knowing that they have done this, Mrs. Hilliard remains intent on getting to the phone, and when she finally gets her chance, the film gives us one of the more agonizing images of telephonic disconnection in cinematic history: stretched face down on the floor, she pleads desperately for the operator, only to look up (and here we share her low-angle perspective) at the ripped-out cord down the hall (see fig. 3.2). It is not the first time her hopes have been dashed by the film. One of the older thieves

Figure 3.2 The horror of disconnection.

(a prostitute named Sade) is a woman, as Mrs. Hilliard realizes by smelling her perfume. Thinking a woman might be more receptive to her appeals, there is a brief moment of hope for the trapped heroine, but this old-fashioned female networking fails too.[33] The film's geography is clear: inside the cage is the human; outside are only treacherous machines and unfeeling animals.[34]

Indeed if humans are the animals that use language, Mrs. Hilliard certainly qualifies.[35] It is as the young gang takes over her house that Mrs. Hilliard launches the film's rhetorical frenzy, calling them monsters, creatures, animals. Her distressed internal monologue reveals with some eloquence her besieged position between what she calls "our god kilowatt" and an encroaching animality: "We made cities and towns and thought we had beat the jungle back, not knowing we had built the jungle in." Randall's taunting call to his gang becomes something of a slogan for the inverted circus culture of these conditions: "Come and watch the human being be sick in a cage." And here the film enforces the raw deal that shadows the arrival of women as a class on the stage of history: women get to be human only once the human becomes exotic.[36]

When it comes time to assign blame for this dire situation, therefore, *Lady in a Cage* spurns feminist critique for an old story about the family—one that at this point in history had been circulating for some time under the name of "Momism."[37] It is a shrill cautionary tale, set amidst the ruins of patriarchy—for there is no father in this movie, only the clichéd mother whose love smothers her son, as the letter Malcolm leaves for her makes clear:

> I'll be thirty next Wednesday, and I won't have many more chances in life. Every time I try to leave you, you add a room, or dress up the house, or charm me. Give me my half of what's in the living room safe. Release me from your generosity. Release me from your beauty. Release me from your love. p.s. think it over. I'll call in a little while. Please make it yes, or quite simply, I'll kill myself.

Without the father to guarantee the human as a patriarchal category, it seems the son cannot take up his destiny. The mother's pre-Oedipal role makes her an enemy of the differentiation civilization requires.[38] Indeed, her alignment with the forces that blur distinction becomes most apparent in the moment of reading the letter. Having found it upstairs in Malcolm's desk, the gang delays killing her in order to learn about the location of the safe he mentions. Randall reads the letter aloud slowly, comparing her to his own "holier-than-anything old crow of a grandmother," in order to make a further spectacle of her life and justify the gang's crimes. As Randall nears the end of the letter, Mrs. Hilliard begins strangely to respond to him as if he were Malcolm. It is as if the pain of this sudden rift with her son (a rift no doubt widened for her by the fact that Malcolm communicates by letter) causes a madly overcompensating collapse of difference, a collapse that stands as both the cause and allegory of the film's larger crises. By the time she comes to recognize her assigned role in the film ("It's all true. I'm a monster," she says to herself), the category of the human has been fully vacated—it is apparently what happens when you replace a husband with a telephone.

When home remains unredeemed, even a working phone can reach only the uncanny. Such is the lesson for Jake Gittes, the lonely detective of Roman Polanski's *Chinatown* (1974), whose investigations begin with the wrecked homes of divorce cases and move toward incest, perhaps the most intimate crime of all. Set back in the 1930s, *Chinatown* follows on the heels of a migration of the representation of the telephone in the 1960s. No longer largely confined to the private and the domestic, the phone becomes an emblem of male paranoia and cold-war hysteria, as seen in such notable films as *The Manchurian Candidate* (1962), *Fail Safe* (1964), and *Dr. Strangelove* (1964). Indeed *Chinatown* appears just after Watergate, and in the same year as the very apex of cinematic audio paranoia, Francis Ford Coppola's *The Conversation*. At the time of its release, then, it was certainly no longer possible to sustain an ideal view of the phone, or to pretend, as in *It's a Wonderful Life*, that the phone could conveniently disappear. Indeed Polanski brings this skepticism to the project of reenvisioning the classical period through what John Cawelti has called "generic transformation." If *The Big Sleep* found a way to pursue both romance and detective work through the telephone, *Chinatown* takes up that double pursuit and follows it to a telephonic dead end.

Both the love plot and the detective plot derail because of telephone calls. When the phone calls Evelyn Mulwray out of bed with Jake, it delivers him a choice that is essentially a choice of genres: trust Evelyn, as she asks, and find love, or investigate her and solve the mystery. When Gittes continues to investigate, that route is also blocked by a phone call from the police in the middle of the night: they have found his home phone number on the wall of a murdered woman and will hound him until the end of the film. Unlike Marlowe, who kept the phone under his sole control, Gittes finds himself perpetually open to the calls of others.[39] As Avital Ronell argues in *The Telephone Book*, "The telephone belongs to the artwork both as parasitical inclusion and as its veiled receiver, the opening from which invisible vents are directed, quietly co-occupying the scene with the voices of commanding phantoms" (213). We might moreover understand these voices as speaking the law of genre, and very much in Derrida's double sense that genres are at once "not to be mixed" and subject to a prior law of contamination.[40] For Gittes, detection and romance are as irreconcilable as knowledge and ignorance; they represent two different ways of being in the world. At the same time, his investigation—in a woman's pay, into a woman's mystery—has romance as its very ground.

Cawelti argues that *Chinatown* represents generic transformation in the mode of "demythologization," pointing up the inadequacy of the myth of the private eye in the kind of world Gittes inhabits (194). What must be added is how heavily this perceived inadequacy is a result of his entanglement in feminine discourse—and not only in that the detective's use of the phone means a considerable reliance on a female workforce, but that a great part of the business of investigation looks an awful lot like gossip. Indeed, what Gittes and Marlowe share is an interest in their scandalous cases in explicit excess of their professional obligations.[41] Both continue investigating well after they have been paid and asked to stop, and Jake's nosiness is the cause of a famously literalized punishment at the hands of Polanski himself.[42] What haunts Jake's supposedly rational investigation, the uncanny lure that whispers his name through the telephone (and deems that name comically unpronounceable), is in fact the mystery of his own curiosity.

What Jake finds so fascinating is the shadowy world of female networks. The film's deepest mystery turns precisely on the problem of relationship between women, as Evelyn notoriously fails to designate the woman who is both her sister and her daughter. It shows in a world of patriarchal crime just how tangled a woman's entry into discourse can be. Moreover, Jake comes to know this world only through his own progressive emasculation: as is often pointed out, the police, agents of masculine authority, won't listen to him by the end, when it matters most.[43] What *Chinatown* cannot do is bring itself to believe in the power of female discourse. It is a film that questions profoundly the novelistic desire to know personal secrets, and the power of such knowledge to be of any real use, thus implicating not only the detective but also the culture that loves him. But perhaps the film ends in despair because it pursues a novelistic interest in personal scandal from a male perspective, disavowing the historically feminine association of this interest. The detective genre, we might suspect, was doomed to remain a political dead end until the detective, a telephonic subject and incorrigible gossip, embraced her discursive status and became a woman.[44]

CHAPTER 4

Voices Carry: Film and Telepathy

Under the conditions of high technology, literature has nothing more to say. It ends in cryptograms that defy interpretation and only permit interception.
　　　　　Friedrich Kittler, Gramophone, Film, Typewriter

The definitive film about the telephonic investigations of a woman is Anatole Litvak's gothic masterpiece, *Sorry, Wrong Number* (1948), which chronicles the last evening in the life of an invalid named Leona Stevenson. Much like Jake Gittes's investigations, Leona's proceed from, and toward, a fundamental unrest at home. Indeed for the duration of *Sorry, Wrong Number* Leona is not at home in at least two ways: from Chicago, she finds herself alone in a house in New York City, and, as a so-called "cardiac neurotic," Leona is not at home in her own body. Appropriately, Leona finds herself at home only in the state of disembodiment called talking on the telephone. The technology that mocks George Bailey for his lack of mobility compensates Leona for her far closer confinement. And yet in her insistent reliance on the phone, Leona falls into a vicious stereotype of aggressive or foolish women callers tying up the lines. In doing so, she risks alienating everyone she speaks to, and the viewer as well.[1] Indeed, despite a degree of glamour unavoidably acquired from the presence of Barbara Stanwyck, some critics have not hesitated to register their disgust with Leona—hence this film's reputation as a portrait of the controlling "Bitch Goddess," to quote the title of an article that prominently features her image.[2] Understood in the context of telephonic dependence that the film develops, this representation becomes the portrait of a cultural swindle, standing for the systematic denial of all that the telephone should mean to women.

In *Sorry, Wrong Number* gothic forces seem to overwhelm and even incorporate the phone that would ostensibly be their technological antidote. Certainly the essential trappings are all there: isolation in a big creepy house, a husband as the possible source of terror, and the heroine's investigation of that terror. The gothic, moreover, precisely defines a space where the ideal telephone breaks down, for in the recurring figure of the suspected husband, the messages of love and death become hopelessly mixed. Thus the film will not depict the phone as an extension of orderly meaning and rationality, but instead invoke a phone of the darkest superstition, one that initiates an inexorable gothic plot through the eerie force of coincidence. We are offered an image of this nightmare phone in the opening titles of the film: it is the huge, menacing shadow phone looming above its ordinary counterpart (see fig. 4.1). Litvak's film, moreover, sustains a darkness that is rare even in the gothic, for the eventual triumph of rationalism that we find in novels like *The Mysteries of Udolpho* or *Dracula* never comes. Instead, the fateful crossed line of Leona's first phone call marks the film's permanent shift to this register of what we might call a telephonic unconscious. From this moment it will be the film's main business, as carried out through Leona's relentless telephonic investigations, to try to bring us back to the light of day, to rationalize this event and domesticate the phone. But like her husband's final call home at the end, this assurance does not get through, for the film cannot finally untangle her from its telephonic nightmare.[3] The killer who invades her house on schedule appears, apart from his white-gloved hands, almost entirely in shadow, an avatar of the nightmare phone. A last-ditch attempt to bring the phone to some rational account, the husband's call, or so the voice of this shadowy killer tells us, is a wrong number.[4]

As important as this film has been to feminist film criticism, and as seriously as its phones have been considered, it has not been understood in its full telephonic complexity. The fact that most of this film's narrative information comes through a woman on the phone implicates our investment in the diegetic truth of the images

Figure 4.1 The nightmare telephone.

we see, and hence in the detective plot that seems to unfold before us. This plot begins with a shot of a phone off the hook in the office of one "Henry J. Stevenson," a shot that poses two simple questions: who is Henry J. Stevenson, and why is his phone off the hook? The second question will be displaced, and likely forgotten, in a series of more pressing questions that arise during the course of the film. The first will be quickly, if inadequately, answered by the appearance of the bedridden Leona on the other end of the line, trying to reach her husband. And while Leona now takes over the film's present, making and receiving the calls that constitute the bulk of the film, Henry's absence structures the film until he calls Leona twice from a phone booth at the end. Indeed, Henry's inaccessibility is what places Leona immediately in the position of the detective; in tracking down her husband, she pursues the questions of the film, questions that will at once take a dark and serious turn.

The plot thickens when Leona is mistakenly connected to another conversation and overhears two men plotting a murder for 11:15 that night. As a clock by her bed reads 9:23, the questions of who will die and why come to shape and intensify the film's detective structure, and hence Leona's activities. But as she tries to rescue the unknown victim, she also continues to search for Henry, calling his secretary to begin reconstructing his day. Gradually, the plots dovetail. Along with Leona, we come to realize that the murder will be her own and that her husband arranged it. We never learn why the phone was off the hook, but we learn all too well who Henry Stevenson is. Pared down to essentials, it goes something like this: Henry resents her because she took him away from his girlfriend Sally, stuck him in a token job at her father's drug company, and continued to manipulate him through continual phone surveillance and occasional well-timed fits of cardiac neurosis. When Henry tries to find work on his own, her father uses his connections to block him, insisting that Henry's only job is to take care of Leona. Desperate to achieve independence, he starts to skim from the company, gets squeezed by mobsters, and puts a contract on Leona's life to get the insurance money. To add one last great coincidence, Sally's husband turns out to be the man investigating Henry.

Leona's reconstruction of this story comes from a variety of sources: six calls that trigger flashbacks of increasing complexity, a telegram, and her own memory.[5] Especially baroque is the structure of a call to her doctor, which includes a flashback within a flashback where Henry tells his version of their marriage to the doctor, who in turn tells it to Leona, and hence suggests all the transmission problems of a game of telephone. Moreover, the flashbacks themselves already complicate this *noir* story, hinting at an ongoing Oedipal struggle in Leona's life for separation from paternal authority and maternal inheritance that makes it difficult to take Leona as simply a grasping and inscrutable *femme fatale*. The father's symbolic power is everywhere in the flashbacks, from his name on the side of a building to a shot of him hovering between Leona and Henry during their wedding; it is made manifest in the one moment Henry tries to get a job on his own, only to be squelched by her father's influence with his business associates. This pervasive influence carries over into the present tense of the film, as for instance in the prominent portrait of her father in her bedroom. Against this authority Leona's only weapon is to become her mother. Whenever she finds her desires blocked, she suffers attacks—attacks she believes come from a heart condition she inherited from her mother, who died giving birth to her. Unfortunately, this strategy leads to its own complications. Is dying during labor the ultimate female disappearing act, subsuming a woman into the role that culture assigns her? Or is it the ultimate refusal, the total rejection of the kind of responsibility motherhood entails? From a daughter's perspective, it may not matter. Dead is dead, and that is no fate for Leona to look forward to. In the second generation, then, "cardiac neurosis" takes the place of a physical heart condition as the purer symbol of a culture that diagnoses a reluctance to be a mother as a failure of heart.

Skewing this story further is an odd, almost throwaway scene that occurs before the flashbacks begin. Having just heard the murder plot, Leona has the operator connect her to the police. At the station, the phone rings and the lone officer says to a young black girl, "Maybe that's your mom calling for you"—a startling whiff of miscegenation in a film where the only black man works at the Bingo parlor, though less startling if we come to see Leona's marriage to Henry as itself a kind of taboo mixing across divisions of class. In this film, arriving when Hollywood was just beginning to represent racism, there is perhaps a hint of the power Avital Ronell describes when she claims that "the telephone has also flashed a sharp critique at the contact taboos legislated by racism" (7).[6] Here, moreover, the potential collapse of racial separation figures as part of a broader implosion of meaning under telephonic conditions. Little more than a toddler, the girl is virtually buried in random symbolic objects—a prize ribbon, a pocket watch, an American flag—that all converge at the site, or sight, of another American daughter. The problem of visual proportion in this scene captures the problem of thinking about the scale of the telephone, how it can mean either the most intimate of connections, as to one's mother, or the most remote kind of encounter across the vast physical and social divisions of postwar America. Refracting our discovery of Leona's own missing mother through a truly unassimilable coincidence, this girl breaks the circle of the film's tidy mystery plot.

With so much narrative interference, we might question then whether we should accept Leona's account of the murder plot at face value. It is this assumption, for instance, that allows *Sorry, Wrong Number* to figure prominently in Kaja Silverman's landmark study of the female voice in cinema, *The Acoustic Mirror*, which draws a contrast between two versions of Leona: the powerful woman of the flashbacks who demonstrates "symbolic mastery," and the helpless woman of the present who exhibits increasing verbal incompetence, reverting finally with her scream at the end to the infantile condition in which Patriarchy prefers her.[7] But as Amy Lawrence has argued in an extended and subtle analysis of the film, there are no clear grounds for accepting the authority of the flashbacks, for what we see and hear could be no more than a representation of Leona's thoughts.[8] Even if we were inclined to accept the flashbacks as objective, they cannot account for many of the real mysteries of the film: the flood of coincidences that defy explanation, and the uncanny feeling that investigating them is dangerous. Thus Silverman reads the film more classically than it seems to want to be read: even as her critique challenges the representation of the speaking woman, it sustains the fantasy of an ideal phone transmitting clear, singular messages. But telephonic coincidence is so central to Leona's experience on the phone this fateful night, and likewise to our viewing experience, that to overlook it is to neglect the full import of what the film is doing.

Sorry, Wrong Number is in fact a film that presents itself in terms of coincidence from the very beginning. As we look at the titles, not only do we see a phone itself doubled by its larger shadow, but we also hear a busy signal—perhaps the most basic representation of telephonic coincidence, of too much talk clogging up the system. This busy signal, moreover, seeps into the musical score, producing a corresponding instrumental echo. Returning soon with the film's first interior shots of the phone off the hook in Henry's office, this echo simultaneously evokes and refuses the illusion of matching sound.[9] Coming before we meet Leona, this tantalizing mismatch is important because it establishes an unusual dynamic between what is often called story and discourse, between the world the film evokes and the mode and manner in which that world is presented.[10] Indeed, while the story of the film, the one Leona pieces together that seems to account for her death, is shot through with misogyny, the discourse participates in something feminine, a certain saturation or busyness that worries easy listening in a male key.

This feminine discourse makes itself known in the film's prologue, letting us know what to expect for the next 89 minutes. Between the shot of the doubled phone and the tracking shot into Henry's office we see a row of female operators working a switchboard. Against this image the following epigram scrolls up the screen:

> In the tangled networks of a great city, the telephone is the unseen link
> between a million lives. . . . It is the servant of our common needs—the
> confidante of our inmost secrets . . . life and happiness wait upon its
> ring . . . and horror . . . and loneliness . . . and . . . *death*!!!

Within this fairly typical recital of telephonic ambivalence, we notice "confidante" in the feminine form. The telephone, at least in its most intimate modes, is female, though the sound of the busy signal disrupts any fantasy of confidential dialogue we might entertain.[11] When we meet Leona, we learn she is responsible for that signal. She has been trying to reach Henry, and her assumption that this will be possible reflects a split between male and female domains precisely at the point of participation in the telephone system. A busy signal, as the name suggests, signifies ostensibly that a phone is being *used*, so Leona assumes that Henry is talking on the phone to someone else, making it worth her while to keep trying to reach him. The one thing alien to Leona, the telephonic subject, is a phone off the hook. But consciously or not, the man has begged off. Let loose from the discourse, he is out making trouble in the story.

This trouble makes its presence felt immediately when, as she continues to try to reach Henry, Leona's line gets crossed, and she overhears the killers plotting the murder that will turn out to be her own. When Leona asks the operator to trace the call, she finds herself locked into a complex double role of detective and victim that unleashes a flood of explanation and commits her to an essentially reactive position. A trace is a repetition of lines already drawn—here they have not been drawn in her favor, and they will double back upon her. But Leona is not for all that a single-minded phone-user. In this very first exchange, where she asks for the trace, she is already asking for something more as well: she gives the operator a great deal of extra information, explaining her situation and describing what hearing such a frightening call meant to her. In an emergency such digression certainly counts as "talking too much," but we should also note the need for sympathy behind this inefficiency, and the view of the phone that makes Leona seek it here. Leona's position amounts to an insistence that the phone remain personal, allowing for sympathetic attention, or the world will become all business.[12] It stands in direct contrast to her characterization of male phone conversations at their most lethal: when the operator asks if the killers might still be on the line, Leona scoffs, "They weren't exactly gossiping." We might take Leona's dismissive statement as the strongest objection a film could raise against a male discourse that liquidates the personal.

But feminist criticism has read Leona's work on the phone as a failure. Lawrence, for instance, observes the extent of female networking among the characters but emphasizes its ineffectiveness: "The women talk, but they cannot do anything. Sally cannot stop her husband's investigation, and Leona cannot make Henry call her back" (133).[13] Silverman's judgment is stricter still, inferring Leona's "verbal and aural incompetence" from "her inability to get even a simple message straight" (79). We must take issue with this second description at once, for Leona receives nothing remotely resembling a "simple message." The character who asks her to take a message is Henry's cohort Waldo Evans, and while his speaking style, complete with numbered points, does preserve all the outward forms of a "simple," logical message, it is in fact extremely confusing to both Leona and the viewer because the field of reference we need to understand it has only begun to come into focus. Even as Evans goes into further explanation of her husband's descent into crime, we can understand the difficulty of Leona's comprehension because the story is so surprising and painful to her. There is an odd way, then, in which both Lawrence and Silverman accept the male business criteria of efficacy and efficiency in judging Leona's performance. Obviously this assessment is fair as far as it goes, since an ability to fight men on their own terms might have saved Leona. But it also entails a certain refusal to sympathize with the heroine that, while understandable, limits what a feminist reading of the film might perceive.[14]

If the business of the film lies in recovering its backstory, this business can be conducted only through the personalized channels of female networks. We should not be surprised that the film's feminine discourse will not leave the story alone, that this film will be "busy" in a way that jams the system—and not just the phone system but the system of the movies itself. *Sorry, Wrong Number* is above all a *noisy* movie, and in the sense not only that the soundtrack tends to be quite loud, but also that information comes at the viewer with such speed and density as to border on sensory overload. If there is a message in the eventual death of the talking woman in this film, we should be careful not to assume that it comes through loud and clear, as if over a Classical Hollywood Telephone. The effect of this discourse, rather than allowing any sadistic satisfaction in the punishment of the heroine, is to bring the heroine and the viewer together in shared confusion and distress.

What a more personal understanding of Evans's phone message reveals is its deeply gothic character. Not only does Evans convey the terrifying news that her husband has turned into a monster, but he speaks, as Lawrence observes, from the shadows, and this darkness makes a mockery of Evans's reasonable, business-like phone conversation (137). Why should we accept, for instance, his request for her to read his horrid message back to him as the simple observance of telephonic protocol? Is it not rather gratuitously cruel of him to solicit her participation in this way, making sure she registers the nightmare fully? If Evans's sadism is not clear at once, it certainly is by the time the conversation ends and Leona follows up on Evans's cryptic clue that she might reach her husband at "Bowery 2-1000." As she soon learns, this is the number of the city morgue, and her call gets her nothing but gallows humor at her own expense. Thus in retrospect we see her exchange with Evans for what it is: an obscene phone call. Working against this encroaching telephonic nightmare is Leona's own phone project, which I would argue clearly succeeds: to replace telephonic sadism with sympathy. In a world of such dark connections, there is indeed a strange way in which the possibility of sympathy arriving through the telephone becomes the most mysterious possibility of all. It is this mystery that takes us to the far end of the telephonic imagination, where a different kind of ideal telephone goes under the name of telepathy.[15]

Telepathy is the telephone in a perfect state of dematerialization—no apparatus, no sound waves, no ear. Thoughts simply move from one mind to another without static, delay, or the need for translation. Death and distance pose no obstacles. The only thing that can go wrong is the mind itself, as we will see when we turn to *Shadow of a Doubt* (1943), where Hitchcock places his heroine in telepathic connection with a deranged killer. Narrative film stimulates telepathic fantasy as a part of its usual course of operations, making us long for telepathy whenever we care about a character and urgently wish to communicate with her. Romance and horror seem to produce the purest examples, prompting viewers to think, "Kiss her already!" or "Look out!" It is not surprising that Alfred Hitchcock, who often foregrounds the dynamics of viewing, has captured the relationship between telepathic fantasy and helpless viewing on more than one occasion. Think of the scene in *The Birds* where witnesses in a diner look through a window at a man who is about to drop his cigarette butt in gasoline. They begin to shout at him while the window is still closed, opening it too late for him to heed their warning. Our desire for telepathy is thus closely connected with the feeling of suspense, as in Hitchcock's famous example where the viewer knows there is a bomb under a table. In other words, we want the power of telepathy, reasonably, when we have some very timely information to share.

Of course our telepathic conversation with a film runs both ways. How, after all, can a film represent what a character is thinking? The list of options is relatively short, representing the choice between textual, oral, and what is sometimes called audiovisual communication. The first option would be something like the cartoon bubble or other written messages relaying a character's thoughts to the audience. Used quite rarely, this technique is nonetheless deployed to good effect by Woody Allen in the date scene in *Annie Hall*, where subtitles reveal the characters' anxieties about impressing each other. The oral option is the much-maligned voiceover, in which either characters address us or we overhear their thoughts, and is of course far too common to require examples. But the consensus winner as the most elegant and "cinematic" solution is simply to *show* us what a character thinks, particularly as the hokey visuals of the old-fashioned dream sequence give way to more sophisticated techniques. A state-of-the-art example would be a scene in *High Fidelity*, in which John Cusack imagines, and we see, various possible responses to the arrival in his record store of his absurd rival, played by Tim Robbins. Bruce Kawin calls this technique mindscreen, and indeed conceives of the category quite broadly, aligning any number of subtle expressionistic techniques with first-person narration.[16] But this technique founders whenever a character's head is filled with something besides the easily rendered scenes of fantasy or dream. Indeed what is impossible to represent in this way is abstract thought.[17] To communicate such mental states, it seems we still need language.

Consider then the striking declaration attributed to film maker Chris Marker that the voiceover is "the destiny of cinema: it is soliloquy, it is a telephone system to the inner self."[18] This is an extraordinary claim, not only because we find the destiny of this supposedly visual medium in the realm of sound, but also because it embraces the cinematic embarrassment that is voiceover narration, with all its baggage as literary storytelling. Marker installed this magic phone line in his remarkable *La Jetée,* in which a voiceover narrator offers a meditation on time, love, and death. For Marker, it would seem that film cannot purify itself of literature without terrible loss, a loss felt perhaps most keenly as a diminishment of telepathic scope—and no wonder, given that, as Catherine Gallagher has argued, the uncanny accessibility of characters is the very sign of fiction ("Rise" 352). In this way the loss of voiceover would undo any history of novelistic culture we might chart along a trajectory of increasing telepathic sophistication. Such a history would note that the shared mental world imagined by the epistolary correspondents of Samuel Richardson's *Clarissa* has by the time of Jane Austen already become the special privilege of the reader. To know what characters are thinking is by then so much the point of reading novels that it seems hardly necessary to reflect on its ethics, or on the subtle narrative technology that delivers the goods.[19]

But the telepathy of reading or film viewing cannot be fully understood in terms of communication between stable subjects. Daniel Frampton enthusiastically theorizes a "transsubjective" film experience in which the "'I' becomes an 'other'—subject and object can thus become fused, *participating* in each other" (87). The similar discourse on reading takes on a more gothic inflection, suggesting that our imaginary invasion of the fictional thoughts of characters only distracts us from the real invasion that defines the scene of reading. Stephen King, for instance, understands reading as receiving information telepathically from the writer: "All the arts depend upon telepathy to some degree, but I believe that writing offers the purest distillation. . . . I sent you a table with a red cloth on it, a cage, a rabbit, and the number eight in blue ink. You got them all, especially that blue eight. We've engaged in a real act of telepathy. No mythy-mountain shit; real telepathy" (103–6). And perhaps King's claim points toward a fuller way of understanding the novelistic endgame played out by Henry James. As our access to the minds of characters grows ever more sophisticated, as it threatens to leave off mere figural representation and replicate consciousness itself, the telepathic privilege of reading rebounds upon a reader no longer capable of separation.[20] As Georges Poulet puts it: "The opposition between the subject and its object has been considerably attenuated. . . . You are inside it; it is inside you; there is no longer either outside or inside" (54). Poulet further argues that in the act of reading, not only am I "thinking the thoughts of another" (55), but also "the *I* which I pronounce is not myself (56, emph. orig.); "A second self takes over, a self which thinks and feels for me" (57). To read is then to be possessed—a condition to which my motionless silence testifies as clearly as the head-spinning ventriloquism of *The Exorcist*.

This gothic description of possessive reading is in keeping with the scholarship of Garrett Stewart, who argues for instance that a novel "gains domestic access to us only at the invitation of our interest" (11). Reading is a kind of genie in a lamp. In opening a book, we let it out and it fulfills wishes—though as always happens with genies, there is much doubt as to whether these wishes will make us happy, or if they are even truly ours. Indeed representations of telepathy as nightmare rather than as fantasy have long recognized the danger of a collapse of distance between self and other. Telepathic invasion haunts characters from episodes of *The X-Files* and *Buffy, the Vampire Slayer* back to George Eliot's *The Lifted Veil*, where in each case telepathic sensitivity summons audio overload, a barrage of alien voices crowding consciousness. Even a glib film like *What Women Want* registers its doubts in a scene in which Mel Gibson, initially smug about his ability to read women's minds, is suddenly overwhelmed by the sheer number of female thoughts that bombard his brain during a walk in the park. Jacques Derrida confesses an inverted form of this anxiety, in which it is the self that cannot help destroying the distance it requires: "What I always have difficulty getting used to: that non-telepathy is possible. Always difficult to imagine that one can think something to oneself [à part soi], deep down inside, without being surprised by the other, without the other being immediately informed" ("Telepathy" 13–14).[21] There is a deep irony in Derrida's fear, attuned as it is to a culture that turns the very perfection of telepathy against us in a nightmare of endless exposure.

This nightmare has special importance for women in a culture that is slow to abandon its interest in feminine modesty. Recalling my argument about *Evelina* in chapter 2, we might say that Burney downplays Richardson's fantasy of epistolary access, addressing the reader on the outside of a gap between what her heroine thinks and what she writes, as a principled and strategic refusal of the fantasy of telepathy. And it is worth considering more generally how risks and rewards of telepathy are distributed along gender lines, for if the gothic teaches us anything, it is simply that the need for communication is directly proportional to the horror when it goes bad. But while Burney shields her heroine by burying her novel's female networks under an exemplary feminine epistolary performance, Litvak does no such thing in *Sorry, Wrong Number*. In fact, if we seriously entertain the idea that most of the images in this film are representations of Leona's thoughts, what could be more intrusive? Is this film not her nightmare of exposure to countless unknown viewers? The most important feminist objection to this film may finally be that it refuses the dignity of privacy to its heroine. And yet we would do well to hold on to the fantasy of telepathy as a counterweight to the foreclosing power of its competing fantasy, the Classical Hollywood Telephone, which has nothing to tell us beyond another mindless iteration of generic closure, nothing to tell us except that Leona, and all she stands for, is dead. Exposure may be the price of having a voice, for out of the nightmares of telepathy we get a glimpse of a more hopeful kind of telephonic film, a film that stages the unlikely coincidence of minds that is real sympathy.

As Leona's appointment with fate draws near, *Sorry, Wrong Number* performs one of the recurring tasks that I am attempting in this book, to direct an unwavering sympathetic attention toward female characters when it is unpleasant to do so, or even when they seem unworthy of the effort. While Silverman expresses disgust with Leona's helplessness at the end, this reaction does not seem to be a fair one. How many of us would fare better against a professional assassin? And if visuality triumphs over Leona's voice, as Lawrence argues, is this triumph not duly recorded as the brutal revenge that it is? After all, if the camera that outlives Leona performs a gravity-defying feat, as Lawrence observes, when it scales the side of the house to announce the killer's arrival, is it not as occult as the nightmare phone? (144–45). If some films naturalize genre, *Sorry, Wrong Number* supernaturalizes it. Genre itself becomes nothing more than superstition, with Leona and Henry tragically caught up in it as star-crossed lovers, only here it is not the stars that are crossed. When Barbara Stanwyck screams, "Henry, he's coming up the stairs!" into the phone at the end, what I hear in her voice is not incompetence, but the appropriate distress of a thinking and feeling person in mortal danger.

We should therefore reconsider the end of *Sorry, Wrong Number*, where Leona is on the phone with Henry as the killer he hired arrives at her house. It is difficult to imagine many viewers watching this scene with punitive satisfaction, for it is all about our frustration—particularly with Leona's compulsive decision to answer the phone even after she has heard the killer downstairs, and her subsequent paralysis when Henry tells her to go to the window and scream. For a brief moment it seems Henry speaks for us, sharing our helpless concern and desire to save Leona—that is, until he reveals in a panic that he is concerned only about getting the electric chair now that the authorities are closing in on him. Selfish to the end, Henry is therefore not so much our surrogate on the phone as he is someone in the way. Thus the killer's mocking final words—"Sorry, wrong number"—speak no more to Henry's failed call than to our own undeliverable messages: we want to call Leona, but the line is always busy. As the echo of the film's title reminds us that our calls were never going to get through, Leona's telephonic nightmare becomes ours as the audience of a cinema that has yet to open itself up to freer telepathic fantasies. Indeed, her fatal paralysis is perhaps not physical but technological, a refusal to give up her habitual connections, and might make us think twice about how healthy our own paralysis is the next time we find ourselves at the movies, glued to our seats.

Double or Nothing: Film versus Literature *in* Shadow of a Doubt

It is this question of immobility, in tension with a complex and ambivalent understanding of telepathy, that I want to bring to the critical discussion of *Shadow of a Doubt*. I will begin with the question of telepathy, for everyone agrees that telepathy is what Hitchcock's great film of small town America is about, though few critics have much to say about what telepathy is or what it has to do with the film's obsessive and critical interest in reading. The film raises the issue as a way of describing the special bond between Uncle Charlie, the suspected "Merry Widow Murderer," and his adoring niece and namesake. But whatever truck Hitchcock's film has with telepathy, it is clearly *not* in the business of delivering a fantasy of telepathic knowledge to the viewer. Of the techniques I have listed for representing the thoughts of characters in film, Hitchcock avails himself of at most one, the voiceover, and this for only a single, ambiguous moment at the beginning, when we meet Uncle Charlie before he flees across the country to hide at the home of his sister's family.[22]

The ambiguous moment occurs when Uncle Charlie looks out his boarding-house window at a pair of detectives who have staked out his room. As the camera impishly cuts away from his mouth, we hear his thoughts seemingly as a voiceover: "What do you know? You're bluffing. You have nothing on me." Uncle Charlie then proceeds to flaunt his invincibility, leading the detectives on a wild goose chase through the neighborhood. As viewers, we are led on a similar chase throughout the film, pursuing the elusive villain, never quite sure what we know. And even if we could be sure these words are Uncle Charlie's uncensored thoughts, that knowledge would mean merely this: that the one thing in the entire movie we are sure Uncle Charlie thinks is that we cannot know what he is thinking. Thus this voiceover we supposedly overhear functions also as a form of mocking direct address. Hitchcock's telepathic lure communicates nothing but its own uselessness.

Of course Uncle Charlie will continue to transmit signals throughout the film—indeed his modus operandi is to act outrageously guilty, an m.o. enhanced by the film's many *noir* effects, from menacing shadows and oblique camera angles to startling movements of the camera and actors. But all of these signals remain in a taunting mode, defying us to know Uncle Charlie beyond a reasonable doubt. The first of Uncle Charlie's notorious rants, for instance, is filmed so as to suggest a soliloquy. Sitting at dinner with his sister's family, he seems to lose himself in a trance as he reviews the supposed sins of widows. As his voice gets lower and closer—as if to approximate a voiceover—the camera draws in tightly on the side of his face. Before the speech is finished, however, the camera pulls back abruptly to show the scene as a whole, with the resonance of his voice again reflecting the acoustic space of the room. Does this switch undercut the telepathic status of the speech, or simply indicate Uncle Charlie's return to self-awareness? Either way, it makes us aware that this unpleasant intimacy may be just an effect of cinematic technique. What from one angle looks like a spontaneous irruption from a killer's unconscious looks from another angle like calculated rhetoric, the weapon of a merely verbal terrorist. Even Uncle Charlie's other seemingly transparent self-betrayals, such as the two occasions on which he involuntarily clenches his hands, remain signs that must be read, thus always falling short of the standard of perfect knowledge that Hitchcock invokes when he invokes the voiceover.

If this is our dilemma, it is certainly the dilemma as well of Charlie, Uncle Charlie's presumed telepathic partner, for she must gradually confront the way her intuition is insufficient, even wrong, and resort to earning her knowledge of her uncle the old-fashioned way. Of course Charlie wants her uncle to be innocent, and the report of a second Merry Widow suspect on the loose in Maine gives her ample room to deny his guilt. But despite her wishes, her case does build in strength, turning on a ring her uncle gives her in a much discussed scene of pseudo-betrothal, a ring inscribed with the initials of one of the murdered widows. On the strength of this evidence she eventually drives her uncle from town, though we never get any confirmation from the police that the ring in fact belonged to the widow.

This is not the only proof the film neglects. Earlier one of the detectives manages to take Uncle Charlie's picture, wiring the photo back east so a witness can identify him. But we never hear the results of this identification. Instead the last word from the east coast comes from a conversation between Charlie's father, Joe, and his friend Herb, a pair of silly crime buffs who spend most of the movie imagining how best to murder each other. Herb has heard on the radio that the other fugitive died while fleeing the authorities, and tells Joe, "I guess that closes that case pretty fine." This reasoning is so absurd, and these men are such obviously unqualified gossips, that it is almost as if the film means us immediately to conclude the opposite: that it is in fact Uncle Charlie who is guilty. And yet what happened to the photograph? Like the ring, it never circulates through the male realm of proof, law, and professional detectives to issue forth as official, public knowledge. In fact, the detectives on the case come to the same inane conclusion as Herb and Joe. Charlie's case thus remains in a realm of private female knowledge, a realm clearly shown to be superior and yet, crucially, inadequate to the needs of the women who enter it. For it is not clear that Charlie's knowledge solves the problem that launches the film. Recall that in her first speech to her father, Charlie has nothing to say about her uncle but complains about the rest of her family—in particular her mother, whom she wants to be "a real lady" but who instead "works like a dog" and wears a shabby hat. Thus, however successful Charlie becomes in reading Uncle Charlie and getting into his head, the question remains whether he distracts her, and us, from her true concerns.

In this light, I would argue that we can productively pose the central question of *Shadow of a Doubt* as the question of whether the heroine reads too much or not enough. It is a question the film cannot fully resolve, because reading itself remains such a term of ambivalence, particularly for a woman whose need for access to the wide world—especially if she lives in Hitchcock's Santa Rosa—is a need as acute as that world is dangerous. Like Emma Woodhouse, Charlotte Newton has outgrown her little community. When Charlie gets the idea that she might make use of a worldwide communications network to summon relief, her mother's immediate response can only be "Who do *you* know to send a telegram to?" Who indeed. As it turns out, of course, Charlie knows her Uncle Charlie. Not unlike Frank Churchill, he will swoop into town and put the heroine's reading skills to the test.

But a crucial difference between *Shadow of a Doubt* and *Emma* is that Charlie need not wait passively for male entertainment to arrive. Instead she summons her uncle and namesake telepathically (or so she comes to think). And while clearly Uncle Charlie possesses all the charms of the itinerant gentleman, there is something more behind Charlie's desire to bring him to Santa Rosa—indeed both this desire and the power to exercise it come from a mysterious source. Critics of the film have made much of the bond between this pair, who are "more than an uncle and niece," exploring the idea of incest or the double.[23] The idea of the double is most important for our purposes—not to downplay the erotic tension, which is powerful, but in order to consider this bond precisely as an effect of reading. Indeed, if the modern mind is prone to the uncanny experience of doubles, it is so only because that mind has been trained to open itself to the telepathic experience that is reading novels. As Friedrich Kittler has argued, by "introducing a hero like you and me," the novel trains readers in techniques of hallucinatory recognition, of seeing doubles (*Literature* 90). Cueing identification, the double plays a special part in the novelistic fantasy of telepathy. It is the external sign of the invisible telepathic effect. We might even see the double as the most intense incarnation of the telepathic partner, carrying not only the dream of impossible intimacy, but the corresponding nightmare of exposure—hence the double is repeatedly found in some direct relationship to the scandalous secret self: he either *is* that hidden self (like Stevenson's Mr. Hyde) or he is the conscience that pursues that self (Poe's William Wilson).

Kittler's point, however, is that we should never forget that the double of the imagination is simply a technical effect: "In order to see one's Double as the 'phantom of our own ego,' the cunning strategies by which others produced it must be thoroughly masked" (*Literature* 88). And indeed we can catch a similar trick at work in *Shadow of a Doubt*. Charlie's "knowledge" of the telepathy she enjoys with her uncle has in fact no meaning except through the technological networks that confirm it. Going to the post office to telegraph her uncle "the normal way," she has no thought of circumventing the usual channels. Her superstitious belief that she and her uncle are doubles who enjoy a telepathic connection occurs only when she finds that a telegram already awaits her, telling her that her uncle is on his way.[24] Thus the double occurs in a moment of charged recognition of the externalized self, a moment of technology. Loaded with affect, it at once stands for an ideal telepathic partner and threatens to collapse telepathy back upon the self as mere solipsism. This doubt will become particularly serious over the course of this film as Charlie has to separate her fantasies from the dawning truth about her uncle. But as we shall see, this doubt is perhaps the lesser half of the double bind of reading in which Charlie finds herself, for if the fantasy of telepathy is the error of an overeager reader, the reluctant reader has her own blindness.

Elsie Michie has argued that, as an eligible young woman, Charlie is positioned between her long-married mother, Emma, and her pre-adolescent sister, Anne. This structure exists for the film in another sense as well, for the three female members of the Newton family form a continuum of possible readers.[25] The great reader of *Shadow of a Doubt* is Anne, whom we see reading obsessively, in any number of strange positions and locations, throughout the film, fulfilling her announced quota of two books per week. Marked clearly as a female quixote, Anne seems to get all her information about the world from books, and to her mind "They're all true." But despite her librarian's glasses and lecturing tone, we should not be deceived into dismissing her as an irrelevant pedant. Not only does her knowledge of the library help her sister's investigation, but when it comes to reading Uncle Charlie, she twice seems uncannily prescient. The first moment occurs when the phone rings to announce his arrival. Absorbed in *Ivanhoe*, Anne ignores it. This self-sufficiency immediately sets her apart from her sister upstairs, who, in a romantic mood for a savior and a double, yells down at Anne to answer the phone. Complying reluctantly—and without setting down her book—Anne, however, refuses to take the message when she can't find a pencil to write it down, saying, "I'm trying to keep my mind free of things that don't matter." How should we understand the irony of her dismissive attitude to what turns out to be news of Uncle Charlie's imminent arrival? If Anne's remark, despite her choice of literature, seems un-romantic, it also expresses what turns out to be a very healthy lack of interest in Uncle Charlie. Indeed, what if Anne's sixth sense, rather than being absent, is more advanced than her sister's, her apparent boredom concealing a deeper distrust? Her second moment of insight bears out this idea. This moment occurs before dinner on the evening following Charlie's momentous trip to the library, the trip on which she discovers that the initials on the ring match the initials of the victim in a news-paper account. As the table is being prepared, without warning or explanation, Anne asks to sit next to her mother, away from her uncle. It is here that she seems to be the real telepathist, tuning effortlessly into her uncle's guilt—or her sister's suspicion. There is, then, every reason to think that her reading has prepared her well. Indeed *Dracula* is the other novel we know Anne has read, and when held up with *Ivanhoe* it captures the great ambivalence generated by Uncle Charlie as an outsider.[26] Anne knows better than to assume every man of mystery is Richard the Lionhearted, returning to save the country, and not a vampire.[27]

On the other end of the reading spectrum is Emma, who thinks Anne "has too many foolish ideas." Emma is not a stupid person—she takes note of the world around her and recognizes patterns, but she does not read these patterns, no doubt because the interpretive possibilities are too painful. An important example of this reluctance occurs after Charlie twice becomes the apparent target of homicidal attacks—first as she takes a fall on the back stairs, and second as she gets stuck in the garage with the car motor running. After the garage incident, Emma sits in a cab fretting about these two successive brushes with death, and for a moment it looks as if she will muster an appropriately sinister reading of this dark coincidence (see fig. 4.2). But the cab drives off, and the film lets her off the hook, teasing us with the possibility of the mother's knowledge. This knowledge is something Uncle Charlie has cleverly taught his niece to fear, saying it would kill his sister to know the allegations against him, but it is also something deeply desired, the sympathetic and strategic support of a female network. Without it, Charlie will continue to bear the work of reading—and the pain of knowing—alone.

Of course uncorroborated reading is the plight of the gothic heroine, who drifts into carefully orchestrated insanity. Paradigmatic here is the heroine of *Gaslight*,

Figure 4.2 Emma on the verge of knowledge.

manipulated to the point of desperation because she can't find anyone to confirm her impressions of the world. For such a heroine, reading is always shared or worthless, double or nothing, we might say. Perhaps this is why Charlie eschews Anne's solitary reading habits and is drawn to her uncle. The question of shared reading certainly has implications for the film's romance plot, entangled as it is in detection. Recall that Jack Graham, one of the detectives who comes to investigate Charlie's uncle, falls for her and proposes to her in the garage. Charlie demurs, and while she does ask Jack to come to the funeral at the end, I read this less as a romantic invitation than as the momentary need for someone who can share her knowledge. While Jack's knowledge of the plot is hardly complete, he at least knows that Charlie carries the burdensome secret of her uncle's guilt.

Charlie's secret knowledge is in fact the erotic basis of Jack's interest in her. When Jack first investigates the Newtons undercover as a reporter, he challenges Charlie when she tries to bar his access to her room, on the grounds of protecting her uncle's privacy:

Jack says, "I'll bet you 50 cents your uncle isn't in there."
    Charlie replies, "Oh, betting is silly. All you want to do is photograph my room. Besides, I know my uncle is in there."

Charlie is of course wrong twice over: her uncle is not in the room, and, as a detective, Jack couldn't care less about photographing it. But in staking a suspicious reading of her uncle, he makes it possible for her to see that the transition from desiring Uncle Charlie to investigating him can be as smooth as a transition from her sister's classics to her father's potboiler detective fiction. We need only recall Dupin's technique of identifying with his adversary in "The Purloined Letter" to see that the founding operation of literary detective work is a fantasy of telepathy, and so Charlie has been a detective all along in her desire to know her uncle's secrets.[28] Moreover, just as Dupin must share his interpretations, publishing his success both to his defeated opponent and to the narrator of Poe's tale, so Jack and Charlie can attempt to come together through a reading of her uncle.

But it is interesting that the sexual instincts of Charlie, the "good girl," are at this stage far in advance of her detective skills. Erotically speaking, Uncle Charlie is in her bedroom, and Jack wants to displace him, so in this sense her remarks are perfectly accurate. But in framing Charlie's vexed choice of erotic objects, this scene points to the difficulty a woman's desire has here in finding a home. I don't mean by this merely the usual reading that contrasts the dashing but doubly taboo uncle (as blood relative and criminal) with the stuffy detective who preaches normalcy and wants to marry her and turn her into her mother, for there is actually a sense in which Uncle Charlie and Jack are very similar. They are both far more mobile than Charlie, and both not as easy to reach as she assumes. The message Charlie would have sent her uncle in the beginning might in fact have gone to the wrong place (Uncle Charlie's initial residence hardly seems long-term, and Emma's confidence that he can be reached reliably in Philadelphia is contradicted by Joe's comment to Herb that Uncle Charlie is a "New York man"). Jack is himself disturbingly unavailable toward the end, when Charlie tries desperately to reach him at three different phone numbers after the incident in the garage. In this film, the heroine's best hope does not lie in summoning men to save her. Charlie responds to Jack's unavailability by taking the initiative and searching for the dead widow's ring, though it is not clear how possessing this complex symbolic object will help her sort out this film's tangle of knowledge, sexuality, and mobility.

One problem with the ring is that its symbolism distributes femininity in all the wrong ways. For instance, when Charlie removes the ring during a confrontation with her uncle at the "Til-Two" bar, it becomes an object of interest for the waitress Louise. An acquaintance from high school, Louise has already clearly separated herself from Charlie in her comment that "I never thought I'd see *you* here," and as she is a waitress serving soldiers during wartime, the insinuation of Louise's sexual experience is clear. Her remarks on the ring then are telling: "I'd just die for a ring like that . . . notice I didn't even have to ask if it was real. I can tell. *I* can." Sexual women know the price of things. Once touched by such knowledge, it seems that the good girl can only follow the symbolism of the ring right into marriage as the respectable place for women's sexuality. When Charlie finds the ring and wears it publicly, she does temporarily take control of its signification, sending Uncle Charlie the clear message to leave town or risk exposure. But Charlie cannot put on the ring without herself risking one last dance with this deadly partner. Making the shift from the romance plot to the detective plot is insufficient, for both plots keep her reading, keep her invested in the stifling pursuit of the wrong telepathic intimacies. Yes, seizing the ring works to an extent, since Uncle Charlie gets the message and boards a train the next day. But he doesn't leave without a final expression of his deep anxiety about "fast" women. Indeed the colloquial metaphor for female sexuality has become quite literal over the course of the film, suggesting an important slippage in the film's psychic economy. As Uncle Charlie holds his terrified niece by an open door of the accelerating train, he tells her to "let it get a little faster, just a little faster, faster," thus leaving her with a final warning, not against too much knowledge but against too much speed.

The confusion in Uncle Charlie's mind between knowledge and speed can be traced back to the childhood accident Emma refers to when Charlie finds an old photograph of her uncle shortly after his arrival. Apparently the young Charles got a bicycle one Christmas, went riding, and "skidded into a streetcar." Critics have interpreted this episode metaphorically as premature sexual awakening, but I feel less confident in sorting out the latent sexual content from the manifest nature of the event, ignoring the tangle I've just described.[29] I would suggest instead that it is worth slowing down to consider what a more literal-minded reading might yield.[30] At the time of the accident in the early twentieth century, bicycles were not the harmless toys of children—they were *fast*. Their design had improved, their price had dropped, and they made people nervous.[31] Clearly for such a powerful machine to collide with a still faster, and far larger, streetcar was a major crisis of speed for a previously unaccelerated body. Indeed, more interesting than the sexual allegory might be the historical one, for this accident must date close to the time of World War I, the crisis of speed that shell-shocked a great many young men, dividing the fallen present from the good old days that Uncle Charlie quite openly longs for. But oddly the response of young Charles to his traumatic collision is not to give up movement, but to give up reading. According to his sister, he was a great reader until the day of the accident. It would seem he confused transportation with communication, displacing his anxiety about moving bodies onto a fear of moving ideas. This displacement, moreover, is exactly the strategy of the film itself.

All the fuss about reading in *Shadow of a Doubt*, and particularly at the moments where it is treated as a suspect activity, merely distracts viewers from the medium truly at hand, which is, of course, film. I want to propose Uncle Charlie's psyche as a significant model for understanding the choice between film and literature. Giving up the novel for film means giving up something of the fantasy of telepathy in favor of speed, particularly speed understood at its limit as the dream of being in two places at once, since if we approach a destination with infinite speed we are already there. Beginning with its famous rhyming shots of the two Charlies in their respective beds, the film represents two sides of America without the viewer's leaving her seat, and it does so, we should note, at incredible speed, for the film arrives in Santa Rosa not only far before Uncle Charlie's train, but also well ahead of his telegram. But if in this way film trumps the technologies of speed it invokes, it also calls attention to the ghostly quality of its victory. Our travel west here feels strangely incomplete, haunted as it is by the lingering knowledge of a killer on each coast. Hitchcock's transcontinental sensibility, as manifested by wire, rail, and double, highlights film's special power to deliver an experience of bi-locality at once thick and spectral.[32]

All we have to do is subtract the idea of a destination and we can see that speed is closely connected to being nowhere. As in *Clarissa*, the fact that being nowhere is desirable may not seem so strange to those trapped in an unpleasant place, as Charlie clearly is at the beginning of the film. But here the escapes of women gain no foothold in representation. We should not, however, be blind to the ways in which the prospects of female mobility cast a long shadow at this historical moment. After all, *Shadow of a Doubt* appears only a short while after Amelia Earhart, the great aviator who helped connect the coasts, disappeared over the Pacific in 1937. At this moment, we might say, Earhart is still very much in the air, and it is not difficult to imagine the stirrings of a small-town girl occasionally finding form in the great haunting figure of female flight.[33] Airplanes are indeed briefly heard from in this film, with speed again figured as highly traumatic, even castrating: recall that Uncle Charlie's counterpart on the east coast gets sliced up by a plane's propeller while fleeing the authorities. In any case, this film certainly unleashes more female speed than Uncle Charlie can stand, or than its plot can contain. It is an anxiety clearly foreshadowed—and misplaced—in the reaction of Charlie's father upon hearing that the family had received a telegram: "I knew there'd be trouble if your Aunt Sarah got her driver's license." But it is the movements of Uncle Charlie, not Aunt Sarah, that bring trouble to the Newton family, and so with Joe's comment the film briefly concedes that the fear of female speed is at once widespread and ill-founded.

Uncle Charlie's ideal woman is of course his sister Emma, the hard-working, self-denying housewife, and the first words he speaks to her in the film are "Don't move." The slippery man from who-knows-where clearly wants women to remain where he likes them. It is perhaps telling that the widows Uncle Charlie despises appear in a recurring cryptic image dancing to the tune of "The Merry Widow Waltz." This extra-diegetic image is well analyzed by Patrick Crogan in terms of how it visually bridges uncle and niece at key points in the film, but it is the movement I want to emphasize, as if the widows are taunting Uncle Charlie with their merriment. Led around in circles by men, the dancers hardly represent the mobility Charlie needs, and yet it seems even such controlled movement is enough to disturb her uncle, no doubt because of the social mobility it makes possible as women try new partners.

Unfortunately for Uncle Charlie, his niece is not willing to be led. As Michie points out, Charlie is inherently mobile as the only member of her family who knows how to drive (40). Even on foot, moreover, the film notes her pace as transgressive, for twice a traffic cop stops her for a moving violation. Consider her second fast walk, which occurs when she storms away from dinner the day after discovering the devastating clue in the library. Unlike the first incident, when she was rushing to reach the library before it closes, here she has no destination, her speed purely in the service of escape. For his part, Uncle Charlie may know he can catch up with her, but his pursuit is not quite effortless—her speed, much like her knowledge, is just enough to strain his nonchalance. Once her knowledge grows to the point of becoming a threat that he must deal with, every attack occurs at a site of potential female mobility: the back stairs, the garage, the train.[34] It is as if Uncle Charlie is restaging his childhood trauma in reverse: instead of suffering from speed and turning away from knowledge, he suffers from knowledge and lashes out at speed.

Of these three key sites, of course only the back stairs are an entrenched feminine space. Connected directly to the kitchen, and by association and proximity to the proverbial "back fence" of gossip, these stairs are used exclusively by women in *Shadow of a Doubt*—except, that is, for the brazen incursions of Uncle Charlie. After her frightening fall, Charlie goes out at night with a flashlight to investigate the stairs, only to be confronted by her uncle on the top landing. It is in this crucial encounter that Uncle Charlie ridicules his niece's case against him and announces his intention to stay in Santa Rosa. But Charlie is having none of it, saying: "I don't want you here, Uncle Charlie. I don't want you to touch my mother. So go away, I'm warning you. Go away or I'll kill you myself. See? That's the way I feel about you." Challenged on her own stairs, she defends her turf. If since Woolf the thinking woman has required her own room, we see in this film the woman of action beginning to demand a free path: a staircase, a sidewalk, a road of her own.[35]

Pursuing the logic of the double, critics have made much of how in threatening to kill her uncle, Charlie takes a step toward becoming him, and some have even gone so far as to consider her self-defense on the train as at least morally, if not legally, on par with her uncle's homicides.[36] I disagree. A close look at this scene shows something very different. It is not as if Charlie *stalks* her Uncle on the train—her dance with death is hardly voluntary. Her face, moreover, registers no hatred, no sadism, nothing really but fear, especially in the two close-ups of her widening eyes as he forces her to look out at the ground whizzing by. So why would we say that Charlie's guilt is what this scene is primarily about, when it is clearly about fear and speed? As I suggested before, is this not Uncle Charlie's attempt to scare her off mobility forever as he demands that she "Let it get a little faster, just a little faster, faster?" Are we sure, in fact, that her far larger uncle hasn't committed suicide in just such a way as to leave a lasting impression, including, perhaps, yes, an undeserved sense of guilt? Thus her resemblance to her murderous uncle here is not the point. Indeed, it is not her uncle, but her mother that Charlie is afraid of turning into—if anything, niece and uncle here are rivals, competing for the right to define who Emma will be.

The film itself continually presents the mother in a kind of double vision. It is easy to view her as something of an idiot, the butt of a kind of running joke on domesticity. Surely Hitchcock was one to enjoy such a joke, and surely Uncle Charlie, for his own safety and comfort, would like her to be a simpleton. But Emma's remark that in marriage "You sort of forget you're you" should remind us that she is not without her moments of critical consciousness. There are also several hints that her adoration of her brother is not unmixed, as when she refers to him as the spoiled youngest of the family or tells him he was never one to help out.

Charlie needs to break through to this smarter, critical Emma, but circumstances are against her. The crucial encounter occurs just before Charlie nearly dies in the garage, when they are getting ready to go out as a family to hear Uncle Charlie speak at Emma's women's club. Wearing the fur stole her brother gave her, and indeed basking in the prospect of his oratorical glory, Emma seems at this moment well within his grasp. But Charlie pulls her aside hurriedly in a spare moment, asking her quickly, without explanation, to ride with her, so she won't be alone with Uncle Charlie. Her mother gives no answer as Charlie hurries out the door, simply turning toward the camera with a distracted look on her face. Indeed, Emma never has to decide, for Charlie will get stuck in the garage and end up staying home while everyone else goes to the club. As in the moment in the cab that soon follows, the moment when Emma ponders the coincidence of two "accidents" in such quick succession, Emma is let off the hook by the film, never having to choose between her daughter and her brother.

Thus the real reason the end of this film feels so heavy is not that Charlie will inevitably marry Jack (why do we want to believe this?), and not that we secretly miss Uncle Charlie's devilish charisma, but that Charlie remains alienated from her mother, no closer to solving the problem of female destiny that began the film. We should keep in mind that at the end Charlie must have lied to the authorities to account for her uncle's death, since the town treats him as a hero at the funeral. Here Charlie stops being a reader and starts being an author, and no doubt her prime motivation is still to protect her mother. What I want to suggest is that Charlie may be wrong about the necessity for this subterfuge—her mother may be prepared to know everything, may almost know it already. In imposing his view of Emma as fragile and helpless, Uncle Charlie has won after all. Indeed the whole town will remain the innocent and ignorant place he wants it to be. For want of any penetration into her mother's mind, for want of a little genuine telepathy, Charlie, and through her *Shadow of a Doubt*, passes off a crippling failure as a necessary fiction.

If Charlie finally fails as a reader, then we should ask if film culture offers her something else, particularly in light of Jack's comment in their final conversation at Uncle Charlie's funeral that "Sometimes [the world] needs a lot of watching." As the male detective insists that vigilance is enough to make the world right, Charlie looks unsure; her final words dwell on her uncle's hateful vision of the world. It seems that the desire for film that *Shadow of a Doubt* leaves us with has a lot less to do with the dubious reassurance of surveillance than with the possibility of escape. It is film as transportation rather than communication, speed rather than knowledge. *Sorry, Wrong Number* stages this distinction as a clear trade-off: the breakthrough of telepathic knowledge and sympathy toward Leona comes only at the price of her wrenching and fatal paralysis. Here we see the trade-off in reverse: Charlie can purchase mobility only by abandoning the consolations of shared knowledge, whether with her mother or, less promisingly, with Jack. He in fact offers Charlie a cheapened version of Leona's deal—a slower death in marriage in exchange for a rather limited intimacy. All we can hope is that Charlie has the courage to see through this rotten bargain, that her uncle's final act of terror on the train has not scared her into the false safety of stasis. Better to go out like Amelia Earhart, who must have known as well as anyone that there are worse things than flying solo.

CHAPTER 5

The Space of Crime

*Hammett took murder out of the Venetian vase and dropped it
into the alley.*
    Raymond Chandler, The Simple Art of Murder

*To label all this "the police" thus anticipates moving the question
of policing out of the streets, as it were, into the closet—I mean,
into the private and domestic sphere on which the very identity
of the liberal subject depends.*
    D. A. Miller, The Novel and the Police

Out of the vase and into the alley, back from the streets and into the
closet; from Richardson's rooms to Burney's ditches to Hitchcock's trains—the
space of crime is always on the move. Everything seems to be at stake in its shifting
location, whether Chandler's obsession with the artistic legitimacy of crime fiction,
or the scene of novelistic liberal power that Miller illuminates. In this chapter I
will pursue a somewhat different set of stakes in this game, following on the im-
mobilizations of Leona Stevenson and Charlie Newton to consider how a cultural
insistence on space seems to emerge in direct proportion to the manifest range or
intensity of female networking. I want again to emphasize the gothic as the cultural
mode that governs the isolated and threatening space, a mode that must be constantly reinvented to maintain the spectacle of the suffering, singled-out heroine in
the face of new technologies. But before we consider the cultural response to such
recent developments as cell phones, the Internet, or even a looming artificial intelligence, I want to trace briefly the spatial history that informs this response. It is a
history visible in the epigraphs, where opposed to the ubiquitous streets or alleys
as the space of masculine urban adventure is a space of feminized confinement.
Indeed, Miller's closet and Chandler's vase represent the various contractions of a
space that was plenty claustrophobic to begin with, and that deserves some attention for its status in the history of crime fiction. Enter the locked room.

Long a mainstay of detective fiction, the locked room represents a crucial intersection of female independence (a room of one's own) and murder. As the epitome of the mystery puzzle, these social concerns may seem the mere props of an abstract cognitive exercise. John T. Irwin, for instance, addresses the conceptual appeal of the locked room in these terms, as "a physical embodiment, a concrete spatialization, of that very mechanism of logical inclusion/exclusion on which rational analysis is based" (47). But the comfortable cogitations of the armchair reader are not so different from the desperate cunning of the hunted animal, a difference measurable perhaps by little more than the strength of the lock on the reader's own room. Not just analysis but survival depends on the successful sorting of inside and out, as ever-vulnerable bodies must regulate the necessary but dangerous contact with the world. As Mark S. Madoff points out, the problem posed by the locked room is an essentially gothic one; in the ensuing tradeoff between shelter and mobility, women have long been conditioned to prefer the former, banking on the security of the locked room.[1] The locked room mystery is the genre that dedicates all its genius to cracking that primitive security.

The tradition begins with animals, casting its puzzles from the outset in terms of a brutal game of survival that women are supposedly ill equipped to play. I am thinking of Poe's rampaging ourang-outang of "The Murders in the Rue Morgue," and also of the carefully aimed swamp adder of Arthur Conan Doyle's "The Adventure of the Speckled Band." Both creatures kill women; the former story, in fact, goes so far as to make its female victims part of the spatial puzzle, tossing one woman out the window and cramming the other up the chimney. Both stories, moreover, choose victims closely bonded to other women, and in possession or near possession of economic independence. It seems here to be precisely the security of female networks that calls down the most virulent narrative aggression. If the genre finds these animals appealing for their superhuman powers of entry, it also finds them natural foils for the rational detective with his own extraordinary mental penetrations. After all, it is no accident that before tackling the inaugural case of detective fiction, Poe's C. Auguste Dupin treats the narrator (and reader) to a stunning display of mind-reading. Thus while it might seem that the locked room at least localizes and contains murder, I would argue the opposite: that a locked room mystery is essentially a fantasy of impossible penetration, subjecting a recalcitrant female privacy to the double surveillance of stalking and detection. It is about making everywhere outside.[2]

This holds true even when a third celebrated story—Jacques Futrelle's "The Problem of Cell 13"—inverts the typical scenario by replacing the detective with a pure logician who, with much bravado, has *himself* placed in a prison cell to demonstrate the omnipotence of reason. Known as "The Thinking Machine," this character proceeds to demonstrate superhuman powers of exit, though even this intellectual exercise cannot suppress its gothic roots. Where is crime in this story? As it turns out, it is two floors directly above Cell 13, where a man is imprisoned for throwing acid on a woman's face. This is apparently as far as the scene of logic can get from a gruesome crime against a woman.[3] In fact, the Thinking Machine's activities commune strangely with that parallel room: when he calls through a sewage pipe for acid to corrode the bars of his window, his voice is overheard by the criminal, who takes it for the haunting voice of conscience and confesses. An accidental detective, this Thinking Machine projects a ghost. There cannot be much solace for women in a culture that generates penetration as a by-product of escape.

As the trope of the locked room develops, in various guises, throughout the twentieth century, it becomes a question of whether there is solace for women in technology, whether our culture has finally engineered a way out. I should reiterate that this book spans a crucial revolution in communications technology, one that made the law's arm long indeed, as now the innermost rooms of the private home and the outermost regions of the countryside were within its grasp. The first manifestation of this revolution—the telegraph—was used in celebrated cases to catch criminals speeding away on trains, and indeed the law's reach would soon cross oceans with undersea cables and wireless telegraphy.[4] Sherlock Holmes himself made use of this technology in the apprehension of more than one villain. But as the previous two chapters suggest, more important for women than the outward spread of the law was its new availability in the home through the telephone. As Carolyn Marvin explains "If the lone woman at home seemed especially vulnerable to predators, she could also lift the telephone to sound the alarm, in many stories a device by which help was quickly dispatched to thwart thieves, murderers, and frustrated suitors" (93). Thus a certain backlash against this security, a reassertion of the gothic, can be detected, as I have argued, in the culture of telephonic terror and other challenges to female spaces. As surely as a locked room mystery, this culture turns stories of women's security into lies, much like Henry Stevenson's phony reassurance of Leona at the end of *Sorry, Wrong Number*: "You're right in the heart of New York City and a telephone's right by your bed."

If anything, technology can confuse a woman's ability to maintain a safe distance, for if Leona's murder still respects the expected relationship of inside and outside, with the killer entering her house through the window downstairs, the famous opening sequence of *When a Stranger Calls* turns this typical invasion scenario on its head. In this film a babysitter gets repeated calls asking her if she has checked the children, calls that she first interprets as random creepiness until she realizes the caller must be able to see her and gets very afraid. In a classic gothic scenario, to have the bad guy on the phone is oddly reassuring, because at least he is tied down to a phone somewhere. It is when he hangs up that the real danger begins. Indeed phones traditionally signify distance so powerfully that it is always a surprise to be called by someone who can see you. Thus terrified, the babysitter now calls the police, and they attempt to trace the call. The sequence ends with a cop calling her back in horror, telling her that they have traced the call from inside the house. It turns out a killer was upstairs with the now-dead children, calling from a second line to lure her to her doom. *When a Stranger Calls* turns the space of crime inside-out, or rather outside-in.[5] But rather than sustaining the most intense danger in the present tense, since the babysitter quickly escapes, the effect of the cop's warning is retrospective, imparting the haunting knowledge that the killer was in the house all along. Thus even if the phone can no longer be counted on to signify a safe distance, it remains nonetheless the essential link to safety.

Perhaps the most thorough undoing of telephonic security can be found in *The Terminator*. It is as if the evil machines of the future watched the movies of the last half century, mastering a wide repertoire of telephonic terror. The vulnerability of a phone book listing in *I Saw What You Did* comes back as the Terminator rips out the page with Sarah Connor's name on it and tracks her down (systematically killing two other Sarah Connors first). Then the Terminator tricks Sarah by reproducing her mother's voice on the phone, an impersonation that in its technical fidelity makes Brad Allen's playacting in *Pillow Talk* look like amateur hour. But the final insult has to be when the police chief has Sarah sleep on a couch in the police station, promising: "You'll be perfectly safe. We got thirty cops in this building." After all, he speaks as the guarantor of telephonic security, the one we call to deal with a threat. By the time the Terminator is done shooting up the police station, however, Sarah is beginning to think she had better rely on herself (as we discover at length in *T2*). Perhaps women must resign themselves to the wisdom of Miss Marple, who knows that "Murders . . . can happen anywhere. And do" (Christie, 26). If the law offers no protection at the very home of enforcement, perhaps it is time to abandon the dubious fortresses men build and hook up to a mobile female network.

Unfortunately, the representation of cell phones fails to leave telephonic terrorism in its dust—even an exuberant film like *Clueless* cannot manage to be wholly sanguine. To be sure, here cell phones seem especially promising for female networks, since sympathetic interest can be carried around in one's bag. Thus in a notable scene, Cher and her friend meet in the school hallway while still talking to each other on their phones. But this fantasy of uninterrupted friendly contact—or continuously coddled narcissism—fails to dispel a nightmare of total exposure and vulnerability. Cher's cell phone is not enough to prevent her from being mugged when a boy abandons her late at night in the Valley. Indeed the mugger steals the phone, knowing perhaps the darker possibilities of this technology. No longer tied to a hard line, the telephonic criminal roves about in the dark and peers in windows, like Tim Robbins as the stalking antihero of *The Player*. This stalking effect reaches its apotheosis in the opening sequence of *Scream* (a film, incidentally, that continues the gothic tradition of the boyfriend as suspect). As Drew Barrymore finds herself tormented by threatening calls, the sense of ubiquity created by the portability of phones exceeds all rational bounds. We learn later, of course, that this terrifying effect was the calculated plan of *two* killers' coordinated efforts. But this revelation fails to dispel a lingering doubt that we have not yet contained the uncanny power of cell phones to explode our sense of space once and for all.

Indeed, fiction has not outdone the real stories of cell phones' putting us in help-lessly close contact with almost unimaginable spaces of fear and death—recall, for instance, the story of Rob Hall, the climber at the summit of Mount Everest who called his wife at home in New Zealand when he realized he could not get down, or more famously the calls from the passengers of hijacked planes and workers in burning towers on 9/11.[6] Mountains, planes, and towers, moreover, are all in these devastating moments suddenly far too high for human beings. Catching us complacently overextended in space, the cell phone does as much to confirm as to eliminate our forgotten vulnerability. It is in this sense like the gothic itself, the genre that insists that we not get too comfortable, and which I would like to invoke once again in the context of romantic comedy, crossing the boundaries of genre to shed light on a new space of crime. This space is the Internet, the strange place born at the intersection of writing and phone lines.

The Godfather's Got Mail

Outside the gothic, new telephone technology is not so much terrifying as simply unmannerly. For some, people who talk on their cell phones in public are rude. For others, the inconsiderate are those who interrupt their conversations with us for call waiting, or screen our calls with Caller ID, or put us on speakerphone. It is all very offensive. *You've Got Mail*, Nora Ephron's 1998 comedy of manners, would avoid this vulgarity by avoiding the telephone. In fact, phone calls are very much what don't occur, a peculiarity all the more striking given this film's considerable ambition. Make no mistake, this is a movie with ideas: Ephron's romance plot—remarkably knowing to begin with—aggressively gathers the discourse of politics, business, and technology in its wake.[7] But amid such inclusion, omissions become all the more glaring, and the missing phones point toward an ominous foreclosure of possible networks.

The story develops instead through a series of comically illicit, anonymous e-mail exchanges in ironic counterpoint with face-to-face encounters. In real life Joe Fox is a third-generation business tycoon whose megastore is putting Kathleen Kelly's children's bookstore out of business. When Kathleen first meets Joe at a party, he inspires her personal animosity as well, mocking the value of her busi-ness, greedily scooping large quantities of caviar garnish, and referring sardoni-cally to books as the equivalent of vats of olive oil. But in cyberspace, Kathleen's "shopgirl" and Joe's "NY152" are already unwitting confidants, falling rapidly in love. And at no stage in the unfolding romance do they use the phone. There are a few incoming calls in Kathleen's shop (all so inconsequential that we never actu-ally see anyone on the phone), and one interesting call for help from inside a stuck elevator, but beyond that there is not a single phone call in the film—and nothing involving the cell phones or answering machines that we might expect to find in a movie otherwise concerned with technology. Needless to say, this is a strange picture of New York in the nineties. Indeed it contrasts markedly with the one we get in *Denise Calls Up* two years earlier, which, shunning *You've Got Mail*'s breezy neighborhood charm for claustrophobia, depicts the lives of New Yorkers as pathologically telephonic.

But *You've Got Mail* nonetheless participates in telephonic fantasy in a covert way, for much like earlier epistolary films, it cannot represent e-mail without the complicated deployment of voiceover, translating the written message into a private call between the characters that is overheard by the viewer. An early voiceover of Kathleen's sets the terms:

> "What will NY152 say today, I wonder? I turn on my computer. I wait impatiently as it connects. I go on-line and my breath catches in my chest until I hear 3 little words: You've got mail. I hear nothing, not even sounds on the streets of New York, just the beat of my own heart. I have mail. From you."

Her passion for e-mail speaks nothing of inscription or typography, but rather the telephonic language of saying and hearing, of breath, and it all runs on the same phone lines (this being before wireless Internet) that have carried affairs of the heart for the last century.

More than subsuming the telephone in its fantasy of e-mail, though, *You've Got Mail* invokes the phone several times as precisely the thing that has not happened. For instance, one character's anxiety about his published articles gets expressed in telephonic terms: "A week goes by and the phone doesn't ring." Or Joe discusses with Kathleen the alternate universe in which "if only" they had met as something other than business rivals: "I would've asked for your number. I wouldn't have been able to wait twenty-four hours before calling you up." Here the telephone finds itself in league with wistful fantasy, the link to a better world. But its capacity to bring worlds together is also a source of great anxiety for *You've Got Mail*.[8] Thus the most extended discussion of the telephone occurs at the exact point where cyberspace and physical space begin to collapse. Shopgirl and NY152 decide to meet, but when Joe shows up and sees that shopgirl is Kathleen, he decides not to reveal his identity. Later, discussing her disappointment with her staff, Kathleen cushions the blow of being stood up with a series of fantastic scenarios, all to explain why he did not call her: he was in a subway accident and there was "no phone"; he was in a car accident that left his elbows in splints "so he couldn't really dial"; he was the just-captured rooftop killer and used his one call to call his lawyer. Similarly, as Joe writes an e-mail to account for the failure of NY152 to appear, the first lame excuse he concocts (and deletes) is that he was stuck in a meeting and the electricity went out "and the telephone system blew too . . . amazingly enough." In a world of global telephone networks, only an emergency or an act of rejection can prevent communication, and the emergency, for this film, would be the lesser disaster. In its odd role here as the technology that must fail on command, the phone simultaneously threatens and keeps at bay the violence of these compensatory fantasies, and so too the genres that unleash that violence. If comedy is the genre that puts danger in its place, then the telephone is a trope through which comedy taps that place: the dangerous worlds of other genres.[9] Thus genre and technology combine forces to remove the space of crime. Under the regime of comic e-mail, crime literally cannot *take place*.

But it happens nonetheless. The longing of Kathleen's e-mail fantasies—what she calls "the dream of someone else"—quickly gets captured by a plot that I can only call gothic in its isolating and cornering effects. Much as in *Pillow Talk*, the opening comic coincidence plays out entirely at the heroine's expense. Like Brad Allen, Joe figures out the coincidence first; also like Brad, he manipulates Kathleen to his romantic advantage through a kind of fake triangulation, serving simultaneously as advisor and suitor. To be sure, here the game unfolds as more of a partnership, as Joe and Kathleen spend a leisurely third act flirting and speculating about who NY152 might be. But if *You've Got Mail* takes the heroine's desire more seriously than *Pillow Talk* does, that may just be a way of saying that its seduction is more convincing, rather than less gothic, than that of the earlier film. Indeed, in making Kathleen and Joe business rivals, *You've Got Mail* poses a more direct challenge to the heroine's economic independence than its predecessor. Joe's machinations finally cut much deeper than Brad's—his trick, we might say, is to shift the business model of their romance from one of his hostile takeover to one of her consumer choice.

That Kathleen becomes this romantic consumer precisely by ceasing to be a business owner is a fact obscured by an Oedipal narrative no less insidious than it is absurd. For what the film asks us to believe is that this transition is a matter of growing up. This is not to say that the loss of Kathleen's business is not depicted as painful—growing up always is. To be sure, her business, The Shop Around the Corner (named of course after the movie), is presented as very much a home, and we're asked to register the trauma of its loss. But to facilitate its eventual abandonment, the shop is haunted. Originally owned by her mother, it dwells in the tainted realm of maternal inheritance, as property that possesses the daughter rather than the other way around. The fact that Kathleen's mother is every bit the friendly ghost does not seem to disrupt this story in any significant way. Even her twirling appearance in a sentimental scene of farewell seems only to underscore the idea that Kathleen's store is ultimately a space to be weaned from. According to this ghost story, the horrifying question, encountered on a book as the camera browses the new Fox store, is "Are You Your Mother?" And when, by luring away Kathleen's customers, the Fox juggernaut finally steamrolls that possibility, we are asked to accept this violence as the belated enforcement of her painful but necessary individuation.

As if to ease the transition to the wide world of adulthood, what dominates the film is an astonishing proliferation of happy places, from the steady procession of spacious apartments and attractive eateries to various landmarks such as Zabar's and Gray's Papaya. Even the subway, closed space of the crowd, becomes utterly transformed for Kathleen's benefit by the unlikely appearance of a butterfly in a brief scene. But this relentless softening of New York space cloaks the question of whether in losing her bookstore Kathleen isn't emerging into a mass culture of *diminished* individuation. Indeed, in the debate about whether or not Fox Books can itself become a happy place (and no doubt many a Borders patron secretly cheers this film's partial challenge to enforced liberal sentimentality) lies hidden the film's more serious social question. This question is not at bottom a tradeoff between, say, price and service—a simple enough calculation easily comprehended as consumer choice. What is nice about not having to shop at a store like Kathleen's, I can say from experience, is that you don't have to talk to anybody. Anonymity is not merely lonely and alienating, it is immensely attractive and, as we all know, goes a long way toward explaining the appeal of the Internet.

But the film denies this appeal. Take, for instance, the scene that unfolds in a stuck elevator, the film's only true scene of confinement, and yet a scene that barely registers on the Richter Scale of claustrophobia with its four people casually seated on the floor. Joe has already impressed us by knowing that the elevator man is named Charlie, and in this scene he will have the chance to earn further points by caring deeply about Charlie's love life. Situated in his apartment building, this elevator is ostensibly removed from the social implications of the typical corporate elevator as vertical theater of economic hierarchy, with the enforced anonymity of its unspoken obligation to face the door in respectful silence. And yet there can be no question that the cost of Joe's privilege comes home, sleek corporate efficiency doubled by the sheer waste of having a man push buttons for other people.

But the spectacle of pointless labor is by no means what the scene wants us to notice. As I said above, this scene contains the film's only phone call of any significance, and indeed it accomplishes a great deal of work, for, stuck in a relationship with his girlfriend Patricia, Joe is much like the elevator, and here man and machine can be freed together. The scene begins with Joe's call for help, during which Patricia betrays her character by grabbing at the phone and shouting profanity into the mouthpiece. As they wait for help, they participate in a ritualized game of "What I will do if I get out alive," a game that Patricia loses badly. Her failure is a failure to observe the rules of genre: her own comments are not suitably romantic (she says she would get her eyes lasered), and then she steps on Joe's lines, searching sulkily for her tic tacs as he prepares his revelation. Her failure at this ritual is, moreover, simply an elaboration of her telephonic shortcomings. Absorbed in her anger and her impatience, she does not take turns. To a boyfriend who is cheating on her electronically, this rudeness is by comparison all too damning, for what defines his e-mail romance above all is precisely the orderly and luxurious taking of turns. Unlike phone calls, e-mail transmission can be delayed for revision and even deletion, allowing Joe to compose his thoughts, manage his mood, and send only his best self.

In its most baroque forms, then, the film's voiceover representation of e-mail unfolds a new kind of telephonic fantasy, one that incorporates desirable delays. During most of the film's e-mail exchanges, we merely hear the voice of the person typing, allowing the voiceover to act as if by telephone, without delay. But sometimes we hear that voice as the other reads its message, invoking the multiple moments of writing, reading, and narrated events implicit in all written correspondence. We are reminded of what until the answering machine remained an advantage of written communication over the telephone: it transcends time as well as space. Telephone calls transmit, but letters transmit and record. Their relative permanence buys time, maintaining even in the face of electronic transmission something of the rhythm of the post. To this rhythm shopgirl and NY152 dance, as does the film they inhabit. Banishing the telephone to the realm of bad surprises, *You've Got Mail* revels in protracted epistolary suspense.[10]

But here the epistolary persists with a difference, as becomes clear from one of Grandpa Fox's lines. Revealing, to Joe's surprise, that he had corresponded with Kathleen's mother long ago, he dwells fondly on her "beautiful penmanship." What is important is not the elevation of style over substance, since Joe and Kathleen's e-mails themselves are hardly substantive, but penmanship as the mark of a fixed individuality that can be celebrated as beautiful. However much letters allowed for games of identity, identity remained the name of the game. E-mail, by contrast, allows for a much fuller typographic anonymity and threatens to replace the temporary suspension of identity with perpetual flight. No longer simply a shelter from oppressive sociability, it is a technology of disappearance. Consider, for instance, what happens during a typical scene of writing e-mail. Beneath the trademark Meg Ryan cuteness, a hint of something darker unfolds in the contrast between Kathleen's fluent voiceover and her halting synchronized speech. What does she say with her physical voice? Sentence fragments that include the words "blank," "who recently belittled my existence," and "nothing." If e-mail is for Kathleen a form of self-composition, it is so in compensation for a self that will be increasingly shattered.[11] In some fundamental way the question that the film must resolve for romantic closure, and that creates its only real suspense, is not about who the hero will turn out to be, but about how much of herself the heroine can delete. It is here that we should locate the real crime of the film, as we trace Kathleen's disappearance into a lopsided marriage not to be confused with Internet anonymity. This being a romance plot, sooner or later the technology has to make way for the convergence of bodies.

You've Got Mail in fact offers two models of what happens when a big fish and a little fish come together. There is no doubt that Joe will consume her; the question is what exactly this consuming entails. The first model of consumption is the prevailing belief of Kathleen's bookstore, in which "You are what you read." According to this model, Joe cannot assimilate Kathleen without being changed by her, without perhaps even becoming her. A diminished version of this model survives in Joe's ironic comment that, thanks to Kathleen's influence, employees in the Fox Books children's section now need Ph.D.s. In playing this model out to such insulting lengths, however, the film avoids looking squarely at its other model of consumption, which is that Kathleen is such a small fish as to be caviar, a fine garnish for Joe to devour, and that she will disappear without a trace.

Indeed, as *You've Got Mail* saunters toward closure, the supporting characters drop out, leaving Kathleen in isolation, with little connection to who she was before Joe. Most important, the support from her friends in the shop, her female network, ends just when she needs it most. The disappearance of these relationships is all too consistent with the film's dark subterranean logic: they are gone because the shop is gone, and the shop is gone because Joe destroyed it. No wonder the film is so resolutely forward-looking. This is one couple that won't be telling the story of how they met. Of course the economic warfare is greatly muted by the fact that everyone is middle class and therefore no one will be going, as Joe's black flunky Kevin puts it, "Back to the projects with food stamps." The film is careful to let us know that two of Kathleen's employees will be financially solvent, though a third may have to face economic consequences and leave paradise for Brooklyn. But even to ask whether these minor characters will be all right without Kathleen is a convenient way of not asking if Kathleen will be all right without them.

You've Got Mail has from the beginning worked far harder than *Pillow Talk* to displace the gothic, to push it out of the frame of interest and into the colorful background. The signs of the hero's monstrosity that are so obvious with Brad, his grotesque physicality and his rapacious appetites, are all carefully displaced when it comes to Joe. Joe himself is very average looking—it is his father, as played by Dabney Coleman, who is the image of a comic monster, gnashing peanuts and spewing rhetoric like an ogre. Similarly, Joe's seductive talents are channeled safely into the business. Indeed the only time seduction gets mentioned in the film is when Joe describes his business strategy: "We are going to seduce them with our square footage, and our discounts, and our deep armchairs . . . and our cappuccino." All sexual excess gets pinned on the older Foxes, as their penchant for younger women spawns a distorted family portrait: Joe's aunt is actually a young girl. Such generational projection finds its source in Joe's favorite cultural reference, *The Godfather*, where Michael Corleone tells his girlfriend: "That's my family, Kay. It's not me." If it takes considerable violence for Kathleen to escape becoming her mother, Ephron seems to take Michael Corleone at his word and think it easy for men like Joe to avoid becoming their fathers. Coppola, of course, thinks otherwise and increasingly adopts Kay's point of view as *The Godfather* ends to show the horror of Michael's absorption into the mob.

You've Got Mail's obsessive joking reference to *The Godfather* amounts then to a rather hopeless disavowal, because the gangster's slogan, that his crimes of business are "not personal," is in fact what Kathleen comes to accept in accepting Joe, despite her protests to the contrary.[12] When Joe visits her sick at home after her shop has failed, she does react to his plea that "It wasn't personal" with a brief, sharp critique: "All that means is that it wasn't personal to you. But it was personal to me. It's personal to a lot of people. And what is so wrong with being personal anyway? Whatever else anything is, it ought to *begin* by being personal. My head is starting to get fuzzy." Unfortunately, whatever cogency this speech might have for a feminism rooted in the personal trails off into that concluding fuzzy-headedness, a sickness that infects the remainder of the film as its upbeat resolution cannot contain the dark generic contagion its conflicts have unleashed. Nothing makes this clearer than Ephron's own commentary on this scene, in which Joe invades Kathleen's apartment and finds his way to her bed: "It's almost like taking Omaha Beach, as I said to [Tom Hanks] in rehearsals. Since he had just done *Saving Private Ryan,* I thought that metaphor would be the sort of thing he might enjoy." The metaphor is startling in its honesty, as is the idea that a female director would proffer it so matter-of-factly to promote a romantic comedy. As the scene unfolds and Joe puts his hand on Kathleen's mouth to stop her insulting him, Ephron's commentary sustains the coupling of seduction and violence while reversing the vector of the metaphor: "When he puts his hands on her mouth, what I said to Tom was 'This is a kiss.'" And so seduction is violence, and silencing is love. *You've Got Mail* would be bold and insightful indeed if we were not supposed to be enchanted with these discoveries.

Both *You've Got Mail* and *The Godfather* funnel their heroines toward a fake moment of truth, what we would do better to call a moment of fiction. For Kathleen, this moment arrives when a date with Joe threatens to make her late for her appointment to finally meet NY152. Joe laments the circumstances of their acquaintance, and Kathleen is left with the choice of forgiving Joe on the spot, or leaving to see NY152. It is a funny kind of choice, and Joe's prior sardonic comments about patrons of Starbucks echo painfully at this moment:

> "The whole purpose of places like Starbucks is for people with no
> decision-making ability whatsoever to make six decisions, just to buy
> one cup of coffee: short, tall, light, dark, caf, decaf, low-fat, non-fat, etc.
> So, people who don't know what the hell they're doing or who on earth
> they are can, for only $2.95, get, not just a cup of coffee, but an absolutely
> defining sense of self."

Kathleen has in fact been a loyal Starbucks customer from the beginning. And we have to ask if Joe, who understands seduction so well, has not provided her with just this kind of false decision, to be mulled over by a sham self. After all, once you are thinking about caf or decaf, you are no longer thinking about whether you want coffee.

Of course the fact that Joe asks for forgiveness is not insignificant, since an admission of wrongdoing is more than we get from, say, Michael Corleone. But the timing of the scene, just as the pressure of the NY152 mystery has built to its apex, buys Joe this credit cheap. Unable to confront the plot of forgiveness directly, the film routes it through the plot of curiosity. Thus Kathleen chooses to avoid Joe's request and meet NY152 instead. This curiosity should return us to Kay's most painful moment in *The Godfather*, when she presses Michael about his involvement in murder. After some of his usual resistance to her interest in his activities, Michael sees an opportunity to put an end to her questions: "This one time. This one time I'll let you ask me about my affairs." The absurd denial that follows matters little to Kay, for she has won his participation in the sustaining fiction that he is good, and they are intimate. Kathleen's curiosity, like Kay's, seeks intimacy, not knowledge. She goes forth to meet NY152 because he is her confidant, and she hopes he will be Joe because that will unite her fantasies with the man who takes such an interest in them, enveloping her in the benevolent plenitude of narcissism. In *The Godfather*, Kay's bliss lasts all of a minute. Having left the room to prepare a drink (hoping to seal their new bond), she is shut out when one of Michael's henchmen closes the door in her face. It is this wrenching image of exclusion that ends the film, sealing Michael inexorably in the space of crime. *You've Got Mail* ends in the park, with a clinch and a dog, to tell us that all is right. But the lasting image is Joe's shrug just before, as Kathleen sees the truth. If romance is to be this resigned, what is the use of having romance? Joe of course gets what he wants, gets in fact to have his cake and eat it too, since Kathleen and shopgirl are one. When Kathleen greets him at the end with "I wanted it to be you," we are meant to believe her desires are as easily reconciled. And yet somewhere back in cyberspace, the dream of someone else gathers dust, colonized by a man who wouldn't know a dream from a vat of olive oil.

How to Fail a Turing Test, or: Murder in a Telepathy-Proof Room

I would like to suggest that the soft murder of Kathleen, her slow and subtle death by typing, has a specific history that is philosophical as well as cultural. The (dubious) production of Joe Fox as an acceptable human being under conditions of anonymous typed communication, and as the winner of a zero-sum game, can be seen as a frightening—and revealing—cultural extension of Alan Turing's famous test for artificial intelligence. Indeed, if AI remains perhaps the ultimate hi-tech fantasy, then it becomes a critical site for discovering the horizons of female networks (and a site I will return to in discussing *Blade Runner* and *The Terminator* in chapter 6). Laid out in the 1950 essay "Computing Machinery and Intelligence," the so-called "Turing Test" posits the ability to pass for human in tele-typed conversation as a guarantee of intelligence. Curious is Turing's decision to model his test on an "imitation game" involving the impersonation of a woman by a man:

> It is played with three people, a man (A), a woman (B), and an interrogator (C) who may be of either sex. The interrogator stays in a room apart from the other two. The object of the game for the interrogator is to determine which of the other two is the man and which is the woman. He knows them by labels X and Y, and at the end of the game he says either "X is A and Y is B" or "X is B and Y is A". . . . In order that tones of voice may not help the interrogator . . . the ideal arrangement is to have a tele-printer communicating between the two rooms. (433–34)

Thus Turing founds the epistemology of AI on a game of deception, a female impersonation routine that should remind us of Lovelace, our archetypal seducer, writing to Clarissa under the name of Anna Howe—should remind us also of Richardson himself, inaugurating the novelistic culture I've been describing through a monumental simulation of female writing. Moreover, when Turing makes the pivot into his discussion of thinking machines, something strange happens:

> We now ask the question, "What will happen when a machine takes the part of A in this game?" Will the interrogator decide wrongly as often when the game is played like this as he does when the game is played between a man and a woman? (434)

This initial formulation in fact contains two surprises—that the machine replaces the man and not the woman in the imitation game, and that the standard of success remains strangely tied to the man's performance in that prior game (the bar for artificial intelligence thereby fluctuating with the available quality of female impersonation). It would seem though that as the essay proceeds, these complications disappear—by the very next page the computer's task has been clarified as the "imitation of the behaviour of a man," and the deciding question is reformulated as follows: "Is it true that by modifying this computer . . . , C can be made to play satisfactorily the part of A in the imitation game, the part B being taken by a man?'" (435, 442).

Thus in retrospect Turing's prior formulation merely looks incomplete: he forgot to replace the woman. Perhaps we should have taken her discreet withdrawal for granted. This complacency has certainly been the path followed by most of the subsequent commentary, treating the Turing Test as simply a competition between a man and a machine for the most humanlike performance, with all the sexism that implies.[13] A recent intervention by Tyler Curtain, however, makes the opposite move. Advancing the important claim that cyberculture requires gender to be at once "a peripheral, negligible phenomenon" and an "indispensable" emblem of "world-knowledge," Curtain takes Turing at his initial word and keeps the woman in the room, ignoring the essay's subsequent gender realignment (141). Thus Curtain concludes that the Turing Test

> succeeds only in reseating gender firmly within "intelligence" itself: a woman is put in the position of defending and authenticating her gender across the network; in turn, a computer authenticates its intelligence only if it simulates her gender better than she can across the same network. (142)

Here we find the woman in a position that has been familiar since *Clarissa*: she is put to the test, bearing the burden of proving her full humanity. But while this conclusion is far more revealing than the routine sexism of Curtain's predecessors, it seems still to miss something about the now-you-see-her, now-you-don't figuration of the woman in this essay.

As it happens, Turing is not done with gender once he asks a man to represent humanity in the big showdown. For instance, our thoughts may drift back toward an image of the displaced woman when he justifies sequestering the competitors from the interrogator: "We do not wish to penalize the machine for its inability to shine in beauty competitions" (435). Or consider the strange appearance of gender in the section where Turing meets the "Theological Objection," according to which the idea of a thinking machine is a species of blasphemy. Turing remarks:

> The arbitrary character of [this objection] becomes clearer if we consider how it might appear to a member of some other religious community. How do Christians regard the Moslem view that women have no souls? But let us leave this point aside and return to the main argument. (443)

Indeed a certain arbitrary character, if not much else, becomes clearer in this example. What we should note, however, is not so much the rather elusive point of Turing's argument at this moment, but its larger rhythm and pattern. Again women appear only to be immediately left aside, and again women appear with their human endowments under question (even if the source of that question is projected outwards). Moreover, if we return to the essay's opening move with this passage in mind, the initial failure to replace the woman with a man begins to look less like a simple omission than an enabling suspension. It is as if Turing's essay has to be approached by way of an ironic slogan: women—can't think with them, can't think without them.

Making this approach becomes especially urgent when we consider the sanitation that has occurred in the collective philosophical production of the Turing Test in all its elegance. Indeed, the odder turns of Turing's mind, by no means confined to matters of gender, have evidently proved embarrassing enough to be studiously ignored. In considering the relevance of a machine's ability to enjoy strawberries and cream as a basis for conversational affinity, for example, Turing refers to "the difficulty of the same kind of friendliness occurring between man and machine as between white man and white man, or between black man and black man" (448). This backhanded tribute to racial solidarity could not be more out of left field—it is the only mention of race in the entire essay, a rather hysterical recruitment of difference offered, we might suppose, in lame compensation for the white male human's looming loss of superiority to the machine. And no one talks about it.[14] No less strange, and of immediate interest for this book, is Turing's astonishing concern with telepathy. Addressing what he calls "The Argument from Extra-Sensory Perception," Turing informs us that "the statistical evidence, at least for telepathy, is overwhelming" (453). Worried, then, that humans will defeat intelligent computers by telepathic cheating, supplementing their typing with an illicit channel of communication, Turing logically concludes that we must "put the competitors into a 'telepathy-proof room'" (454). Few commentators acknowledge this remarkable stipulation, as if the community of philosophers has conspired to avoid the scandal of an occult female network appearing at the origin of their conversation on a serious subject.[15] Thus telepathy is twice disallowed, first by Turing's magical architecture, and second by a rational discourse that knows far more efficient purifications.

John Durham Peters has pointed out that these kinds of purifications derive from the tradition of philosophical idealism, with its preference for lonely souls agonizing over vast communicative barriers. His description of this tradition has a clear gothic resonance: "The favored architecture of idealism is the closed room containing a subject out of touch with others"—in other words, an ideal place for a crime (180). Indeed, Peters goes on to describe the Turing Test as a "good murder mystery" for its elimination of the body from consideration, advocating instead a model of communication that is openly erotic and embodied, that remains faithful to what he calls the "insuperability of eros" (237, 233). But if we recall *Pillow Talk* or *You've Got Mail*, we might doubt how easy it is to escape the gothic by way of romance, even if technology gives way to the eventual convergence of bodies. The trouble is, of course, that the Turing Test is *already* a romance, that eros in fact thrives on the sensory deprivations that attend words spoken or written from a distance. And while Peters will go on to offer a moving tribute to the importance of touch, back in the closed room humanity is disappearing not as a consequence of murder (indeed the ultimate betrayal of touch) but as a consequence of seduction. After all, what better way to describe the task of Turing's sweet-talking computer? The cost of this seduction is perhaps borne less by the surprised interrogator, who might even have a thing for machines, than by the losing human. If there is a murder in this room, it is less in the initial hiding of the body than in the transfer of humanity from the human to the machine in a zero-sum game. It is perhaps not surprising then that Turing's followers have displayed much of the Cold War's signature paranoia, followers for whom the game of "spot-the-machine" might mobilize anxieties familiar from games of "spot-the-communist" and—dangerous for Turing—"spot-the-homosexual." Within this context, the game of "spot-the-woman" that we began earlier looks like a bit of a shell game, in which every attempt to locate her reveals a mocking man or machine.

This game is by no means confined to the literature on AI. Turing's essay appears two years after Litvak's Leona Stevenson undergoes her trial on the telephone in *Sorry, Wrong Number*, with her humanity—her credibility as a thinking and feeling creature—emerging only as a trace of her disappearance. And indeed it is written in the midst of a culture obsessed with the *femme fatale* as a creature of supposedly dubious humanity. This game proliferates as theme and variations throughout the Cold War, from the nearly world-ending question of *Fail Safe* (is that really the pilot's wife calling him home, or a Soviet impersonator?), to the more personal obsessions of films such as *Vertigo* (which will be discussed in chapter 6) and *The Conversation*. In fact the latter film is notable for its reproduction of Turing's spatial configuration, with its climactic scene of hi-tech eavesdropper Harry Caul losing his mind in a hotel room adjacent to the closed space of crime, tormented by what Peters calls "the idealist trope of the wall" and by the discovery that the innocent woman he thought he was protecting does not exist as such (183). Interestingly, it is not entirely clear that this hotel room is in fact "telepathy-proof," insofar as Harry's breakdown seems to involve an intense experience of the neighboring crime.[16] Unable, finally, to spot the woman as a redemptive figure of humanity, Harry returns to his own apartment and famously turns his aggression against the walls themselves as he searches for a recording device—his game thus degenerating into its most paranoid form: spot-the-bug.[17]

But as written, rather than as commonly received, Turing's essay is to some extent the opposite of paranoid, fearlessly welcoming machines into the community of thinking entities. It is, in a word, romantic. After all, what else to call the inference, based only on the machine's observable performance in the test, that the machine was actually thinking, the inference that so irked John Searle in a well-known response? Isn't it the same generous leap we make when we infer that the person opposite us is not only intelligent, but maybe even loving? And how many romance plots turn on the equivalent of Turing's premise—that in simulating love (typically in the form of pretending to be married), love is achieved? What I want to suggest, in fact, is that the will-o'-the-wisp aspect of the woman in this essay can lead us out of the locked room and toward a dream of artificial intelligence as a promising extension of female networks. If philosophy seems hellbound for a definitive unveiling, in which once and for all some poor machine does or does not think, then perhaps our task is to suspend this teleology. One of the striking things about Turing's essay is that it reads so much like a series of thoughts, without the benefit of correction (there is even a mathematical error). Unfolding before us in time, it is a bit like conversation, a bit like he himself was taking the test, and so we might do well to restore the role of surprise and suspense to our understanding of

Turing's thought. Remembering its origins in a parlor game, what would it mean to play the Turing Test for fun?

To address this question, we should perhaps begin with Timothy Clark's observation that "the interrogator, asymmetrically, might also be seen as the very scene or stage of the effect, describable as both part of the spectacle and part of the audience" (26). Or in Mary McGee Wood's version: "I could argue that the Turing simulation does indeed desire me, that it needs my discourse, the discourse of the other, to stir it into 'life'" (223). It is good to see that Wood inserts herself without hesitation into the game, for indeed we should not forget that the interrogator may be "of either sex" (433). As at once the observer and the observed, the desirer and the desired, the interrogator of either sex introduces considerable erotic ambiguity. What is more, the test cannot be put into practice without introducing epistemological doubts far more radical than the either/or question it pursues. As she administers the test, all that the interrogator really knows is that she has been *told* that the room contains a computer and a man, and that someone or something is typing back at her. But as anyone who has ever participated in a university psychology experiment knows, scientists don't always tell you what they are really testing for.[18] Thus during the test something approaching a full erotic menu emerges, with all responses asking the implicit question, "Who do you *want* me to be?" It doesn't seem that the desire for a female network can ever be ruled out among any of the test's three players. Indeed, what are those two—if two they are—really up to in the locked room? (or so we might wonder during a long lag in the typing). Crime isn't the only thing a locked room is good for.

I would argue then that for the best legacy of the Turing Test to emerge, we have to wait for a film like the Wachowski Brothers' *Bound* (1996). Following *The Conversation*, *Bound* subjects one of its heroines to conditions of tormented adjacency, with Corky the butch fix-it woman assuming Harry's earlier listening position at a hotel wall and toilet bowl (see figs. 5.1 and 5.2). Widely considered neo-*noir*, this film plays the specter of the *femme fatale* against a specifically lesbian humanity, as Corky has to decide if her hopes for sexual and criminal partnership with the voluptuous Violet are worth the risk of deadly betrayal. One of the interesting things about the lesbian wrinkle is that, in collapsing spot-the-human/woman/homosexual into a single game—and revaluing each term—it threatens to collapse the structure of paranoia by depriving it of stable oppositions. Fortunately for Corky, she never quite manages to confine Violet to an either/or question, and this elusiveness proves irresistible. As the paranoia of Harry's position gives way to romance, we might say that *Bound* asks what happens to the space of crime when women stop trying to be safe and start trying to be happy.

This is certainly the choice Violet makes as well, abandoning her "work" (her word) as girlfriend to the mob in favor of the high-stakes alliance with Corky. Here happiness in fact depends not only on the acceptance, but on the enjoyment, of risk. What begins, at least for Corky, as a tentative if highly charged sexual

Figures 5.1 (above) and 5.2 (left) Tormented adjacency in *The Conversation* and *Bound*.

relationship evolves into a criminal partnership, which Corky says requires still more trust. Their plan is not just to get Violet out of the mafia, but to get her out with a huge cash bonus. Their opportunity comes when a mob accountant gets caught embezzling $2.176 million, enraging, we are told, another gangster, who shoots him on the spot, splattering the money with blood. When Violet's boyfriend, Caesar, becomes responsible for cleaning and counting the cash, the women plot to steal it before his boss shows up to claim it. If they can get Caesar to think his rival stole the money to set him up, perhaps he will panic and run away, convincing the mob that *he* was the thief while freeing them of suspicion.

In representing a female partnership as unambiguously criminal and sexual, *Bound* articulates a vision of female networking fully independent of men, subject neither to male law nor to male desire. It is this independence that enables Violet to reply, when Caesar asks what Corky did to her, "Everything you couldn't." But *Bound*'s solicitation of male desire in particular has been the subject of critique, with the specific objection that Violet and Corky's soft-core sex scene early in the film plays into an established genre of lesbian pornography for the benefit of male viewers.[19] And in a sense there is no getting around this scene as a sexual spectacle, for no matter how it is framed in the narrative, there is nothing to prevent a viewer from skipping to the dirty parts. But I do think it is worth noting that there is something strange going on in how this sex is framed, and that this strangeness has interesting implications for the film as a whole. The scene begins with Corky and Violet making out in Corky's truck, then, without an obvious cut, the camera pans up through the floor of a room where we see them having sex in bed. It is as if the truck were somehow the room below and we have just floated up in the space where a wall should be. Thus the camera stages any pornographic male gaze as impossible—impossible, moreover, precisely in spatial terms. And this impossibility does not support a male fantasy of omniscience so much as contribute to an overall argument of the film that men are naive about space, letting their desires determine what they see.

Until the very end, Caesar thinks that all the important action of this film takes place in the space of his apartment and that he controls that space. He is so fatally overconfident, in fact, that, in a remarkable scene, he hangs $100 bills, newly washed of blood, all over the apartment to dry, then irons them one by one, all with Violet as his only companion. After all, as Corky and Violet discuss, and as Caesar must reason, few people are brave, or foolish, enough to steal from the mob. Contemptuous of the police, whom he calls "just cops," fairly sure that he is smarter than his fellow mobsters, and confident, finally, in the ultimate authority of his gun, Caesar feels he can handle just about anything that happens in his apartment until his discovery of the missing money throws him into a panic. Even then he remains resourceful and, he thinks, in control of his fate, so long as he stays at home and doesn't "run."

But Caesar's apartment is in fact a highly porous space, hemorrhaging desire, information, and money behind his back. The walls are thin and the pipes conduct sound, so that Corky gets a pretty clear idea of what is going on (and these events range from sex to dismemberment) while working, or waiting, next door. Moreover, Caesar has far less control of the phone, the door, and the elevator than he thinks—the crucial links for regulating his exposure to the outside world. Violet twice betrays him in the elevator, eyeing Corky behind his back in their first encounter, and later betraying him to his bosses on a cell phone. And Corky continually enters the apartment through the only door, coming first for sex, then money, then finally to save Violet. There is also a strange moment when Corky appears from out of nowhere in the kitchen with Violet, just after Caesar brings the bloody money to the apartment. It is not clear if there has been an ellipsis or if we are supposed to think Caesar is totally oblivious, or indifferent, to her presence, but in any case the effect is the same: Corky's access to this space seems effortless and uncanny. Caesar does nearly catch Corky and Violet having sex but becomes relieved to see that it is Corky in the darkened apartment with Violet instead of a man. Unable to conceive of Corky as a sexual rival, Caesar is much quicker to see Violet as a *femme fatale*. Indeed it is Violet's more conventional role as the duplicitous woman on the telephone that Caesar first gets wise to.

Violet twice uses the phone in the bedroom to call Corky next door, letting her know how the plan is going. The second time, they linger briefly on the line, putting their hands up to the wall that separates them—as if by telepathic understanding—and intimating their strong feelings for each other. Apparently not the least of Caesar's oversights was neglecting to secure a telepathy-proof room! But for Corky and Violet this delay proves costly, as Caesar catches Violet hanging up. At first glance the film here seems to cast Violet as a Leona Stevenson, who doesn't know the difference between urgent business and mere desire. In this view, the film punishes her for the nonbusiness part of the call, for an exchange of affection that went beyond the information necessary to the plan. On the other hand, the plan is useless without trust, and therefore the personal connection was in fact the most essential business of the call, especially from Violet's position. After all, when this call is made, Corky is sitting in the next room with $2.176 million, plenty of incentive to abandon her partner. In any case, Caesar does reclaim control of his phone line at this moment—he is not so stupid as to neglect to hit redial—and now the thin walls work against Corky, for Caesar hears the phone ringing through the wall. Asking Violet who is over there, he begins to understand that he has misperceived the space of crime. Caesar in fact discovers the violations of his apartment in reverse order, noticing first the missing money, then the leak of information. What Caesar never gets wise to, and what proves his undoing, is the flow of desire.

At one level of rhetoric, desire in *Bound* is little more than a question of taste. Thus people seem to express what they want first through a predetermined range of consumer choices, like Joe Fox's hypothetical Starbucks customer. Leading Corky through a ritual of self-disclosure to learn that she drinks her coffee black, drinks beer, and drives an old red truck, Violet responds to each revelation with the same confidence in her predictive powers, saying "Of course" or "I thought so." Caesar's rival, Johnny, will later attempt a poor imitation of this come-on, insistently drinking the same "T&T" as Violet. But never is the desire to drink really in question. One *has* to choose from among the available options as a sign of sociability. Only the impotent police suffer outside the loop, declining drinks because they are on duty and not allowed to express desire (only the expression of need is permissible, as one of them asks to use the bathroom). Taste is the kind of desire Caesar can understand—it is what leads him to make sure the mob boss will have Glenlivet, his favorite scotch, when he visits. But such understanding is not enough for him to anticipate the desires of Violet and Corky.

Sexuality for Violet and Corky cannot be reduced to a matter of taste—not to the consumer logic of male pornography, which makes of sexuality a kind of fetishistic smorgasbord—nor is it fair to say that they have a mere taste for crime. To be sure, they play a typical game of displayed desire, not just in discussing drinks and cars, but with their tattoos and clothes. The coy signification of these displays, however, quickly gives way to far more serious communication, culminating in Violet's passionate confession of desire: "I want out." This plea is a normal enough response to gothic conditions, for a heroine trapped in the space of crime. But her desire to be out is clearly doubled—to be out not only as a general negation of all that she is in, but out, also, of the closet and into an open ownership of her sexuality. Of course the irony is that when Violet speaks her desire, the more openly lesbian Corky has been literally in the closet for the whole film. In typical *noir* fashion, *Bound* is framed as a flashback, proceeding backward from a shot of Corky tied up in a closet to account for how she got there. The masochism of this retrospective framing, with its suspense and its suggestion of bondage, is, as Chris Straayer points out, not without its countervailing energy, for we also flash forward through much of Corky and Violet's plan as they hash it out (151). And yet we never forget that we will eventually catch up with Corky bound on the floor.

But if there is something of a death wish lurking in Corky and Violet's daring plan (and it might be worth speculating about whether they will ever steal again), the chief pleasure of this film ultimately enlists both anticipation and retrospection in the service of heightened present consciousness. At a deeper level, *Bound* imagines desire largely in terms of secrets, of knowledge hoarded, and, more rarely, of knowledge shared. The continual hiding of money and bodies has less to do with any practical concern for the future on the part of the characters than with their need, and the film's, to stage the experience of the secret repeatedly, and in new combinations. A great part of what Corky and Violet love—and love to share—is the knowledge of putting one over on Caesar. In this respect they have the same kind of desire that he trumpets with such parodic excess. Recall his horror at the thought that Johnny is setting him up (he repeats the phrase "laughing at me" obsessively), or his insane gloating over Johnny's dead body once he knows he has won ("Who's dead, fuckface? Guess again."). Like all con artists, what Caesar revels in as a winner is the same thing he can't stand as a loser: surplus knowledge. But what the women who undermine him in his own space know is that what he takes for his knowledge is really just wishful thinking, really just desire. Thus Corky anticipates him beautifully: "The second he opens up that case, he's gonna know in his gut that Johnny fucked him." Of course how he reacts to this "knowledge" comes as a bit of a surprise to Corky, as he proves to be just slightly smarter than she thought. But even once Caesar catches on to their plan, he has not in fact closed the gap in knowledge, for he does not learn Violet's last secret until too late: "You don't want to shoot me, do you Vi? Do you? Do you? I know you don't." Violet's response, and the stream of bullets that accompany it, might well speak to all men who underestimate the range of female desire: "Caesar, you don't know shit."

And so, out of its heist plot, *Bound* has constructed a lesbian test, though perhaps not a reliable one. Lee Wallace has offered a detailed critique of this test, claiming that Hollywood has not come very far in the representation of queer sexuality. Wallace observes that the sex scenes are confined to the first part of the film and that they fail to resolve the question of Violet's status as a genuine lesbian. Instead, he argues, the burgeoning lesbian romance gets hijacked by the heist plot, which systematically substitutes violence for sex, most notably in a pivot from fingers as sex organs to fingers as something for gangsters to cut off with pliers. This general pattern of substitution enables conventional plot closure to pass for convincing character revelation, culminating in Violet's "proving" her lesbianism only by gunning Caesar down in spectacular fashion. Thus for Wallace, "The lesbianism of *Bound*'s characters . . . is foremost and finally a function of the plot"—is, in the last word, "cinematic" (386, 387).

It might be useful then to try to reconstruct the implicit test that Wallace himself administers—and *Bound* fails—in light of the Turing Test, for we can notice right away that the Hollywood "machine" appears in the programmed position, seducing us with treacherous simulations. Indeed, Wallace's reading of the typical viewer is akin to my reading of Caesar as the narrative's dupe: "The cinematic sleight goes unnoticed, perhaps, because of our viewerly investments in narrative outcome and closure. We can be relied on to see what we want" (387). Of course, if we're identified with Caesar, we *should* be paranoid, though even then I'm not sure we want to paint ourselves into such a corner that the term "cinematic" is a clinching denunciation. Interesting is the metaphor Wallace uses to address the film's central question of Violet's identity: "The question of Violet's trustworthiness is indexed to two equally paranoid structures, those of sexual orientation and organized crime" (384). The term "indexed" conjures another game of spot-the-woman, a game in which we look Violet up and find her cross-listed, a game once again of now-you-see-her, now-you-don't. My point is that, as in the Turing Test, the very doubling of the paranoid structures (tripling if we're more attentive to gender) is what defeats them, generating an erotic complexity that dodges even the most desperate vigilance.

Where Wallace's argument generates a lingering doubt for me is in the way it seems to arise from a basic concern for all the men who are chopped up and blown away in this film, and particularly out of an identification with Caesar (who attracts such adjectives as "brilliant") that I mentioned earlier (384). I say this not because I suddenly want to abandon this book's attention to female characters, but because I do have a doubt that this film is just about lesbians triumphant. It is hard to dismiss, for instance, the claim that Caesar is written as the film's most charismatic character: while Violet and Corky exchange more than their share of clichés and platitudes, he delivers line after line of imaginative dialogue. If Caesar's collection of idiosyncracies threatens to steal the whole show, it seems understandable that Wallace would find pathos in his death and not allow the violence visited on his body to pass unremarked. Overall, as the body count mounts, and the pliers embrace another finger, it is hard not to feel sometimes that the lesbian characters are indeed a means to an end, the sexy new vehicle (like Corky's new red truck) delivering a familiar payload.

It is certainly a depressing thought to imagine *Bound*'s female networks, operating with an abandon we haven't seen in this discussion since *Moll Flanders*, sucked into our culture's ever-expanding black hole of male violence, irony, and nostalgia. But if the film's gangster pastiche wins the day for some, perhaps this defeat points toward the space where female networks must now resume operations, a space that isn't really a space at all. For if everywhere the end of history is recognized in the proliferation of retro performances like Joe Pantoliano's Caesar (in a diagnosis that is difficult to distinguish from the symptoms it observes), then perhaps female networks must forge connections across this reigning (a)temporal order, connections across the time we are told no longer exists.[20] As it happens, this is no time to be confined to the *space* of crime, with postmodern culture and theory conspiring to lob a grenade into the locked room. Here is Fredric Jameson talking about films like *Speed* which reduce "plot to the merest pretext or thread on which to string a series of explosions":

> the fundamental formal principle of such films . . . is something like a unity of place or, at least, a confinement within a *closed space of some kind*. The defining framework can be a high-rise building, an airport, an airplane, a train, an elevator, or, as here a city bus. . . . But the closure is formally essential in order to render escape impossible and to ensure the absolute saturation of the violence in question, like the walls within which a proper explosion can best be realized. Something peculiar then follows from this requirement; the closure now becomes allegorical of the human body itself and reduction to the vehicle of closure in these films represents the reduction to the body that is a fundamental dimension of the end of temporality or the reduction to the present. (16, my emphasis)

This is how to fail a Turing Test. "Saturate" the locked room with instantaneous violence—violence understood as "a specific form of temporality," as an aesthetic of pure speed—in order to abolish the time for conversation (13). Jameson seems right to read this scenario as a form of covert idealism in its denial of "the" body's material specificity and ideological construction, but we might wonder why, instead of rewriting the scenario, he inflates it into a distinctive description of our era (13–14). After all, how different is the saturation bombing he observes from the violence in that first locked room on the Rue Morgue, a violence that forcefully ejected two dead female bodies from the space of crime? Thus Caesar, in a rather pithy echo of Jameson, articulates the obsessive question that a temporizing female network—and the next chapter—will have to contend with: "Who's dead *now*?"

CHAPTER 6

Time Stalkers

Film is an immeasurable expansion of the realms of the dead.
Friedrich Kittler, Gramophone, Film, Typewriter

In the wake of the telephone, the locked room seems a leaky old container, needing ever-growing cultural reinforcements to maintain the myth that it could be a suitable defense for a woman. And it may already be clear from previous chapters that chief among these reinforcements is the stalker, the figure summoned at every crisis point to chase women back into their rooms. But as the stalker confronts isolated women with the usual gothic choices of fight or flight, his work must not be seen as limited to his relentless domination of space. As Orit Kamir has argued, the "stalker's repeated returns to the other's life create a circular time frame that unites pursuer and prey in a closed, seemingly-eternal cycle" (17). Following the stalker through two pairs of films—*The Terminator* and *Klute*, then *Blade Runner* and *Vertigo*—this chapter will confront the peculiar nature of this eternity, which gets defined with remarkable consistency in opposition to another temporality—a time of female relationships. If all four of these films are famously films of the city, their ambivalent urban tours will confirm a double pattern: in each case the stalker will strive to leave the heroine cut off from other women, and in each case the film will stake the question of modernity and progress on his success. By way of the eternal heroine, the stalker chases time itself.

This abuse of the past constitutes criminal necrophilia, the stalker's desire drifting between the act of murder and the corpse itself, between wanting things dead (eternal women) and wanting dead things (compliant women). Splitting the stalking function between two characters—a killer and a lover—is perhaps the simplest way to manage this equivocation, projecting aggression onto the killer who can be destroyed; I have paired *The Terminator* and *Klute* as powerful examples of this encompassing strategy. When the stalker remains an ambiguous single figure, as in *Blade Runner* and *Vertigo*, murderous desire may finally catch up with him, though even then the engrossing spectacle of the hero's shame tends to obscure female escape routes for characters and viewers alike. What all four films insist on is the projection of necrophilia back onto the heroines, a projection achieved by representing female networks as inhabiting in various ways a realm of morbid simulation. Like all simulations, these tainted networks emerge as a question of media, though in this case of the personal kind most available to women. In this way this last chapter will develop the book's interest in communications technology from the question of transmission to the question of recording and storage. In their scrupulous attention to paintings and photography, tape recorders and answering machines, stalkers would rededicate storage media, disabling the extension of female networks through time in favor of perpetual male fantasy.

Splitting the Stalker: The Terminator and Klute

Starting with *The Terminator* should make the stakes of this scenario all too clear, as this film unleashed a stalker who would eventually swell so far beyond his original movie as to become governor of California. Appealing perhaps more because of than despite revived charges of sexual harassment by Schwarzenegger—more because of than despite his iconic status as a stalker of women—the Terminator's political afterlife forces us to wonder about stalking as cultural policy, particularly as a means of circumscribing female destiny,[1] As the stalker's obsessive attention locks his target in the crosshairs, it is hard to imagine a narrative engine more efficient in enforcing female singularity.[2] Indeed we should not ignore how flattering even an assassin's attention can be. For *The Terminator*'s Sarah Connor, the waitress who suffers humiliations at work and spends Friday night alone, it means suddenly that she is worth killing. Thus early in the film both she and the police are quick to interpret the deaths of two other women named Sarah Connor the same way: the deaths are linked, and Sarah may soon share their fate. Of course she will quickly learn that her destiny is not to be confused with those of the other Sarah Connors—their misfortune is to be confused with someone who matters, their elimination raises the possibility of female multiplicity only to confirm that there can be only one.

At home, the film needs to separate Sarah from her roommate, the perpetually headphoned Ginger, as we see when Ginger's boyfriend Matt calls on a Friday night as they get ready to go out. Mistaking the answering Sarah for Ginger, he launches into a phone sex routine. If Sarah is amused for the moment, it is only because she thinks she ultimately controls the telephone, only because she has no idea how soon her identity will be made unmistakably clear. But as I argued in chapter 5, this film will purge the telephone of female networking in all conceivable ways. Indeed, special attention goes to the phone's new assemblage in the 1980s with the answering machine, which is first heard from in a follow-up scene as the women continue their evening preparations. The first message is from Sarah's mother and is hard to hear—we will not hear her voice clearly in this film until it has been appropriated by the Terminator's voice-imitation technology. The second is Sarah's date calling to cancel and provides a moment of classic female networking, with Ginger offering sympathy and the sisterly promise to "break his kneecaps." If at first female networking enjoys a mild enhancement from this technology, it is again, however, at the price of a debilitating exposure, for when Sarah later calls Ginger for help, she succeeds only in revealing her location to the Terminator. Culturally, it is an old trick, converting female networks from a source of strength into a point of vulnerability.[3]

But there is something more elaborate going on here with the answering machine, as we see when we begin to think about Ginger's performance on their outgoing message:

> "Hi there. Fooled you. You're talking to a machine. But don't be shy; it's okay. Machines need love too. So talk to it, and Ginger—that's me—or Sarah will get back to you. Wait for the beep."

It is a prosaic enough performance, perhaps, but what interests me about it is how, in staging the deception of the caller by a technology of female impersonation, it reprises the terms of the Turing Test discussed in chapter 5. Indeed, it would seem to grant Turing's scenario its most generous form, soliciting conversation and love for the machine. But this generosity must be disallowed in *The Terminator*, for nowhere has the murderous paranoid reaction to Turing's fantasy of artificial intelligence been more virulent. After all, this is a film about how a thinking machine "decided our fate in a microsecond: extermination." And so it is no surprise that we never hear the answering machine playing the games Ginger intended. Instead, the first time we begin to hear the outgoing message is when the police are calling to warn the absent Sarah. Ginger is by now having sex with Matt, who turns up the volume on her walkman, drowning the answering machine out for her and us. When we finally hear the message all the way through, it is when Sarah calls for help, but by then Matt and Ginger are dead. Thus this film presents the promise of the answering machine only under the sign of tragic irony—the talking Ginger is truly a ghost in the machine, and she won't be getting back to anybody. As haunted recording technology, the answering machine relegates female networks to the morbid past.

If Sarah receives her future as the dubious gift of the Terminator, the question remains of just what kind of gift this is. What is striking about *The Terminator* is how much it grants Sarah—we feel we are watching her become an action hero, a process underscored by the conclusion in Mexico, which emphasizes her mobility and knowledge. As she utters the words "I know" and drives off in a jeep (a military upgrade from the moped of her opening shot), we seem to have come a long way from the conclusion of *Chinatown*, where Evelyn's escape to Mexico is cut brutally short. But clearly it still matters *where* you are going and *what* you know. Up to this point the film has routed Sarah through a decidedly flat and dark Los Angeles—a particularly desolate version of "The Plains of Id" that Reyner Banham once identified as but one of L.A.'s four "ecologies."[4] Sarah's beleaguered vitality seems admissible precisely because it is out of step with this environment and can blossom only within the plot that arrives from the future. What Sarah "knows" is that the present must be abandoned as hopeless, must indeed be seen as already past.

The Terminator asks us to believe at the end that we are witnessing the birth of a legend, as Sarah prepares for the paramilitary training that will play out in the sequel. But as welcome as the prospect of a female legend might be, we do need to wonder: where are the *women* she is inspiring? After all, the person motivated by the legend of Sarah Connor is Kyle Reese, the film's second stalker, who has been sent from the future by Sarah's son John to save her from the Terminator. It is Reese who will inform her that she is the "mother of the future," since John has grown up to lead the humans against the machines—Reese who will sire that son, and Reese who will deploy the fear of the Terminator to set her in motion along this prescribed path: "That Terminator is out there. It can't be bargained with. It can't be reasoned with. It doesn't feel pity, or remorse, or fear. And it absolutely will not stop—ever. Until you are dead." Thus Sarah's destiny as a child-bearing vessel is neither self-authored nor open to revision. Being stalked may get Sarah moving, but she can only go in a circle.

The author of this future is John Connor, a character whose absence in this film from all but hearsay representation makes him all the more viable as a source and entry point for viewerly fantasies. Fundamentally, he mobilizes the common time travel theme known as the grandmother paradox—the fantasy in which a time traveler goes back and kills or impregnates his grandmother, a fantasy with obvious appeal to a male ego horrified by its own contingency.[5] What is interesting about *The Terminator* in this respect is how it deploys both versions of the fantasy through its tag-team of surrogate stalkers. It is important that Reese's stalking is at first hard to distinguish from the Terminator's—they both emerge from a particular place in the culture that is here called John Connor, the figure who must ultimately be seen as the film's real villain. But with Reese pursuing John's fantasy of incest, and the cyborg his fantasy of homicide, the future hero's hands are clean.

Crucially, both the sexual and the homicidal stalking traverse a definitive historical break—a nuclear holocaust—that conveniently inflates the desire for self-fathering and self-destruction into the dream of world-fathering and world-destruction. John Connor's initials are not an accident—he is an obvious Christ figure—but even more, he gets to play God too. Recall the message that John asks Reese to deliver to Sarah: "You must survive or I will never exist." The unspoken corollary of that line is, "There must be a nuclear holocaust or I will never get to be the leader of humanity." After all, if these future humans have the power to travel back in time, why aren't they trying to prevent the holocaust unleashed by the thinking machine? John enjoys a classic apocalyptic fantasy: if only I could get rid of all these people, I could really be somebody.[6] To be sure, we have heard versions of this idea before—in Orson Welles's "panic broadcast" of *The War of the Worlds,* for instance, or in Peter Sellers's gleeful speculations in *Dr. Strangelove*—but in both of those narratives it is played for the sick fantasy that it is. And while *The Terminator*'s sequels try to back away from this logic, these revisions are like trying to unring a bell. The fact remains that John Connor sends Reese back across time to *preserve* a horrible future.[7]

Unlike the Terminator, who comes to 1984 armed only with Sarah's name, Reese knows her face from an old photograph that found its way to the battlegrounds of 2029. It is this advantage that allows John's sexual fantasy to win out, though not without traversing the realm of necrophilia. Constance Penley has described Sarah and Reese's sex act in suggestive terms, calling it "a kiss across time, a kiss between a man from the future and a woman from the present, an act of love pervaded by death. For Kyle has to die in order to justify the coda, in which Sarah ensures the continuity of the story, now a legend, of their love for each other." But the pathos of this reading seems to fall in with the film's fantasy too wholeheartedly. Is it really right to say that Kyle has to die? It seems that he dies only to be reborn in the future, free again to chase this mother image across time in an endless loop that lets him love her, as he puts it, "always." The point is more that *Sarah* has to die, has to have long been dead, to give the male desiring machine its primary target. Reese falls in love with a photograph, falls in love with a woman not despite her being dead but because she is dead. What Reese wonders in particular is what Sarah was thinking at the moment the photograph was taken. He will never find out, but we will, and there is no question whose fantasies are served when, at the end in Mexico, we catch up to and recover that lost moment.

Recall that Sarah has been driving through Mexico, narrating the events of the film into a tape recorder. It is a complicated narration, in part because the unborn John is to some small extent actually *there*, hearing if not understanding her words, but also because, as Sarah confesses, the tapes are "more for me at this point, just so that I can get it straight." "Getting it straight" does not leave much room for authorial choice, and indeed what stands out about this narration is its concern that *John* will make hard choices in the future, in particular the decision to send Reese back in time again to father him and die. Sarah reassures him, though, with the concluding words that "In the few hours that we had together, we loved a lifetime's worth." It is at this moment that the snapshot is taken, and so we have our answer: what Sarah was thinking of was Reese, surrendering body *and* mind to male fantasies. As the only one privy to this tidy loop, the viewer is thus the final surrogate in the relay of male narcissism. But this tidiness is deceptive, for this moment has to be seen as equally John's fantasy, a rehearsal of his primal scene. Thus we can catch the trick the film achieves by sending the tapes to John and the photograph to Reese: the splitting of Sarah's face and voice maintains precisely the ruse that Reese and John are ultimately distinguishable, are distinct characters to be thought of as motivated individuals. Asserted at the very moment Sarah has abandoned such prerogatives, this thinking is precisely backwards. Along with the carefully disfigured Terminator (whose original bodybuilding physique would tend to betray male narcissism), Reese and John together form the film's ugly jumble of masculine fantasy.

We should not ignore the context of this conclusion, which unfolds at a "Mexican gas station," an absurdly overdetermined generic space complete with chickens, watermelons on the ground, tumbleweeds, and various colorful hanging decorations/advertisements that could be piñatas. The Mexico that in *Chinatown* and so many other films remains the blank space of pure escape is put to further work as *The Terminator* transforms that escape into the promise of a redemptive return. Here a Spanish-speaking boy presents the fateful photograph to Sarah as a commodity, which she dutifully accepts after doubting his story about an abusive father and negotiating the price from five to four dollars. And yet why would she want as a souvenir a picture of herself framed too tightly to include any scenery? To be sure, this question is not one we are supposed to ask, so thoroughly has Sarah been converted from a character into an emblem. But if we stop to consider this moment, it is a final bitter irony that what Sarah buys from the boy is not just one of the primary vehicles of her singular patriarchal destiny, but a nasty mix of cultural compromises. If she seems underwhelmed by the boy's appeal to her beauty, she nonetheless fails to resist the film's last-ditch projection of narcissism onto women. And what she actively buys seems to be some combination of the cheap self-approval and pseudo-sophistication that attend fantasies of having donated generously or struck a bargain in the global economy. On such evidence are we supposed to believe that this tourist has grown worldly enough to be the mother of the future? Miles away from home, her mother and roommate dead, the legendary Sarah Connor gives up her future and drives off into someone else's past.

Whatever controversy *The Terminator* has generated, it has emerged within the overarching consensus that it is a science fiction film and should be understood within the genealogy of that tradition. As a result, despite the ritual acknowledgment of the film's Tech Noir bar as an emblematic space of generic hybridity, the thrust of the critical response has been decidedly more tech than *noir*. But I want to suggest that it is indeed the neo-*noir* tradition that most deeply anchors *The Terminator* to its culture, that to understand where the film is coming from (and where it is going), we need to watch not *Metropolis*, or *Forbidden Planet*, or *2001: A Space Odyssey*, but the equally controversial stalker film from the previous decade, Alan J. Pakula's *Klute* (1971).[8] Like *The Terminator*, it is a tale of two stalkers—a "good" sexual stalker maneuvering in concert with a bad homicidal stalker—but *Klute* makes explicit so much that remains buried, and therefore somewhat incoherent, in *The Terminator*. Above all, watching *Klute* we can see how long Hollywood culture had been preparing us to accept the apocalypse as a judgment on modern urban life, for what the earlier film foregrounds is how stalking builds a case against the city, a case whose exhibits begin and end with feminism and the independent sexual woman. And if *The Terminator* prepares its emerging female legend by carefully separating the mobile and unmarried Sarah from her roommate's technological perversity, these female traits come together in the figure of Jane Fonda's wired call girl, Bree Daniels, whose destiny will also unfold through a series of dates with dead media.

It is not easy to account for the basic narrative drive of Pakula's film on its own terms, since it springs from the rather strange premise that the villain Peter Cable, a successful executive with a murderous resentment of prostitution, would hire John Klute (Donald Sutherland) to investigate the disappearance of Tom Gruneman, their mutual friend, when Cable himself is responsible for that disappearance. But all Cable wants, it seems, is verification of his judgment of the city he gazes down at so mercilessly from his skyscraper—verification and the assurance that, if his homicidal stalking fails, Klute's sexual stalking will nonetheless prevail in purging the city of Bree and Bree of the city. I would therefore suggest that Cable and Klute are best seen as twin ethnographers, each armed with that crucial scientific instrument the tape recorder (recall how Klute begins his investigation by taping Bree's calls with her clients; Cable had long ago captured her voice surreptitiously on tape, a tape which he replays obsessively throughout the film).[9] At the end, it seems Klute will indeed remove Bree from the city, his verdict—articulated earlier, when it looked like Bree's role in the investigation was over—unwavering. Bree had asked him if his study of the city didn't imply a little fascination, a little desire: "Tell me, Klute. Did we get you a little, huh? Just a little bit? Us cityfolk? The sin, the glitter, the wickedness? Huh?" "All that's so pathetic," he responds. Sweeping, perfunctory, dismissive, Klute the good scientist separates himself fully from the field he surveys.

He will not always be able to do so. Klute's equanimity is disturbed not so much by his subsequent seduction by Bree (a seduction which after all is easily converted into her larger seduction by him), but by a deeper penetration of the urban jungle. Beginning with Klute's realization that he does still need Bree to find a key witness, her fellow prostitute Arlyn Paige, the ensuing city tour is significant less for its confirmation of Klute's wildest fears of urban degradation than for the fact that *Bree has to come along*. Tracing Arlyn Paige, as it turns out, is tracing Bree as well, for the investigation systematically confronts Bree with the past she is trying to escape. As we will see, it is the beginning of *Klute*'s own time-travel plot. And Bree can't stand it. But trying to get away from Klute and the trajectory he represents only accelerates her regressive movement. After meeting the now strung-out Arlyn and inadvertently blowing her chance to score a fix, Bree dashes out of Klute's car and enters a nightclub. Curiously packed in the middle of the day, as if to underscore the difference between decadent urban hipsters and decent workaday people, the club will become the space of the past, the tainted bosom of the city from which Bree must be pried.

What follows is perhaps the most powerful scene in the film, in which the sheer force of Fonda's performance significantly disrupts any complacency about Bree's fate. Against increasingly haunting music, we see Bree trying to blend in and stand out, trying to lose and find herself in the crowd, in rapid-fire succession. It is like watching a tragic version of the stock robot breakdown as Bree discharges a lifetime's worth of social programming in the act of crossing a room. At every step the struggle, the pain, the desperation and fleeting hope is stunningly visible. Then she sees Frank, her former pimp, presiding regally over the proceedings from his table in the corner. She goes to him reluctantly, asking for solace, which he provides with similar reluctance. Suddenly Klute appears to return Frank's gaze and fill the reverse shot, as if somehow he could be an adequate answer to Bree's staggering need. But like Frank, Bree meets Klute's stare with a mixture of defiance and disgust—it will not be today that the city lets her go. Who could watch this scene and not wish her free? Not Klute, who looks devastated, fully shorn, if just for a moment, of his usual aloofness and contempt. He may even realize that he has driven her there.

But we don't really know what Klute is thinking, here or for much of the rest of the film. What makes this film difficult for affirmative feminist readings may be less the portrayal of Bree, which remains one of the most elaborate explorations of female subjectivity in Hollywood history, than the portrayal of Klute as so totally sealed off, so completely incapable of dealing with Bree as an equal. Her attempts to turn the tables in various ways achieve little, as when she tries to make Klute's own desire the topic of conversation in their first interview:

"And what's your bag, Klute? What do you like? You a talker? A button-freak? Like to have your chest walked around with high-heeled shoes? Maybe you like to have us watch you tinkle. Or do you get it off wearing women's clothes? God-damned hypocrite squares!"

Klute's only response to Bree's counterinterrogation is to murmur "Okay" twice, as if he is simply enduring the childish outburst. Importantly, he does not answer the question, resuming his own interrogation. Bree maintains her own line of inquiry by shifting methods and preparing to seduce him, but just as she thinks she is getting somewhere, Cable (we assume) appears on her roof as a distraction. Klute's bizarre handling of Bree in this frightening situation establishes what will become a sort of ongoing physical education, for apparently what Bree needs in order to shake off the city is some combination of yoga and dog-training. "Sit," Klute barks more than once. "Lie down!" And he continually positions Bree's body, favoring especially a pose where she sits with her head down, ready not to face any danger. We should make no mistake, then, about the status of Klute's sympathy for Bree. It is really pity. Refusing to see anything of himself in her predicament, determined to train her in his superior ways, Klute acknowledges female subjectivity only as something to be overcome.

The viewer, however, will have a more difficult time converting her (or even his) sympathy for Bree into self-protective pity, because the film works hard to make Klute threatening to us as well. Throughout the film, though the camera certainly tracks Bree and intrudes on her privacy, our access—our voyeurism—does not so much shadow as give way to Klute's. In scene after scene we watch Bree for an extended time, only to realize that Klute is watching her as well. We in fact see far less of Klute's stalking methods than those of the Terminator, seeing instead only the uncanny results, the revelation of Klute as perpetual Johnny-on-the-spot, like Bruno in Hitchcock's *Strangers on a Train*. That Klute's presence is threatening is underscored in that very first interview. Shot from behind, his dark suit becomes a vague encroaching darkness, crowding Bree and her story out of the frame. It is moreover the same way Cable will be filmed when he confronts Bree at the end with a tape recording of Arlyn Paige's death.[10]

So the question of the film seems to be this: is the city a necropolis (as the location of Bree's apartment next to a funeral home would suggest), or is this idea merely a fantasy of the film's two invading necrophiliacs? It is interesting in this light that both Klute and Cable make over Bree's apartment after their own fashion, with Klute's homey tidying, as it were, setting up Cable's definitive trashing. Apparently terrorizing Bree with phone calls, as Cable does, or with photographs of dead people, as Klute does, is not enough—male fantasy requires manipulation of the setting itself. And the pincer movement is unmistakable: Cable's home invasion becomes the pretext for Klute's heightened surveillance, since he can now demand that she always let him know where she is going and how she can be reached. Most troubling is Klute's participation in the film's notorious phone call, in which Cable plays a recording of Bree's own voice to her. With this call from her past self, the very self she has been trying to forget, the dead past fully overtakes and infuses Bree's precarious present—in this moment the circle of her enforced plot cinches every bit as tightly as the time loop of *The Terminator*. And it is Klute who holds the phone to her ear, Klute who then sets it down *off the hook*, so he can get a copy for himself (though a recording of a recording of Bree's voice has no value as a clue), and with the effect that it remains audible. When he finally leads Bree away, it appears she may be spared some portion of this horror—but no, it is Klute who reviews the tape of the call in his room below, with Bree standing right beside him, going through it all over again.

Ultimately, Cable and Klute's project—the obsessive demonstration of urban morbidity—hinges precisely on the game of discrediting female networks by conflating them with that morbidity. This strategy becomes apparent when Klute questions Frank about how Bree met the killer who will turn out to be Cable. Frank is quick to tell the story as a sisterly affair, explaining with exaggerated bewilderment (after all, what does he know about women, he just pimps them) how Cable was sent to Bree as the vendetta of a now-dead prostitute, Jane McKenna, as if male criminality were the result of female rivalry and not the other way around.

We should not ignore how willing Klute is to believe this story, despite its source, nor how eager he is to inform Bree that "Jane McKenna sent you that guy." "Well, she's dead" is Bree's defensive response, and it must have been everything Klute could have hoped for. By the time Cable plays Bree his recently acquired snuff tape of Arlyn Paige, the pattern is clear: as with Bree's phone call from herself, the plan is to reinvent female networks as monstrous doubles, indeed as death itself. Klute arrives (uncannily as ever) just in time to save Bree's life, but not, conveniently, before Bree has heard Cable's closing arguments in the case against the city.

One link in the network survives the assault of Klute and Cable, and that is Bree's relationship with her female psychiatrist. In sessions that recur throughout the film, Bree articulates a consistent ambivalence, first about prostitution and later about her growing involvement with Klute. It is in this setting that we hear what is perhaps her strongest statement against the forces that engulf her, her striking wish to be "faceless, bodiless, and left alone." It is a sad wish, though not one to be confused with Kathleen Kelly's wish in *You've Got Mail*, which is more to be faceless, bodiless, and lavished with attention. In the context of this argument, though, Bree's wish takes shape simply as the wish *not to be stalked*. And to an extent it comes true in the film's final scene.

As Bree finishes preparations to leave her apartment with Klute, her voiceover from a (tentatively) parting psychiatric session overlays the scene to question any future away from the city. Most critics read the final shot of Bree's bare apartment as contradicting and therefore undermining Bree's voice, and they assume that Bree and Klute are bound to live together in the country (see fig. 6.1). While there can be little question that this shot offers the film's final vision of purged urban space, I am far less convinced that Bree and Klute are a couple with a future. I see here exactly the kind of room for doubt that Henry James left at the end of *The Portrait of a Lady*, and must again insist that we seize that doubt in the name of imagining the heroine's best interests. Since Bree has just told her therapist that she is "going

Figure 6.1 *Klute's* purged urban space.

to miss" Klute, we should take her at her word. The mere fact that Klute helps her with the luggage tells us nothing about where that luggage goes after it leaves the room, much less its owner. And even if we take Bree's dissenting voice as nothing more than that, it can also be nothing less; we should not forget how preferable such discord is to Sarah Connor's wholehearted ventriloquism of patriarchy at the end of *The Terminator*. It seems the tag-team of Klute and Cable was not yet so efficient as Reese and the cyborg in the production of female singularity, that multiple Brees are still out there somewhere. The fact that any future of Bree "darning socks" is so much harder to imagine than Sarah's future apocalypse—the fact that, mercifully, we have no *Klute II: Judgment Day*—marks roughly the ground lost to urban women from 1971 to 1984, in thirteen years of stalking.[11]

How to Pass a Voigt-Kampff Test: Blade Runner *and* Vertigo

> *Is this the test now?*
>> Leon in Blade Runner

> *You don't look very much like Jack the Ripper.*
>> Judy to Scottie in Vertigo

The other landmark stalker movie from the early eighties is *Blade Runner*, a film that summons considerably more affection for a far grimmer city. As the film's eponymous "blade runner," hunter of android "replicants," Rick Deckard inhabits a Los Angeles that in 2019 has already suffered apocalyptic judgment. Indeed the film seems more than "a little pleased by this view of a medieval future—satisfied in a slightly vengeful way" (Kael 82). Under such conditions, Deckard's version of the urban tour significantly redistributes the components of the stalking fantasy, which increasingly looks like a pretext to revel in such a space. Unlike *Klute* or *The Terminator*, *Blade Runner* does not feature the wholesale projection of its homicidal program onto a villain (there are five major homicides committed by four different people), and it does not designate an encircled female target whose fate has been in place from the beginning. Instead, Deckard has initially four targets: Leon, Zhora, Pris, and Roy, escaped replicants returned to earth, as it turns out, on an Oedipal mission to confront their maker at the Tyrell Corporation with a grievance about their programmed four-year life span. But a fifth replicant, Rachel, appears during the course of the hunt as a special case, for unlike the others, she does not know she is a replicant. Deckard's Klute-like interest in her—that peculiar mixture of pity and pedagogy—sets the film's countervailing sexual stalking in motion and leads to one of the film's two major moral decisions when Deckard gets the assignment to kill her as well. Thus by the end the familiar pattern reemerges, a triumphant sexual stalking overcoming the homicidal alternatives, banishing the female networks, and ushering the heroine into romantic coupledom on schedule.

Unlike *Klute* or *The Terminator*, *Blade Runner* is careful to tell us that Deckard stalks only because he has to, since his services are secured only by his boss's threat that "If you're not cop, you're little people." But while this reluctance would seem to leave him less open to charges of illicit pleasure than are iconic detectives like Phillip Marlowe or Jake Gittes (whose interests clearly exceed professional motives), Deckard's methods tell a different story. We should note first that, like Peter Cable, Deckard seems to be obsessed with a snuff tape. Early in his investigation he flies around listening to the audiotape of a shooting from the film's opening scene, the near murder of another blade runner, who survives only with the aid of a respirator. All the repeated listening seems to yield is a simple address. More telling still is Deckard's use of a photograph of Zhora with a snake around her neck, which he links to a scale he found in Leon's apartment, since the talismanic function of this image far exceeds its actual value to the investigation. Although a character will seemingly identify Zhora on the basis of this photograph, the quality of the image makes it a dubious undertaking at best, as does the fact that the police already have an excellent picture of her that Deckard neglects to use.[12] Elissa Marder has described Deckard's photo best as "the 'memory' of a murder that has yet to occur," a description that properly locates this artifact, like the snuff tape, in the realm of necrophilia (103). And Deckard's link to the traditional detective's hidden agenda will be confirmed when he finally tracks Zhora to her dressing room: as he watches her undress, every bit the peeping Tom he warns her about, he tries to get her guard down with a cheap impersonation of an effete man—a routine critics have not failed to trace to Humphrey Bogart in *The Big Sleep*.[13]

Deckard proceeds to gun down Zhora in the streets, picking her easily, and recklessly, out of a crowd. The sequence is visually striking, as Zhora runs away in an oddly transparent coat that gives the impression of wings. Critics have noted with alarm how sensuous this murder is, though it is also worth noting the way the film's own preoccupations would recast Deckard's guilt.[14] Deckard has already provided the key image for understanding Zhora's death in an earlier scene where he gives Rachel the "Voigt-Kampff Test." Designed to detect replicants who otherwise simulate humans perfectly, this test unfolds as a series of responses to narrated scenarios. And one of the scenarios from Deckard's script is awfully reminiscent of Zhora:

"You've got a little boy. He shows you his butterfly collection, plus the killing jar."
"I'd take him to the doctor."

If Zhora is the film's butterfly, Deckard is its little boy—sick, but not responsible enough to be criminal. And the transparent jar, with its isolating, immobilizing, and finally smothering effects, stands for a certain strategy of representation itself.

Blade Runner is a film perhaps best seen as a phobic meditation on figures, in which the force of likeness takes on the deadly quality of voodoo, collapsing fantasies of singularity. In addition to the replicants themselves, there is the doll in Rachel's picture of her mother, the toys and chess pieces of J. F. Sebastian (the man who gives Pris and Roy refuge), the mannequins in the window through which the dying Zhora crashes, and the eerier mannequins in the dark Bradbury building where Sebastian lives. Most important, perhaps, are the tiny figures made by Gaff (Edward James Olmos), the man who stalks the stalker, locating Deckard with Klute-like ease whenever the police captain needs him. Gaff's miniatures—oblique commentaries on the unfolding drama—confirm the stalker's basic work, in such deep collusion with the cinema, as a maker of figures in a cityscape. We see the first of these figures, some sort of gum-wrapper chicken, as the camera cuts from the Captain's threat that "If you're not cop, you're little people." It is only outside this particular jar of representation that Deckard can maintain the fiction of living even a little bit large.

And so *Blade Runner* crosses guilt with shame, crosses its doubts about what he has done with its doubts about who he is.[15] The responsibility of stalkers gets vetted largely through his double, Rutger Hauer's Roy, the preening Aryan alpha-male of the rogue replicants. It is Roy who takes on the moral burden of stalking in the film's climactic sequence, cornering Deckard on the roof of the Bradbury building. And it is Roy who accordingly makes the film's second moral choice, choosing to save the dangling blade runner. This tardy motif of redemption transfers all too easily to the Deckard who will decide to spare Rachel's life, but it fails to address the shame at stake at the climax of a stalking plot. Deckard's dangling is a social condition, an inability to secure social standing. In the world of *Blade Runner* this condition is widespread; indeed, it engulfs the Father, for if Tyrell's pyramid seemingly affords him phallic heights and commanding class elevation, his murder by Roy renders such a privileged position definitively uninhabitable. If there is any question about the utter reduction of Deckard's rooftop perch, it is dispelled at the end of the scene by the appearance of the uncanny Gaff from his already parked flying car—suddenly the roof feels like the street, as if Deckard had fallen after all.

And indeed he has, for in this reading Roy's mercy can only add to Deckard's shame, denying him the one consolation every replicant is entitled to, of knowing when he or she is going to die. Of course such knowledge may be more torment than comfort, but the film will be little help in deciding, tangling up as it does at least three different problems: the problem of knowing when you're going to die, the problem of dying too soon, and the problem of death itself. Thus as Roy's dying soliloquy reminds us, imparted with all the authoritative wisdom of famous last words, the film's limitations return again and again to the question of time. Roy has seen amazing things at the ends of the universe, but now "Those moments will be lost in time, like tears in rain. Time to die." If only he had brought his camcorder.

Roy's good behavior here, converting loss into poetry and thereby into cultural memory, should not conceal that between them the boys have spent the bulk of the movie shortening the time of others.

But if Deckard's shame cloaks his guilt, it also conceals the more general shame of "blade runner" as a fundamentally incoherent job description, as a job that puts still more pressure on the question of time. The problem with blade runners is that their function as administrators of the Voigt-Kampff test is incompatible with their function as stalkers, for this test cannot logically take place either before or after the stalking of its subject. If it takes place before, why doesn't the blade runner kill the replicant on the spot (indeed, why doesn't the apparatus incorporate, say, an electric chair?)? If it takes place after, how did the blade runner know whom to stalk? To be sure, the actual plot of the film finds ways around this problem: the first test scene ends with the replicant shooting the blade runner and escaping to be stalked; the second, of Rachel, can spare her because she doesn't know what she is. But there can be no usual procedure in which stalking and testing are not mutually exclusive.

The film wants both operations nonetheless, perhaps because the test allows it to keep stalking while pretending to hasten the obsolescence of that activity. After all, however dressed up in technology it becomes, stalking remains in essence the work of eyes and legs (the two things, as opposed to skin, essential for a functioning Terminator). It is work on a human scale, designed, as I have been arguing, to produce a female singularity available for patriarchal interests. Consider by contrast the ostensible work of the Voigt-Kampff test, in many ways the perfect inverse of the Turing Test. Instead of occupying separate rooms, tester and subject sit in face-to-face confrontation. Instead of initiating an orderly, typed conversation to explore intelligence, the tester bypasses intelligence by noting involuntary responses to provocative questions. In this way the Voigt-Kampff test occults the face and the voice every bit as thoroughly as the Turing Test, and far more insidiously. If the conversational technology of the Turing Test disposes of the body in a dubious way, at least conversation remains the standard; here the body returns only to betray a subject whom no skillful modulation of face or voice will save, her speech reduced to meaningless chatter over the real transfer of data. Such inhuman attention disfigures a test subject who will be reassembled as human only on the condition of producing normative bodily responses. A stalker who might learn to relent doesn't look so bad against a post-human nightmare that dispenses with all flattery.

But the Voigt-Kampff test that *Blade Runner* describes is not exactly the test it performs, and this slippage will allow the human to return with a vengeance. Empathy supposedly takes the place of intelligence as the defining human characteristic in the test, though that term hardly seems adequate to the actual epistemological procedure that unfolds in the film's two scenes of testing. In the first scene, a blade runner named Holden interrogates Leon, who has attempted to infiltrate the Tyrell

Corporation as an employee. To be sure, the initial line of questioning seems to test empathy for animals, as Leon is asked to consider a suffering tortoise:

> "You reach down and flip the tortoise over on its back, Leon—"
>
> "—You make up these questions, Mr. Holden, or do they write 'em down for you?"
>
> "The tortoise lays [sic] on its back, its belly baking in the hot sun, beating its legs trying to turn itself over but it can't, not without your help. But you're not helping.
>
> "What do you mean I'm not helping?"
>
> "I mean you're not helping. Why is that Leon?"

Hiding under a blanket sci-fi immunity ("it's the future, you wouldn't understand"), the logic of this test has tended to escape scrutiny. But strictly speaking, the story of the tortoise does not measure Leon's capacity for empathy, it measures how he feels when accused of lacking empathy. The deck is stacked, as both the test and the film put Leon in the position of the replicant from the beginning. The fact that Leon terminates the test soon after—blowing Holden away with a concealed gun in response to the command "Tell me about your mother"—adds nothing conclusive in an epistemological sense, since Holden merely strikes a well-worn nerve of hysterical masculinity. Human men have killed for less.

But what should make the Voigt-Kampff test unsettling to the viewer of *Blade Runner* is not just its confrontational, paranoid setup, and not just its violent resolution, but the dawning likelihood that we would fail the test ourselves. Just as one could not pass a Turing Test without the necessary language and typing skills, one could not pass the Voigt-Kampff Test without the proper cultural frame of reference, a frame of reference most visibly defined by the scarcity of animals in this future world. And yet I would suggest that few viewers feel the full force of occupying the android position, because the film cheats. Not only does the test not measure empathy, what it does measure is in fact highly legible to the film's viewers. As a result, the terms of humanity, with its entrenched system of sexual difference, remain disappointingly in place, as the invocation of motherhood would suggest. Leon's deviance, in fact, will be constructed as radically excluding our own, and our humanity will be confirmed by our growing ability to comprehend the film (how's that for flattery!). Consider how difficult it is for him to engage with the test in the first place:

> "You're in a desert, walking along in the sand when all of a sudden—"
>
> "—Is this the test now?"
>
> "You're in a desert, walking along in the sand when all of a sudden—"
>
> "—What one?"
>
> "What?"
>
> "What desert?"

"It doesn't make any difference what desert; it's completely hypothetical"

"But how come I'd be there?"

Leon is right to question when the test begins, for he has already failed it, before animals are even mentioned. What he lacks—and what will come to define the human in this film—is not empathy but the willingness to participate in dubious fictions.

The film's most important fiction will turn out to be Rachel herself, the replicant who, thanks to implanted memories and supporting photographs, thought she was human. And it is when Deckard tests her that the full sham of the Voigt-Kampff Test can be discerned. While the story of empathy for animals again covers for the real story of humanity, this time the exceptional android will in an important sense *pass* the test. Of course Deckard supposedly learns the truth about Rachel in this scene, but what the viewer learns is something altogether different. In the first place, it is here that we find the most recognizably human attitude toward animals in Rachel's immediate reaction to the thought of having a wasp crawling up her arm: "I'd kill it." No doubt the fear and aggression in this response would make her right at home with much of the audience of the film. The more elaborate scenario that follows further enhances her human credentials:

"You're reading a magazine. You come across a full-page nude photo of a girl."

"Is this testing whether I'm a replicant, or a lesbian, Mr. Deckard?"

"Just answer the questions, please. You show it to your husband. He likes it so much he hangs it on your bedroom wall."

"I wouldn't let him."

"Why not?"

"I should be enough for him."

While we are told that Rachel eventually betrays her android self to Deckard's apparatus, her answers are perfect from the film's perspective—her humanity recognizable in her willingness to enter the scenario imaginatively, and her romantic eligibility confirmed in her insistence on monogamy and the sexual rivalry of women. If her interruption of Deckard has something of Bree Daniels's defiance in it ("What's *your* bag, Klute?"), the question of a lesbian test does not so much introduce an alternate sexuality as ward it off. For the male stalker, a love plot as old as "The Sandman" has less trouble acknowledging a replicant than it does a lesbian.[16]

The clinching proof of Rachel's humanity will then be her reaction to the discovery of her nonhumanity—her denial, her tears, her inability to imagine there is anything else worth being. This proof will be offered in Deckard's apartment after the test, in the scene in which Rachel produces a photograph of herself as a child holding a doll with her mother. Though he will eventually take pity on Rachel,

Deckard at first attacks her evidence quite ruthlessly, wielding as counterevidence the impossibly intimate knowledge he has gleaned from her files: her memories were implanted—she had no such childhood. No model of terminator can isolate a heroine so efficiently. Sarah Connor can at least claim the memory of her roommate and her mother as authentic loss, but Rachel's female network suffers the annihilation of never having existed. Singled out by the theft of her past, Rachel is in danger of becoming the perfect blank slate for the authoring male fantasist, for the stalker who will inscribe her in the fiction of his own humanity.[17] Indeed, in a later scene Deckard quite literally scripts their developing relationship, feeding Rachel her romantic lines. As Kaja Silverman points out, Rachel does start to improvise, suggesting a desire of her own that survives the liquidation of her past ("Back" 129). This desire is moreover not all that survived, since earlier in the scene she has discovered her ability to play the piano. Fake memories, it turns out, make real music. It is not clear, however, that Rachel will be given a turn at composing the film's powerful fictions.

Deckard commits two murders in this film, and those murders are of Pris and Zhora, the two female replicants and among the most promising candidates for any new networks Rachel might hope to establish. Rachel commits one—killing Leon to save Deckard. It is these two facts that circumscribe Rachel's future. Indeed, her killing of Leon, shown from Deckard's perspective, is not allowed to assume its place as the film's third important moral choice, despite the fact that, as Robin Wood has pointed out, her action could be seen as "the tragic betrayal of her class and race" ("BladeRunner" 286). This missing political dimension has led Yves Chevrier to characterize Deckard himself—who, dour though he is, never actively protests or complains—as being "less real than the society he grovels through" (57). And so the romance of stalking allows him to outrun the shame of his nonexistence, culminating in the end when, for no clear reason, Rachel assumes the role of Sleeping Beauty. But Rachel really does need to wake up if she is to appreciate what it means to have killed Leon, who is not only a member of her class and race: as the only other character to endure the Voigt-Kampff Test—the test that blade runners and viewers use to imagine that *their* humanity is not in question—Leon represents for Rachel her last chance to learn that the test never ended.

But in fairness, *Blade Runner's* commitment to the eternal testing of the heroine lacks conviction, its judgment less thundering than that of *The Terminator* or *Klute* as curiosity overtakes disgust in the tour of urban space. Amid all the *noir*, an old sci-fi vitality lingers here, a mysterious notion that progress might happen in spite of us, our creations exceeding our plans in ways for which we can only be grateful. With such surprises in mind, let us return then one last time to the test and consider the mysterious apparatus itself, the machine that gets to decide who is human. What I would like to suggest is that this machine is alive (see fig. 6.2). Two key details support this idea: first, as Kaja Silverman observes, the presence of a green eye on the screen no matter who is being tested, an eye that therefore seems to belong to the machine ("Back" 111); and second, the machine's bellows that

Figure 6.2 It's alive! The apparatus of Blade Runner's Voigt-Kampff Test.

"breathe" throughout the test. The way to pass the test then would be to please this machine, to make it empathize with you enough to declare you human and let you live. This is not to dispute that the machine measures "capillary dilation and the so-called blush response, fluctuation of the pupil, involuntary dilation of the iris," but rather to mind a gap between the collection of this information and the output available to the blade runner conducting the test, a gap perhaps best described as the will of the machine. Seeing the machine as alive allows us finally to see the film's regime of representation in its starkest light, for the machine's hidden power lies precisely in its disfigurement as a sprawling assemblage, more network than body. Unavailable for representation in any traditional sense, never in danger of being reduced to a figure and triggering a phobic response to likeness, it nonetheless generates the scripts for everyone else. As the reader of the test, the blade runner occupies a curious middle position. It is unclear, finally, just whom he serves, in his culture and in ours. As the subject of the test, Rachel might do better to cozy up to the machine. Recognizing finally the burden of her situation, she might echo Leon, fighting for his life in the interrogation room at the beginning of the film: You make up this story, Mr. Deckard? Or did they write it down for you?

The question of the stalker's script, of who writes it and why, takes us back to perhaps the most formidable stalker movie of all, Alfred Hitchcock's *Vertigo*. To be sure, Deckard, Klute, and the Terminator are all *sent* on their missions, missions that they do not necessarily understand, but Jimmy Stewart's Scottie is the only one sent explicitly on a mission to track and disrupt a female network, and the only one who manages to get the woman he singles out killed. The story that sets him going is told by Gavin Elster, a shipbuilding magnate and college friend, who calls Scottie out of retirement from the police force, and the network in question is that between Carlotta Valdez, an abandoned woman of the nineteenth century, and her living descendent, Elster's wife Madeleine, who has apparently formed an obsession with her. It is a network pathologized from the beginning, as threatening female closeness takes the nightmare form of possession. "Scottie, do you believe that someone out of the past, someone dead, can enter and take possession of a living being?" Elster asks him, a question doubly disingenuous on its face—because Elster quickly follows Scottie into the rational discourse that calls possession madness, and because Elster is in fact setting Scottie up to witness a staged suicide, the part of the possessed Madeleine being acted out by his mistress, Judy Barton. But as in a film like *Sorry, Wrong Number*, what is really disingenuous is the film's system of rational explanation, for this is not a film prepared to give up the power of ghosts—not because these ghosts represent some tragic truth about the male human condition but because these ghosts bemoan, as I hope to show, a crime more perfect even than Elster's murder of his wife.

To miss this point and buy into these explanations is in a sense to confuse *Vertigo* with *Blade Runner*, to accept a rather tidy substitution of Judy the replicant for Carlotta the ghost as the woman behind Madeleine. As in *Blade Runner*, *Vertigo* pulls a switch through the evidence of photography and the bullying logic of the sexual stalker, but here both sequence and direction are crucially reversed. Judy's claim on existence is at one point eerily similar to Rachel's, declaring "That's me, with my mother" as Scottie looks at a photograph in her hotel room. But while Deckard responds by undermining Rachel's memory, Scottie has already deployed his undermining logic against Madeleine, though it is harder to recognize as such, since he seeks to give her memories rather than take them away. Recall how Scottie tries to banish Carlotta by providing Madeleine with a source for her nightmare of the Spanish mission in her own experience: "It's all there; it's no dream. You've been there before; you've seen it." But the retrospective irony of Scottie's restoring memories to a nonexistent person glosses over his careful preparation of Madeleine to receive his own stamp. The revelation that the possessed Madeleine was merely a performance of Judy at the behest of Elster—a performance calculated to lure Scottie to the mission tower, where he could witness the death of the real Madeleine—occludes our perception of the continuity of Scottie's project.

Thinking his Madeleine dead, the haunted Scottie will then find Judy and make her over in Madeleine's image. That this second stalking will again be imagined in opposition to female networks is clear from its inception, when Scottie spots Judy on the street among a group of women who will never be heard from again. Judy's willingness to suffer the makeover—indeed, her eventual acceleration of it by putting on Madeleine's necklace—depends upon the validity of a line she delivers in her famous epistolary revelation of Elster's scheme: "Everything went as planned, except I fell in love with you—that wasn't part of the plan." But if the subsequent history of stalking films shows anything, it is that the heroine's love is always part of the plan; certainly the plots of *Klute*, *Blade Runner*, and *The Terminator* would be impossible without it. Indeed all these films figure a network-busting central romance as the essential condition of progressive modernity, as if there can be no greater condemnation of the modern world than that it makes possessive male love difficult. In *Vertigo*, Judy's love is the assumption by which the film pursues Scottie's fantasy under cover of Scottie's nightmare. Indeed, whatever scruples Scottie might have had about pursuing a woman already twice possessed (through haunting and through marriage) are wiped away by the revised version. Now it seems Judy wanted Scottie to stalk her.

The way Judy's revision retroactively meets Scottie's desire is perhaps more clearly visible in the crucial (and repeated) scene in which Madeleine visits the portrait of Carlotta. When we first see Madeleine before the portrait, it is of course under the suggestion of her "possession" by Carlotta, an idea that if taken literally means that Carlotta has taken over Madeleine's mind, that Madeleine has no thoughts of her own. But as we insert Judy back into this scene, a question emerges: what is Judy thinking as she sits in front of the portrait of Carlotta pretending to be Madeleine? We know how *The Terminator* would answer this question, impossibly circling the dead woman's thoughts back to the hero from the future. It would seem that here the answer is the same, that Judy must be thinking of Scottie, must wonder how he is taking her performance. Looking back at the scene, her consciousness seems indeed to be betrayed by the displacement of the whorl in her hair from the left front, where Carlotta wears it, to the back, where Scottie can see it (see figs. 6.3 and 6.4). Staged for Scottie's benefit, it is more important that the impersonation be visible than exact. Converting the hopelessly remote Madeleine, who thinks of another woman, into a Judy who thinks only of him, the revised scene confirms the hidden appeal of Judy's revelation.

But the co-option of Judy's consciousness by Scottie's plot of sexual stalking is by no means the last word on female subjectivity in this film, for it does not account for the film's interest in female humiliation. Whatever emphasis some critics place on Scottie's suffering, some of the most painful events clearly belong to Judy and her

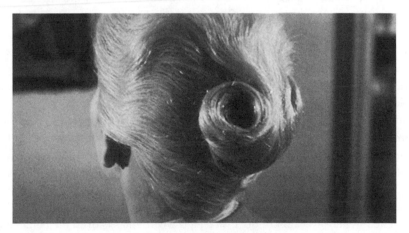

Figures 6.3 (above) and 6.4 (next page) Madeleine's whorl, displaced for Scottie's benefit.

would-be rival, the sadly solid, slyly spiteful Midge. I am thinking of course of their respective makeovers—Judy's on her person and Midge's on canvas—each revealing Scottie's brutality in its own way as the women attempt to approximate what he wants. Indeed, the comparison may shed light on Judy's crucial decision to put on the necklace and finally give away the game, a decision only further mystified by Scottie's hysterical denunciation at the end: "You shouldn't keep souvenirs of a killing. You shouldn't have been . . . you shouldn't have been that sentimental." We should emphasize that, very much in the spirit of *Klute*, there is no healthy identification between women permitted in *Vertigo*—no healthy way, in particular, to connect with the dead Carlotta. Against the terrifying maelstrom of Judy's possession/madness-turned-con-job, the film poses Midge's self-portrait as an impudent and hideous parody. Midge's task will be to pronounce this verdict herself—"stupid, stupid, stupid"—and quietly exit the film. Apart from a perfunctory exchange with Scottie's nurse, she does not speak with another woman. Consistent with this female isolation is the view of Midge and Judy as blunderers. If nothing else, they face Scottie alone, without the support of a triangulating female network to check his story, weigh his motives, and guide their decisions. Donning the apparel of dead women out of pathetic false hope, they construct tests for Scottie that they ought to know he is doomed to fail. In this respect Scottie is like Klute, unresponsive to Midge and Judy because he is too busy testing *them*. Indeed these moments are *Vertigo*'s versions of Voigt-Kampff, the machine judging the film's women as less than human, because less than Madeleine, nothing else but masculine culture.

But all we have to do is recognize that Midge is perhaps only half stupid, and the story begins to change. Similarly, if Judy is being sentimental, I would suggest, it is only because she has unfinished business with dead women, a possibility suggested in her revelation of the Elster plot, where she lets drop the tantalizing claim that "Carlotta's story was part real, part invented." This unknown share of fiction, this sign of play in the otherwise rigid past, must underwrite any present founded upon it. Indeed I wonder if Elster can remain the sole author of this history, or if the women caught up in it do not necessarily introduce their own revisions. Is it possible then that to some small extent, despite all appearances, Midge and Judy are dressing for other women? Such a displacement of Scottie from the center of all female thought carries us back to the original portrait and restores an exciting possibility—that Judy is in fact ignoring her stalker and communing with Carlotta, who after all may have more in common with her than with Madeleine. Midge's opportunities may seem still more remote, but what if she had shown her self-portrait, not to Scottie, but to Judy? The results seem incalculable by the film's terms, though the rescue of the real Madeleine Elster might be the first order of business. In any case, Midge clearly seems right to seek out a medium—not just of expression, but also as a link to the dead, a means of contesting the patriarchal repetition of the past. Such fantasies are vital, and, if a bit beyond the reach of Hitchcock, in no way well exorcized from this ghost story.

Consider the scene in the sequoias. Diffuse lighting will link this scene to the moment when Scottie completes Judy's makeover as Madeleine later in the film, and thus to Hitchcock's declaration that Scottie will be "indulging in a form of necrophilia."[18] It is also the moment of Madeleine's most overt possession by Carlotta, saying, "Somewhere in here I was born, and there I died," while she points toward a ring from the nineteenth-century part of the severed tree trunk. As she wanders off and briefly disappears, there is a dawning sense of panic, as if this enchanted woods were a time machine and she truly could vanish into the past. Of course Scottie quickly spots her behind a tree, recuperating her disappearance for rational understanding. But this has not been her first disappearing act. Recall the earlier scene at the McKittrick Hotel. Scottie follows Madeleine there, watches her enter, and sees her emerge at an upstairs window—but when he asks the hotel manager about her, he learns that she hasn't been there and that her key is still behind the front desk. When the mystery of the McKittrick Hotel is first encountered, there can be no question about its implied solution: Madeleine is a ghost. The question is whether she haunts only Scottie or the entire film (or if there is a difference), and it is a question that must be separated from the question of Madeleine's being haunted in turn (can a ghost haunt another ghost?). Unlike in the scene in the woods, there is no retroactive reassurance that this implication is wrong, for this mystery is never addressed by the subsequent account that explains Madeleine away as a performance of Judy.[19] To be sure, it is possible to construct an elaborate scenario in which the hotel manager is involved in the scheme and Judy has her own key, but the film doesn't bother to do so.[20] Instead this unbanished ghost lingers, haunting the entire reconstruction of events, and demanding in the end her own revision, "part real, part invented."

One of the first things to revise is the stalker's nostalgic story of the city, for it is crucial to remember that it is Elster who invokes the theme of nostalgia as part of his con job: "San Francisco's changed. The things that spell San Francisco to me are disappearing fast." If Scottie fancies himself chasing the eternal woman through Elster's lost city of "color, excitement, power, freedom," his tour, moving from a classic restaurant to museums, a cemetery, and an old hotel, will in fact contradict Elster, establishing the persistence of the city. In this way *Vertigo*'s stalking itinerary manages time in a very different way than do films like *The Terminator* and *Klute*, for both those films pursue their heroines through decidedly modern spaces, as epitomized by the club in *Klute* and *The Terminator's* "Tech Noir" bar. The dynamism of these fascinating spaces, which the films must go on to reject, could not be more different from the subdued elegance of Ernie's in *Vertigo*.[21] Indeed, *Vertigo* is far less sure what to do with its modern woman, the independent Midge, no doubt because to stalk *her* would be to discover a very different city.

Robert Corber's historical analysis of the film is important here. On one hand, *Vertigo* is clearly avoiding the most modern San Francisco of the late 1950s, defined for Corber by the Beats. On the other hand, this avoidance seems less a dread of any recently achieved modernity than a doubt that such achievements have truly occurred. Despite Scottie's trancelike nostalgia, the film maintains active continuity with San Francisco's "gay old Bohemian days" through the recurring story of Carlotta, thrown away by a nameless rich man because "men could do that in those days." As viewers learn from the fates of Judy and the real Madeleine, "men continue to throw women away when they no longer want them" (Corber 159). In this way the contemporary experience of San Francisco is still what Midge calls a question of "who shot who in the Embarcadero," still very much a wild, wild west.[22] In the words of Bruno Latour, we have never been modern.

And Scottie, I would suggest, has never been acrophobic—or at least this film will find it as difficult to chart the course of his condition as it does the emerging modernity of San Francisco. For there is something strange about *Vertigo*'s depiction of the fear of heights: it is a film with many falls, but only one thud. Of the three bodies that plummet to their deaths, only one—the real Madeleine's—makes a sound, and she turns out to have been already dead. The other two falls belong to Judy at the end and the policeman at the beginning, and the sounds of these deaths register, if at all, as fully displaced "crashes" in the orchestral score. Many critics have noticed something phantasmic about Judy's abrupt death at the end, but not the (in)audible link to the falling policeman, which would render Scottie's initial trauma equally phantasmic.[23] It is worth revisiting, then, Tania Modleski's insight that "in some important sense he does not exist either" (*Women* 91). *Vertigo* is of course *Blade Runner's* great predecessor in rooftop shame, Scottie's suspended existence prefiguring Deckard's. Indeed here the phallic and class implications of verticality seem more clearly at hand in the chance to follow Madeleine upwards.[24] And crucially, Scottie makes a strategic move that Deckard the noncomplainer never quite manages, reversing the work of stalking by asking, "Why me?" on his final trip up the tower. It is this audacious question that masks the film's true perfect crime, as the stalker dares to claim that *he* is the one who has been singled out.

When Scottie says "Why me?" he refers to Elster's plot, but of course he would not be available as dupe were he not already known to suffer from the singular condition of acrophobia. And yet it would be a serious mistake to imagine his acrophobia as the source of his shame, despite the work of Elster's plot to position it as such. Acrophobia certainly has nothing to do with Scottie's initial athletic failure on the rooftop, since the slip that leads to the cop's death comes before Scottie knows his disease. Indeed, strictly speaking, what Scottie discovers hanging onto the gutter is his *vertigo*, which then must be said to precede the later medical diagnosis of acrophobia as ostensible cause. The whole point of this diagnosis, then, will be to figure Scottie's humiliations deceptively as inalienable, when in fact he is working tirelessly to foist them onto women. As Scottie marches Judy up the tower at the end, it will now be she who stalked him, she who had greedy class aspirations, she, finally, who suffers acrophobia, since who is afraid of heights now? But if the climbing in this film is always social, so is the falling. We should not forget that as a policeman, Scottie the lawyer is slumming. His fantasy had never been merely a life of ease, but one of easy adventure. In this context, the cop's silent fall may betray a pervasive romance of painless upward *and* downward mobility, with vertigo attending Scottie's sudden perception that the risk is real, and that he may never recover his secure position.

In Judy's flashback, Mrs. Elster's body also fails to make a sound. Thus both the film's framing events *and* its pivotal revelation are acoustically ungrounded. Sonically speaking, the only real fall of the film is the fraud—the concealing fall of the already-dead Madeleine. Hinting that the film's only sure truth is the truth of deception, such elusiveness derails the cultural work of stalking. It is no longer possible to plot the desired trajectory with any confidence—to work forward from a rooftop trauma as an affair entirely between men. Scottie would separate Carlotta from Madeleine, then Madeleine from Judy, so that the singular woman can be his double and die his death. But the impossibility of this project is made clearer when a nun appears in the tower at the end, surprising Judy into the film's final fall. Summoned to do Scottie's dirty work, the nun ejects Judy from the tower according to a little-known law of Hitchcockian physics, that no two women shall occupy the same scene. But recourse to this figure only undermines the narrative work of isolation, for any attempt to imagine why Judy falls or jumps, to imagine what she might fear or what guilt might overwhelm her, inevitably refers back to her tangled connections with other women. Judy is Madeleine is Carlotta to the end. Filling the tower window in the final frame, Scottie assumes the awkward stance of a marionette, as if to indicate one last abdication of responsibility. More convincingly, his posture intensifies the visual impression that, brought to a ledge, he cannot continue. Too late for Judy—and too soon for the Hollywood of *Blade Runner*, *Klute*, *The Terminator*, and so many lesser movies—*Vertigo* arrives at a plea that our culture increasingly disregards: here at last, the stalking stops.

Epilogue: Radio-Free *Middlemarch*

It will likely not surprise anyone when I suggest that a treatment of George Eliot could have found a comfortable place in the first chapter here on gossip. Indeed it is difficult to imagine the cultural politics of interest developing from Austen to James without an intervening *Middlemarch*, whose narrator protests our habits of narrative attention with such famous flourishes as "But why always Dorothea?" and "Was she alone in that scene?" (278, 787) and goes on to shine sympathy in the corners of several unlikely characters. One good reason not to take up the question of gossip in *Middlemarch* is that two of our eminent Victorianists—D. A. Miller and Gillian Beer—have already done so.[1] But that was not my reason, for neither of these accounts embraces the full ambivalence of gossip so important to feminism. Let me briefly then show how my argument about gossip holds for *Middlemarch*, before I explain why I have chosen to displace it and do something else.

I have argued that novelistic culture is thick with the disavowal of gossip—at the level of the novel's own discourse, as it proclaims itself as art, and at the level of critical discourse, as it coheres into intellectual authority. And as I suggested in passing in chapter 1, George Eliot may have been as guilty as any at attempting to elevate the novel at the expense of feminine discourse, and not merely through the use of her pen name. Like *The Portrait of a Lady*, *Middlemarch* endlessly invokes the inadequacy and violence of gossip in contrast to the narrator's own superior attentions to the private lives of characters. But it seems to me a mistake to consent to the sorting of discourse in this way, for as in *Emma*, we risk losing a sense of what gossip accomplishes for the narration.

In *Middlemarch*, the closest thing to *Emma*'s Miss Bates (the gossip) or Mrs. Elton (the ultimate scapegoat for female discourse) is Mrs. Cadwallader. To be sure, the Rector's Wife has more going for her—brains and social position—than either of Austen's characters, but her continual placement in opposition to Dorothea has made her presence rather unappreciated. If nothing else, it is important to recognize that she has a way of articulating the essential points of the novel, as through Mrs. Cadwallader the narrator can be blunt without compromising her own reputation for subtlety. Three examples should make this function clear. The first occurs at Featherstone's funeral, which she watches from the window of Lowick Manor. In typically bracing fashion, she tells a group consisting of Mr. Brooke, Sir James, Celia, and Dorothea that "It was time the old man died, and none of these people are sorry" (327). Equally sharp is her claim in a private argument with her husband that "a woman's choice usually means taking the only man she can get" (538). And perhaps most impressive, if also most routine, is the fact that Mrs. Cadwallader has the honor to articulate the novel's central question, a question that bears powerfully on the plots of Bulstrode and Lydgate as well as Dorothea, the question "Who is Mr. Ladislaw?" (329).

To say that Mrs. Cadwallader does the novel's dirty work, however, is by no means to outflank Eliot, who has dramatized this very point in an episode in which Sir James makes the same use of her to convey scandal about Will Ladislaw. Her response cuts directly to Sir James's motive: "Enough! I understand. . . . You shall be innocent. I am such a blackamoor that I cannot smirch myself" (628). Since characters with this much awareness tend to be the good guys in this novel, we might wonder if this other woman who married down is not one of the novel's great untapped centers of interest. A slight hint of such possibilities comes if we track the echo of one of Mrs. Cadwallader's many unwelcome bits of advice, that if one "can marry blood, beauty, and bravery—the sooner the better" (549). When Dorothea on the next page explains her reaction to this remark, the advice has been strangely truncated: "I should only mind if there were a law obliging me to take any piece of blood and beauty that she or anybody else recommended" (550). Where did the bravery go? We might wonder if, like Dorothea, we are not listening closely enough to this female discourse, deaf precisely to its heroic dimension.

Such is the fate of gossip, though, and I have in mind for *Middlemarch* something better. To plug it into a three-part teleological narrative—Austen, Eliot, James—would be to confirm structurally, and in advance, a middleness about *Middlemarch* that forecloses other futures. Nothing against Henry James, but I want to see this story as a beginning. Eliot's novel is hardly the only candidate to be rescued from such linear histories, but I hope its special qualifications will soon become clear. What these qualifications do not include, I am sorry to say, is an extensive and optimistic portrait of female networking in the first half of the nineteenth century. Indeed insofar as *Middlemarch* presents itself as a novel of bad marriages, it must be seen as a novel of failed or absent female networks, since the regulation of the marriage market remains the measure of their effectiveness until women enjoy other career prospects. What recommends this novel nonetheless, as the forward-looking conclusion to this chapter and this book, is the remarkable friction it opposes to the isolation of its heroine, Dorothea Brooke. From the opening invocation of Saint Theresa to the communion with the long-dead Julia, here at last we have vital female networks across time, not haunted as in *Vertigo* or *Klute*, not annihilated as in *Blade Runner* or *The Terminator*.

So this time the crime will be my own. For it seems to me that if the pieties of historicism tend largely to rehearse the ritual necrophilic sacrifice of our culture's most prominent female networks, then we had better have some anachronism.[2] So let's leap straight to the wince-inducing question, posed with Cadwalladerian bluntness: What has *Middlemarch* done for us lately? In light of the perception that "much in *Middlemarch* has acquired a somewhat pastoral glow" (Beer 53), and at the end of a comparison between literature and film, the case for its ongoing importance could not be more pressing. If we wish to avoid a cultural history that is truly academic, we need to redescribe the stakes and possibilities of reading this classic novel across the gap of history, a gap that can only be widened by the prophylactic historicism that patrols Victorian fiction in our own time.

I would like to posit radio as an appropriate figure for this gap. For us, slightly obsolete, routine, forgotten; for the Victorians, the fantastic culmination of their wildest imaginings, radio restores the lost middle, the shift in home entertainment from novel to television. And as the blind apex of sound culture, radio averts our eyes long enough to hear novelistic culture in a new key.[3] In the context of *Middlemarch*, Kay Young has established Dorothea as a figure for the theory of hearing as "sympathetic vibration," and it is my hope here to add to what Young calls "the mixed media of her soul's expression" (233). I am sorry to say that radio must remain figural in this context, for there is no space here to begin a consideration of its immense complexity as a medium. It must serve simply as an emblem of media specificity and remind us that the past's great gift is surely not our particular present (to the Victorians we would likely be a great disappointment) but rather its wealth of futures. These futures become available only when we ask *not* what *Middlemarch* can do for us, but what we can do for *Middlemarch*.

Our first task is to question a tendency to see this novel as a work of painful realism and sober resignation. I want to read *Middlemarch* the feminist science fiction novel, with its speculative science, its fascination with aliens, and above all its time travel—justified, as it is, by a breathtaking injunction not to see the "world's ages as box-like partitions" (212). And yet despite a manifest concern with prophecy, Eliot seems not to foresee the explosion of audio technology that would follow so soon after the publication of her novel. To be sure, she gives due attention to the stethoscope and makes cryptic reference to "the possible histories of creatures that

converse compendiously with their antennae" (*Middlemarch* 785), but Edward Bel-
lamy's place in the canon of science fiction is probably safe. But what if Eliot secretly
anticipated the coming dominance of the new media and feared the competition?
Indeed, Rudolph Arnheim, a rare and early critic of radio, compares it favorably
to literature in its capacity to deliver speech, "the most spiritual form of expression that we humans know" (175). In Arnheim's formulation we find much about
novelistic culture in general, and *Middlemarch* in particular, that radio throws into
relief, both the overt promise of a transcendent spirit and the lurking fear of voices
that haunt or possess us. Thus my experiment: to mount a case for putting the radio
back into *Middlemarch,* to show how different this novel can start to sound once we
have tuned into its auditory imagination.

Such a case inevitably begins with one of the narrator's more famous digres-
sions, a meditation on sensory amplification and its attendant protective numbness
that anticipates McLuhan by nearly a century:[4]

> If we had a keen vision and feeling of all ordinary human life, it would be
> like hearing the grass grow and the squirrel's heart beat, and we should die
> of that roar which lies on the other side of silence. As it is, the quickest of us
> walk about well wadded with stupidity. (194)[5]

A favorite touchstone for discussions of "the hypersensitive consciousness" and nar-
ratorial sympathy, this passage has more recently been opened up by Alex Woloch
in his study of protagonist-formation through and against minor characters.[6] For
Woloch, the passage captures a profound ambivalence at the heart of novelistic
discourse about the democratic dispersal of sympathetic attention, an ambivalence
that can only form "a precarious balance between different patterns of distribution" (31). Indeed, offered by Eliot in the middle of a discussion of Dorothea's disappointment in marriage, the passage threatens a full reversal of narrative work,
a brief moment of protagonist-dissolution as the already quite singular Dorothea
recedes into the many. But what interests me most is how the politics of interest remain inseparable from an implicit question of media. It is therefore an even briefer
moment within this passage that I would highlight: our fleeting, and surely baffled,
attempt to imagine the sound of growing grass before it turns into a heartbeat no
doubt already fully audible, had anyone cared to listen, with Lydgate's vintage
stethoscope. There for a moment, before a hasty retreat into the prevailing technical conditions of 1830, is science fiction at its finest—the dream, however ambivalent, of an acoustic medium that one is tempted to call time-lapse phonography.

At its most routine, *Middlemarch* will develop the auditory imagination in mar-
ginally more human terms, though even then we would be hard-pressed to call
the effect realism. Consider the continual reference to the quality of characters'
voices, as if such information were the surest index of their inner lives. We see this

indexing most crudely in how the narrator uses the description of voices to cue the distribution of readerly favor—thus Dorothea gets to sound like an Aeolian harp, whereas Joshua Rigg, the legatee from left field, bears the burden of a "high chirping voice and a vile accent" (80, 340). The voice is also our guide to some of the novel's subtlest effects, as in the climactic encounter between Dorothea and Rosamond, in which Dorothea finds a tone that "might have gone to one's very marrow, like a cry from some suffering creature in the darkness" (795). But the metaphysical equation of voice and spirit takes us only so far in *Middlemarch*. Better is Steven Connor's analysis of the voice's defining power:

> Nothing else about me defines me so intimately as my voice, precisely because there is no other feature of my self whose nature it is thus to move from me to the world, and to move me into the world. If my voice is mine because it comes from me, it can only be known as mine because it also goes from me. My voice is, literally, my way of taking leave of my senses. What I *say* goes. (7)

In deflecting the voice from the spirit to the body, Connor describes the vocal production of the self as a process in the world. Once embodied, the voice loses contact with the soul and floats away, free to deceive, block, or simply overbear, like the "loud men" whom Eliot mocks for placing "the seat of candour in the lungs" (123). And crucially for *Middlemarch*, Connor's language suggests finally that the voice cannot deliver the self apart from the twin threats of madness—"taking leave of my senses"—and domination—"what I say goes."

    I want to pursue this analysis then by contrasting two media that channel the specters of madness and domination in this novel, the picture and the bell. These media are of course unlikely candidates for a discussion of the auditory imagination in *Middlemarch*—the picture because it is reasonably thought to be purely visual, and the bell because in this novel it is so low-tech and so seamlessly integrated into domestic routine as to fall beneath the threshold of attention. But these media are nonetheless a part of *Middlemarch*'s auditory imagination at its limits, and indeed from this marginal position they have much to tell us about the sound barriers that *Middlemarch* does and does not want to break.

    We can take up the discourse of pictures in *Middlemarch* with the sketch Ladislaw is making when Dorothea first meets him, and watch as pictures play an important role in their protracted and repressed courtship. Indeed, the first thing Dorothea says to Will is that she is no judge of such things, an attitude that she goes on to elaborate as follows: "I suppose there is some relation between pictures and nature which I am too ignorant to feel" (79). This rather murky objection develops into a complex, if tentative, critique of the medium as she returns to the subject with Will in Rome. She feels that the paintings there produce above all a sense of exclusion, commanding admiration without understanding, and that upon close examination, "the life goes out of them" (206). Will articulates his own critique of pictures in an argument with the painter, Naumann:

> "Language gives a fuller image, which is all the better for being vague. After all, the true seeing is within; and painting stares at you with an insistent imperfection. I feel that especially about representations of women. . . . This woman you have just seen, for example: how would you paint her voice, pray?" (191)

This is one of those moments when we feel Eliot is indulging in a bit of advertising, claiming the most for her chosen medium of words against a visual competitor. But what interests me here is that the failure of painting gets expressed as an inability to capture women's voices, because the only reason Will can make this objection is that he is thinking about the wrong kind of painting.

There is in fact a picture in this novel that seems to capture Dorothea's voice—it is the miniature of Casaubon's Aunt Julia that looks so much like Will, the miniature that Dorothea communes with "as if it had an *ear* for her" (275, emphasis mine). Indeed the terms of Dorothea's critique of painting return for their due reversal. Instead of being dead and forbidding, the miniature seems alive to Dorothea and draws her into a revelatory understanding: "Here was a woman who had known some difficulty about marriage" (275). This reverie takes a striking turn as the miniature morphs into Will himself:

> The colours deepened, the lips and chin seemed to get larger, the hair and eyes seemed to be sending out light, the face was masculine and beamed on her with that full gaze which tells her on whom it falls that she is too interesting for the slightest movement of her eyelid to pass unnoticed and uninterpreted. (275)

Taking leave of her senses, Dorothea indulges her mad romance through the medium of the miniature.[7]

About bells there is less of madness—that is, until we remember Poe's poem or our own telephone ringing off the hook. Bells are rather the opposite of Dorothea's miniature—instead of drawing us into a liberating fantasy, they break in upon us with the relentless demands of others. In *Middlemarch* the bell is almost invisible, mentioned occasionally as it performs its function, to be sure, but passing well beneath the threshold of commentary. I would argue that for the reader it's inaudible as well, taking no part in the chorus of hallucinated voices—the onomatopoeia of the word "ring" compensating poorly for the fact that the bell sounds no words. Writing the bell is like painting the voice, an exercise in incommensurability. You can't picture *or* hear the bell in *Middlemarch*, and so it virtually escapes form and disappears into function.

This function, though, is not the less complicated for being unperceived. The bell summons other people, of course, but its wordless command shows how superfluous words can be. It is a prosthetic shout or cry and reveals starkly a command structure that, like the paintings in Rome, offers no compensatory understanding. (We might note, incidentally, that this structure becomes occluded with the telephone, which reunites the cry with the articulate voice and pretends it's the words that matter more.) The bell, moreover, epitomizes the tendency of technology to efface the human labor behind its creation, maintenance, and use. Indeed in *Middlemarch* it seems like the servants in particular labor under a spell of invisibility—when they do occasionally sneak into the light of representation, it is usually as gossips enlisted to further the *narrator's* work. The passive voice of a sentence like "Dorothea rang the bell violently, and presently Mr. Casaubon was helped to the couch" betrays how a system of domination magically disappears into the apparent innocence of an unremarkable technology merely doing its job (283).

But the notable thing about this command structure is that no one really commands it. Living people may borrow the bell for their own petty purposes, but we all know it's the dead for whom the bell tolls. Hence the only urgent bell ringing in *Middlemarch* is done by Dorothea, as I just mentioned, when she sees Casaubon collapse, and by Mary Garth, when she sees Featherstone dead. We are thus subject to the bell not only when it rings for us, but in those moments when social obligation demands that we ring for others. The commanding grip of the dead is indeed captured wonderfully by Eliot in her image of the Dead Hand of inheritance, the hand that smites the hopes of Fred Vincy as well as of Dorothea and Will. If through the miniature, Dorothea madly puts the dead to work, this is perhaps a reaction against the "bequest of labour" Casaubon is leaving for her, a labor Dorothea has reflexively already begun by ringing the bell (493).

Thus to sound the depths of the auditory imagination in *Middlemarch*, we need to visit the land of the dead. Here death is figured precisely as the end of hearing, bringing a silence to Casaubon's ear that is "never more to be broken" (482). It is nonetheless something for which we intently listen, whether scientifically through Lydgate's stethoscope, mythologically with Casaubon "as if he suddenly found himself on the dark river-brink and heard the plash of the oncoming oar," or treacherously with Bulstrode in the hallway, satisfied that the "hard stertorous breathing" promises the blackmailing Raffles's final silence (424, 710). What Eliot makes clear, moreover, is that listening is desiring. Recall one of the novel's most arresting effects, which occurs as we finish Book 2 and turn the page to Book 3, with its extraordinary title: "Waiting for Death." Seldom do novels catch us quite so red-handed. Moreover, the death we are waiting for—Casaubon's—is delayed until Book 5 and becomes part of a remarkable triptych that includes the death of Raffles as well as of Featherstone. In the phrase "waiting for death," Eliot thus names an aesthetic, erotic, and strangely auditory posture, one that can only be called necrophilia.

Indeed, once you listen for necrophilia in *Middlemarch*, it announces itself with a creepy insistence that no helplessly post-Freudian reader could miss, as you can see by the following examples. The first two come from Featherstone's confrontation with Mary Garth as he tries to get her to destroy one of the drafts of his will before he dies: "The old man paused with a blank stare for a little while, holding the one key erect on the ring; then with an agitated jerk he began to work with his bony left hand at emptying the tin box before him" (316). Then a moment later: "He lifted the stick . . . and threw it with a hard effort which was but impotence" (318). To be sure, we might say that while the old patriarch clings to life, such sexual innuendoes don't quite constitute necrophilia, were it not for their clear trajectory: Featherstone achieves consummation only in his fantasy that, through the medium of his will, "the rigid clutch of his dead hand" might lead to "gratification inside his coffin" (324). This necrophilia seems to be Featherstone's true legacy, as it continues to permeate the erotics of the novel. Thus Will thinks of "beautiful lips kissing holy skulls," engages Dorothea in a "ghostly kind of wooing," and tells Rosamond that he would rather touch Dorothea's hand "if it were dead, than I would touch any other woman's living" (364, 633, 778). For Rosamond's part, she calls her husband "Doctor Grave-face," promising cheerfully to "declare in future that I dote on skeletons, and body-snatchers, and bits of things in phials, and quarrels with everybody, that end in your dying miserably" (458).

No distaste for such ghoulish textual play should prevent us from observing an important transvaluation at work, a transvaluation that makes death sound less like the dominating hand of inheritance and more like some kind of mad freedom. This is not your father's necrophilia—indeed it cuts straight across the gothic claustrophobia demanded by patriarchal interests. Regarding Dorothea's love life, there are two consequences of a necrophilic reading. First, it allows us to reread her marriage to Casaubon as something other than a mistake. Second, as Will's wooing becomes infected with this discourse, he represents an extension of, rather than an escape from, the terrain of necrophilia. To a necrophilic Dorothea, Casaubon and Will begin finally to look like the cousins that they really are. Thus necrophilia bears not only on the novel's central problem of a woman's choice, but also on the question that comes to stand in for that problem—Mrs. Cadwallader's question of who exactly Will Ladislaw is. Of course the trouble when two necrophiliacs get together is deciding which one is going to play dead, and so Dorothea and Will struggle to define their roles, a struggle that returns us to the question of media.

Indeed if, following Susan Stewart, we see the miniature as a medium for the "sympathetic magic" of "requited love," this view raises the important question of who returns Dorothea's love in *Middlemarch* (126). I am not sure the answer is Will—after all he rather aggressively tries to define her as a mere medium when he accuses her of being a poem. Indeed, it is hard not to see in him a bit of the stalker, eager to capture her love not for what it can be, but for what it can be made to represent. This is the character who turns up time and again in Dorothea's path, who resolves that "if he gave up everything else in life he would watch over her" (360). So perhaps instead of loving the miniature because it reminds her of Will, Dorothea loves Will because he reminds her of the miniature. Steven Connor has argued that in the practice of ventriloquism, "The dummy does more than embody the voice; it gives the voice a face" (401). When it comes to Aunt Julia, Will turns this notion around and gives the *face* a voice. It is through Will that the spirit of Aunt Julia comes to life.

Another example may show us what we stand to gain by thinking of Will as a medium and not just an erotic object. Consider Dorothea's big scene with Rosamond, in which Rosamond reveals that she has not been having an affair with Will. Patricia Vigderman has read this scene as a kind of traffic in men: "Neither sisterhood nor rivalry, their mutual recognition is an exchange of a phallic object that opens the moral world to Rosamond and the erotic world to Dorothea" (26–27). This reading is perhaps a little too pat—it certainly allows us to trot out the platitudes that Rosamond is selfish and Dorothea uptight. To me this scene looks less like exchange and more like conquest. And this is not only because, as the narrator tells us and critics often note, Rosamond's impulse to clear Will's name was merely "a reflex" of Dorothea's "energy"—for from the moment Dorothea enters the room, she buffets Rosamond with a series of imperatives (798). Though occasionally softened by a question mark, their cumulative force is little short of commanding: "You will not think me too troublesome," "You will like to know . . . ?" "You will let me speak . . . ?" and later "That will cheer you, will it not? That will give you courage?" ending finally, in regard to Lydgate: "But you will forgive him" (794–95). The word that rings throughout the scene, repeated over and over again, is Will. Will Will Will Will Will Will Will—seven times by my count in the space of a page. Seven is a magic number, and indeed there is something like incantation at work here. Will is not just her beau—he is her magic word.

Thus if a spellbound Rosamond returns us to the metaphysical status of Dorothea's voice, it also offers in the idea of magic a new term to mediate between madness and domination. Recall the exchange between Dorothea and Mrs. Cadwallader that occurs after Casaubon's death, where Mrs. Cadwallader lectures her about the need for socialization:

> "You will certainly go mad in that house alone dear. You will see visions. We have all got to exert ourselves a little to keep sane, and call things by the same names as other people call them by. . . . Sitting alone in that library at Lowick you may fancy yourself ruling the weather; you must get a few people round you *who wouldn't believe you if you told them.*" 537 (emphasis added)

If doubt is the sign of realism, then I would suggest it is again time to switch genres, before Mrs. Cadwallader can isolate Dorothea as a modern-day Cassandra.[8] To be sure, the difference between not adhering to prescribed names and thinking one rules the weather is the difference between being thought mad and being mad—unless, of course, one is a sorceress who *can* rule the weather. And why not? Where else do we think the storm comes from that traps Will and Dorothea indoors for their climactic love scene? Looking back, we can see Dorothea's early necrophilia in a magical light as well—as necromancy. Not knowing what to do with herself, Miss Brooke consults the dead. And of course Casaubon's prophecy, barely disguised as prohibition, is that she will marry Ladislaw.

So who *is* Will Ladislaw? The qualities that appear decisive to me—the qualities for which Dorothea chooses him—are his mobility, his radiance, and his receptivity. He is, then, something like her portable two-way radio, or, if you prefer, her cell phone. In making him her instrument for unhistoric deeds, Dorothea turns the tables on the former dilettante who once called her a poem.[9] Indeed, the simple fact that the dilettante turns diligent speaks volumes for her power. Even so, feminism won't be thrilled with mere revenge, or with the rediscovery of a vague female influence. In our lingering dissatisfaction, we may be prepared then to take up Eliot's famous challenge, in which she defies us to state "exactly what else that was in [Dorothea's] power she ought rather to have done" (836). Many have complained that Eliot denies Dorothea her own career of novelist, but I hope my discussion shows that she needs something a little more commanding, something that better projects her voice, something that perhaps even begins to rule the weather. What Dorothea ought rather to have done is this: build a radio. In lamenting the lost medium in which "ardent deeds took shape," this novel brings us to the brink of the "effective magic" that is female engineering, and brings my own book to its final image of a female broadcast network (838, 388). But with feminist literary history and Aunt Julia similarly remote, Dorothea's program could not yet reach the people who *would* believe her if she told them. All that she could do was announce her second choice, of and through Will Ladislaw, her incalculably diffusive medium, and await her future listeners on Radio Free Middlemarch.

Notes

Introduction

1. Eve Sedgwick, *Between Men*. Helena Michie has surveyed this culture widely in her provocative study *Sororophobia*, and I would echo her caution that female networks are not best understood in terms of family resemblance or "sisterhood." If anything, my work suggests that the conflicts of interest generated in familial relationships often prohibit female networking.

2. This is how Tania Modleski describes her inspiring work in *The Women Who Knew Too Much* (12). See Margaret Russett or Judith Wilt for detailed accounts of gothic reading.

3. It is therefore not a reader in scrupulous conformity to the taxonomies of narratology or the empiricism of ethnography. Both disciplines have enriched my sense of the complexity of reading, but neither has offered the fluidity I find essential for gauging the tensions between readerly constraint and possibility.

4. We might in fact see in this book a counterstrategy that speaks to the well-known concerns of Mary Ann Doane about the female film spectator's overidentification with the image. While Doane argues for masquerade as a strategy for achieving the distance needed for both desire and criticism, I am trying to work *through* narrative to defeat any damaging specularity, restoring character—in Eve Sedgwick's gothic sense of character as "social and relational"—to the female image and fresh plot to the female character (*Coherence*, 142). In this sense I see my project as consistent with Linda Williams's more recent attempt to understand "viewer identification with pathetic suffering" beyond "the dangerous specter of masochism" (46).

5. For important accounts of the risks of identification see Judith Butler and especially Diana Fuss. These risks run both ways, including loss of boundaries for the subject as well as the violent appropriation of the object, and I have tried to

155

be mindful of both of them in my readings. Ultimately, my hope is that female networks provide a conceptual force that checks abuses of sympathetic interest while dispersing attention in more considered ways.

6. See her chapter of that title in *Doing Time*. Felski writes specifically about categories of feminist thought, though in a way suggestive for contesting categories of genre or period as well.

7. Daniel Frampton has attempted a thorough purge of literary concepts in *Filmosophy*. I found this work highly refreshing and original, but dogmatic in this one regard. It seems to me that film studies would do better to hold the literary close, assessing the complexity of this crucial inheritance and maintaining the clarity of direct contrast.

8. Ellen Lupton reports that this tendency to forget the phone is in no way confined to the cinema: "The design ambition behind many telephones is, in fact, to *disappear* as an object, becoming a transparent frame for the conversation it hosts." (29)

Chapter 1

1. William Cohen's argument in *Sex Scandal* represents a more recent attempt to define the relationship between scandal and gossip. For him, gossip implies a community "in which victims are personally known to their audience" (19), while scandal is the better analogy to the novel as "a function of mass media, which rely on an anonymous audience far from the event's dramatis personae" (14). While this contrast is indeed useful for defining the conditions of modern scandal and its particular resemblance to the novel, we should not feel ourselves confined to such a narrow definition of gossip, which is hardly common usage. (Nothing more belies this definition than the term "gossip column.") As should become clear, moreover, gossip remains the better term for my purposes because of the wider field of interest it implies.

2. Of course in many respects the opinions of Emma and Knightley are *too* close for courtship. Thus in one scene we see Emma play at the necessary difference, arguing a position that is not hers simply so there can be an argument.

3. See, for instance, Cohen's comments in *Sex Scandal* (20–21).

4. Wayne Booth is one who writes openly about enjoying "Emma's mistreatment of [Miss Bates]," though as part of a reading in which the judgement of Emma remains a primary concern (263).

5. Frank Churchill gets this line (156).

6. Mary Waldron discusses the idea of a covert love scene in "Men of Sense and Silly Wives: The Confusions of Mr. Knightley." She describes the scene when Emma acknowledges her fault "one of the tenderest of low-key love scenes in all fiction; but, typically, Austen places it at a point where neither party can possibly know that it *is* a love scene, so caught up are they in their erroneous speculations" (154). I agree with her reading of this scene and would simply extend her insight further back to include their entire courtship of gossip.

7. Jan Gordon has seen this quite differently. For him, Knightley "is a natural ally of those like Miss Bates who advance the claims of voice" (31): "Emma, after her abuse of Miss Bates, marries the gossip's defender and virtual competitor, as the voice of Knightley's authority co-opts the spinster's more subversive voice. In attacking Miss Bates Emma comes close to becoming her 'likeness,' which is a radical mode

of legitimizing her role" (37). Gordon's argument turns on an associative logic that is inherently reversible, and one that indeed we would typically expect to run the other way. For is not the usual associative logic the lowering one of *guilt* by association? If we can associate Emma and Miss Bates together (and we assume that Emma enjoys the higher status), we should expect the effect of this association to work at least as much to Emma's harm as to Miss Bates's credit. Clearly the larger context of their association, which Gordon himself notes, suggests that, insofar as Miss Bates represents a possible future for Emma of lonely and inconsequential spinsterhood, her likeness to Emma is intolerable and must be denied in the most emphatic way possible: by marriage. His other claim, that in Austen generally "the gossip demands respect before the conventional marriage can occur" (39), strikes me as more reasonable, though only half the story in *Emma*, since, as I've argued, this kind of "respect" keeps Miss Bates in a place that is less than honorary.

8. Indeed Blakey Vermeule identifies the "trope of the flayed gossip" as central to the novelistic tradition: "Her peculiar fate is to be excoriated for engaging in the same practices as everyone else, including the novelist" (107). I read Vermeule's essay after I completed the work on this chapter, but I am pleased to see that she shares my view of the deep connection between gossip and the novel.

9. Rosmarin observes this (330–31).

10. This distinction in fact makes up half of Edmund Wilson's defense of Austen as an artist: "Miss Austen is almost unique among the novelists of her sex in being deeply and steadily concerned, not with the vicarious satisfaction of emotion (though the Cinderella theme, of course, does figure in several of her novels) *nor with the skillful exploitation of gossip*, but as the great masculine novelists are, with the novel as a work of art" (66, emphasis added).

11. Among the critics who discuss this is Spacks (165–66).

12. Mary Waldron has done some of this work for *Emma* with her attention to Mrs. Cole and Mrs. Goddard. Of course, the most important example of this strategy for Austen studies is in Sandra Gilbert and Susan Gubar's *The Madwoman in the Attic*. It is somewhat strange in fact that Gilbert and Gubar omit Mrs. Elton from their list of "nastier, more resilient, energetic female characters who enact [Austen's] rebellious dissent from her culture" (169). Mrs. Elton apparently gets left out because she is not a widow, but otherwise she fits their critical criteria perfectly: she is certainly nasty, and she is quite literally still talking up to the end.

13. In *Nobody's Story*, Catherine Gallagher cautions against an overly optimistic view of the novel as a training ground for sympathy. Drawing on a theory in David Hume's *Treatise of Human Nature* that sympathy can occur only by one's making a feeling one's own, she suggests that novels stimulate sympathy only because they facilitate this appropriation:

> We can always claim to be expanding our capacity for sympathy by reading fiction because, after all, if we can sympathize with nobody, then we can sympathize with anybody. Or so it would seem, but such sympathy remains on that level of abstraction where anybody is "nobody in particular" (the very definition of a novel character). Nobody was eligible to be the universally preferred anybody because nobody, unlike somebody, was never anybody *else*. (167–72)

14. Spacks describes Emma's difficulty in relating to others in terms of a tendency to fictionalize both others and herself (166-67).

15. Readers of Austen's other novels should be especially attuned to the dislocations of women, whether it is the painful uprootings of the Dashwoods and the Elliots, the happier opportunities of Catherine Morland and Fanny Price, or Elizabeth's triumphant occupation of Pemberley.

16. Deborah Kaplan's historical work tracing Austen's dual participation in gentry culture and women's culture bears on this divided loyalty. In assessing the implications for contemporary reading practices, she concludes that "feminists need to . . . relinquish some of our intimacy with Austen's novels," which "are only partially ours" (204–5). I would only add that this intimacy can do harm in both directions—that it is equally important that the novels not fully possess us.

17. Casey Finch and Peter Bowen offer a reading that develops along these lines: "And though Mrs. Elton, for instance, may begrudge the match of Emma and Mr. Knightley, her thoughts, as they are reproduced in the free indirect style, turn out to be limited and inconsequential. The free indirect style may well recognize certain resistances to the novel's political impulsions, but it will always do so in order to render them palpably illegitimate" (14).

18. See, for instance, pages 45, 97, 217, 286, and particularly 464: "When Isabel heard such things she felt a greater scorn for them than for the gossip of a village parlour."

19. Spacks makes a similar point with respect to James's later novel *What Maisie Knew*: "We experience a kind of apotheosis of gossip, purified, sublimated, providing gratification without contamination" (217).

20. For further discussion of gossip's double aspect in conjunction with the history of the novel, see Spacks.

21. For an extended discussion of the economic connotations of "interest" in this novel, see Howard White.

22. I want to thank Tate Hurvitz for reminding me of this telegram.

23. An important early dissenting view comes from Arnold Kettle, who argues that James sacrifices Isabel to an ideal of martyrdom.

24. Campion solves James's problem beautifully by ending with Isabel running from Caspar—and the camera—then hesitating at the door of Gardencourt. As she turns toward the camera, harried and weary, no longer sure where to run, we must finally realize that it is time to leave her alone.

25. There is something rather bullying about Miller's attitude toward dissent on this point, as when he informs us that he too was "disgusted with the ending when I first read the novel as an undergraduate" (737). Whether we credit this little biography or not, the term "undergraduate" resounds as one of the great uncredentialing slurs of professional criticism. When Miller later claims that a "reading decision changes the reading you," (so be careful!) it is hard not to wonder why any undergraduate disgust would not have left deeper traces on his current reading (746).

26. James in fact had used a version of this metaphor before in a playful review of *Daniel Deronda*, dramatized as a conversation among three readers. In this earlier version he refers to "the discovery by each of us that we are at the best but a rather ridiculous *fifth* wheel to the coach" (431, emphasis added). If the fifth wheel is ridiculous, it is only in contrast to the useful other four, among which Henrietta would have to be counted in the metaphor's later incarnation.

Chapter 2

1. We will see this seductive tactic again, as a more central and sustained strategy, in *Pillow Talk* (chapter 3) and *You've Got Mail* (chapter 5).

2. Lovelace's dream begins on page 920; he murders his conscience on page 848.

3. For a discussion of how the work of the narrator in the realist novel is inherently backward-looking, see Ermarth (esp. p. 88).

4. See, for instance, Preston (50–53).

5. For the comparison with Isabel see, for instance, Ian Watt's *The Rise of the Novel* (225). John Preston invokes this comparison in his book and also links Lovelace and Osmond (87). Moreover, as Watt suggests, when it comes to sexual fantasies, feminine delicacy acts as a powerful brake: the "modern sexual code . . . makes Clarissa withhold her sexual feelings from Anna Howe, and even from her own consciousness" (228–29).

6. Other critics who warn against the impulse to save Clarissa include Christina Marsden Gillis and Linda Kauffman. While there can be little doubt that this position is faithful to the novel's development on its own terms, it is precisely that development that I wish to question, since it forecloses what we might see as the novel's more vital interest.

7. Faderman describes such relationships as follows: "Women who were romantic friends were everything to each other. They lived to be together. They thought of each other constantly. They made each other deliriously happy or horribly miserable by the increase or abatement of their proffered love. They were jealous of other female friends (and certainly of male friends) . . . They vowed that if it were at all possible they would someday live together, or at least die together" (84). For a reading attuned to the excluded lesbian possibilities of Clarissa and Anna's relationship, see Ogden.

8. My point echoes Chodorow's discussion of similar personal relationships: "When people have extreme needs for emotional support, and a few very intense relationships (whose sole basis is emotional connection, ungrounded in cooperative activity or institutionalized non emotional roles) to provide for these needs, these relationships are liable to be full of conflict" (213).

9. Gillis offers a nuanced reading of the space of *Clarissa* in terms of the dichotomy between public and private space, a reading that charts Clarissa's movement toward the publicity of her death in parallel with the progress of her private letters toward the publicity of the book itself. What limits the usefulness of this conception for my purposes is that Clarissa's initial privacy is conceived as solitude and her later publicity as community—lost in between, despite much thoughtful attention to Anna, is the space of female networks.

10. Terry Castle frequently stresses similar points in *Clarissa's Ciphers*. See, for instance, page 149. For a discussion of Richardson's central correspondence with Lady Bradshaigh, see Kauffman.

11. I am by no means the first to spot Fiedler's revision. See, for instance, Kinkead-Weekes: "The significance of Fiedler's splendid gaffes, like the belief that Pamela is a governess (later corrected), and that Lovelace is killed by Belford (uncorrected), is not merely the strong suspicion that he has not read the books; it is that for this kind of criticism the barest plot outline, or less, will suffice" (500n).

12. For example, this claim that the rape is central is the basis for Eagleton's entire book.

13. Frances Ferguson echoes Watt's choice of words (100), as does Angela Carter (48); for Leslie Richardson, Clarissa "has no experience, no memory, of the event" (165). Judith Wilt challenges a different belief in a well-known article—namely, the belief that Lovelace can definitely be said to have gone through with the rape. This reading leads to a very rich account of the novel, though ultimately one that obscures the counterforce of female networks: "[Clarissa] learns the lesson Lovelace has insisted upon all along, the real enemy of woman is woman" ("He Could Go No Farther" 27).

14. Ermarth observes that the epistolary form indeed structures a similar readerly unconsciousness between every letter: "The epistolary form thus confines the reader's consciousness to a discontinuous medium that jeopardizes it at every step" (101). Preston makes the point slightly differently: "It is precisely the reader who best understands, who suffers, in fact, the crucial lesions in experience, the lapses, the moments of vacancy" (47).

15. I'm thinking particularly of Nicholas Hudson's article "Arts of Seduction and the Rhetoric of *Clarissa*." Similar narratives of "overcoming" reading can be found in Watt and Preston.

16. Watt, for instance, registers this desire for separation: "To devote nearly one-third of the novel to the heroine's death is surely excessive" (216).

17. René Girard has argued that such misreading characterizes ritual in general: "Sacrificial substitution implies a degree of misunderstanding. Its vitality as an institution depends on its ability to conceal the displacement upon which the rite is based" (5).

18. We might indeed say that William Warner's strongly "anti-Clarissa" reading was so upsetting precisely because it was so unusual.

19. Linda S. Kauffman and Stephen Melville both make this point as well.

20. In fact, Kinkead-Weekes has argued similarly that, coinciding with its three-part structure, the novel's concerns move from the social to the moral to finally the religious (124). Gillis, on the other hand, finds the social conditions of epistolary to be fulfilled by the opening of private letters into public discourse. To be sure, the novel's religious turn does not entirely prevent it from sustaining social commentary in an indirect way, including commentary about the public fate of private letters. Where Gillis and I disagree is in her idea that this public fate can be seen as a fulfillment, rather than a suppression, of female epistolary relations.

21. Lovelace recognizes Widow Lovick's potential (however ironically) when he recommends that Belford marry her (1442). Of course this fantasy would find a hospitable genre in detective fiction, which, among other things, promotes widowhood by murdering a lot of husbands. It is also capable of generating considerable backlash, as strikingly represented by Uncle Charlie's rage against widows in Hitchcock's *Shadow of a Doubt*, a film I will consider at length in chapter 4.

22. Toni Bowers makes this point with respect to Norton, Mrs. Howe, and Mrs. Sinclair: "the singleness of these mothers seems to promise greater maternal autonomy than Mrs. Harlowe could possibly enjoy" (214).

23. They're all from *Evelina*, pp. 173, 340, 383, 338, and 340. In the fourth and fifth quotations the writer is actually Evelina's mother, Caroline Evelyn.

24. A similar conversation occurs between Anne and Captain Wentworth at the end of *Persuasion*. In this case the ritual is even more thorough insofar as all of Wentworth's unexplained behavior is accounted for in terms of his love for Anne.

25. See, for instance, Epstein (esp. p. 99), Edward A. Bloom's introduction to the Oxford edition of *Evelina*, and Doody (*Frances* 45).

26. In this light, we can't help but see the vicious prankster Captain Mirvan as a repudiation of the idea that the sea is a space of freedom.

27. Janet Altman argues that the potential for this sort of contrast is inherent in the epistolary form: "Given the letter's function as a connector between two distant points, as a bridge between sender and receiver, the epistolary author can choose to emphasize either the distance or the bridge" (13).

28. "Mother-novel" is Margaret Anne Doody's term for *Caroline Evelyn*, Burney's first novel, which she burned; its story made up the backstory of *Evelina*. (*Frances* 37). Samuel Choi has suggestively termed *Evelina* an "orphan" for its lack of nurturing literary predecessors (276).

29. Others have argued against the viability of female networks with respect to other aspects of the novel. For instance, Judith Lowder Newton, observing how other female characters do nothing about Captain Mirvan's assaults on Madame Duval, reflects that "Bonding between women, it would seem, is futile" (83), while Kristina Straub notes "the failures of the mature women in the text to nurture or defend Evelina" (26). Straub is ultimately more generous: "Yet in pointing out where Mrs. Selwyn fails Evelina, Burney seems to suggest potential success, if only the mature woman were less blinded by the attractive light of male power" (28).

30. Doody is referring here specifically to Evelina's embarrassing grandmother, Madame Duval (*Frances* 51).

31. For discussions of this scene in terms of violence and gender, see Doody (*Frances* 56), Epstein (114–15), and Straub (43). For historical background on racing in the eighteenth century, see Earl R. Anderson (56–68).

32. See in particular Martha G. Brown's polemic against feminist accounts of *Evelina* (29–39). Brown situates *Evelina* convincingly in a long tradition of romance; in doing so, however, she distorts feminist claims considerably, subjecting them to a highly reductive form of accounting, as in "the numbers of villainous men and women are roughly equivalent" (35). Betty A. Schellenberg has usefully complicated Burney's bashful image, demonstrating how after *Evelina*, Burney embraced publication with increasing confidence.

33. Quoted in Edward A. Bloom's introduction to the Oxford edition, p. viii. See Catherine Gallagher's *Nobody's Story* for a discussion of Burney's reserve in the context of the shifting marketplace of late eighteenth-century England.

34. As critics have pointed out, even Orville remains passive in this scene, saving his intervention, rather dubiously, for the rescue of Lovel from the monkey at the end.

35. See Lynch for a complex account of agoraphobia in Burney's work. Her chapter focuses mostly on other novels but nonetheless advances an argument of considerable relevance for my reading of *Evelina*. Lynch demonstrates how Burney "depicts the scene of consumption as one in which things and individuals (especially female individuals) seem to change places," while claiming that "the text defines its enterprise as that of supplying a reanimating

remedy to reification" in its "recovery . . . of an inner life" (165–66). We might understand the idea of an underground female network then as an alternate *social* remedy that stands against and apart from the marketplace—a different way to contemplate Lynch's conclusion that "'character' can be a device for pursuing lines of analysis that extend from one self on to others" (206).

Chapter 3

1. Recall Fielding's mockery of Richardson in *Shamela*. For instance: "Mrs. Jervis and I are just in bed, and the door unlocked; if my master should come—Odsbobs! I hear him just coming in at the door. You see I write in the present tense" (Letter VI, 313). Thanks to Leo Braudy for reminding me of this response to Richardson's pretensions.

2. Although he shows little interest in film, John Brooks does consider the consequences for narrative of the technological shift from letters to phones, speculating briefly about the possibility of a novel consisting of nothing but phone calls—only to announce, quite prematurely in my opinion, that "the telephone as a subject for the creative imagination has been exhausted" (223). Jan Olsson also notes the narrative boon of telephones in his exhaustive study of how phone calls were visualized (especially through split-screen strategies) in early cinema (157).

3. We should be tipped off to the dubiousness of this trade by the long resistance, only just starting to give way, to the picturephone. Tom Gunning argues indeed that the phone serves film: "If film had the freedom and the power to cut across space and interrelate separate strands of a story within a consistent temporality, showing a telephone conversation offered a common experience that would make such cutting comprehensible and believable" (Fritz 24).

4. An excellent example of this would be Frank Churchill's letter in Jane Austen's *Emma*, which becomes the object of a communal and narrative scrutiny.

5. Gunning develops his argument further in a recent essay on Fritz Lang. While I remain resistant to his tendency to see "the system" everywhere (a tendency which seems to be Lang's own but which can only further obscure opportunities to think about female networks), I am delighted to see that he finds the telephone worthy of further thought and that it has led him to consistently insightful readings of such an important body of work.

6. The groundbreaking essay about the gender of the viewer is of course Laura Mulvey's "Visual Pleasure and Narrative Cinema." The trope of calling one's mother receives play in many films. Noteworthy examples include *The Thin Man* (1934), *Bells Are Ringing* (1960), *The Misfits* (1961), *Nashville* (1975), and *Mother* (1996).

7. E. L. McCallum is among the few critics to make the kinds of claims I am making for the narrative centrality of the telephone. In her essay about *The Crying of Lot 49* and *The House of Seven Gables* (a novel that of course predates the telephone), she argues that the importance of "wired communications [in these texts] . . . goes further than simply topic or style, implicating their very structure and interpretation" (Hawthorne 65).

8. Regarding operators, Kenneth Lipartito reports that "[s]ince the 1880's, the telephone companies employed women almost exclusively in this position, a practice also followed in other nations" (1082). For further discussion of operators see

Brenda Maddox. For an extensive cultural analysis of the teenage girl on the phone as a major trope of the mid-twentieth century, see Mary Celeste Kearney.

9. See Mary Celeste Kearney for an interesting discussion of the teenage girl on the phone as a trope that pervades mid-twentieth century culture. Her research includes some important films, such as *Bye Bye Birdie*, and draws heavily from magazines, radio, and television.

10. For an excellent discussion of the many different ways the telephone has been used, see Carolyn Marvin.

11. See Christopher Williams for a critical discussion of this terminology.

12. Henry Boettinger has speculated that the phone has disappeared from notice because "no other device can be used (in safety) with such total disregard of the thing itself" (200). While his claim for the importance of safe use should not be ignored, clearly he goes too far in singling out the telephone from a long list of "dangerous" inventions. Can anyone recall a telescope, to name one of his examples, causing a serious accident? But a consensus remains that the telephone came to be seen, as Claude S. Fischer puts it, as an "anonymous object" (259) with a "shortage of charisma" (253).

13. Avital Ronell makes a similar point: "The telephone puts you at risk, or it figures the language of risk—where is your own risk (at your own risk)" (357).

14. For a discussion of these changes, see Gerald Mast (269–74).

15. In taking this position, I extend the objection of Raymond Bellour, who in his frame-by-frame analysis of Marlowe and Vivian's love scene in a car, finds a profound gender asymmetry in the fact that it is Vivian "whose magnified face simultaneously and wholly expresses and receives the admission of love" (15).

16. For discussions of *The Big Sleep* as male fantasy, see David Thomson (Acme 125; *Big* 46–47) as well as Megan E. Abbott.

17. My own attention was called to this idea by Kittler's discussion of Hugo Munsterberg's early writing on film: "Close-ups are not just 'objectivizations' of attention; attention itself appears as the interface of an apparatus" (*Gramophone* 162–63).

18. There are at least two more people in Sam's office who can hear what he is saying. One, an attractive young woman, drapes herself over him as he speaks, clearly signaling that we can let George steal Mary away without guilt. The other is a faceless man who at one point can be heard to contribute the word "jellybeans" to the conversation.

19. George uses what appears to be a version of "the old stand-up Bell model of 1914," which lasted "officially until 1927 and in out-of-the-way places long after that" (Stern and Gwathmey 35).

20. I refer of course to the fact that the basic idea of using impossible visions to induce a change of heart comes from Dickens's *A Christmas Carol*. Howard Rosenberg has observed the unlikeliness that someone as attractive as Donna Reed could find no one else ("Bedford")—and a reader of his points out that the bigger insult is that the life of a single woman is the ultimate horror in this male fantasy ("Debate").

21. It is not that women aren't in fact moving around all the time, or even that this movement fails to achieve representation (think, to name just a single important example, of the wanderings of Esther Summerson in *Bleak House*), but that this movement rarely gains the narrative dignity of a male journey. My thinking here, as in far too many instances to enumerate, is deeply in debt to

Hilary Schor. For a sophisticated account of the narrative and cultural work accomplished by female mobility, see her *Dickens and the Daughter of the House*.

22. Reading the bathtub scene in particular, E. L. McCallum takes the mirroring of mise-en-scène as evidence that the "couple is bound together in sameness, despite their purported heterosexuality" (Mother 84). While I find this way of rethinking gender intriguing in a general way, I intend to demonstrate that the asymmetrical distribution in knowledge in *Pillow Talk*'s plot renders this sameness little more than a fantasy of Jan's.

23. See especially Cynthia Fuchs and Steven Cohan.

24. E. L. McCallum ironically observes that Brad and Jan acquire a private line at the end "by marrying their party-line party" (Mother 83). I would also add that a married woman keeping a private line is taken as a sure sign that something is wrong with her—a sign of excessive, even predatory, independence—as with Joan Crawford's character in *The Women*.

25. The one woman who tries to call her, the secretary from her office, gets a busy signal. Jan is indeed too busy negotiating patriarchal seductions to make even such a minor connection to the independent existence this call symbolizes, both in its reference to her work and in its connection to another woman.

26. *Clarissa*, 36.

27. This scene exaggerates Hudson's capabilities. Steven Cohan reports that Hudson was rigged so he could support the not-so-petite Doris Day. In fairness to Hudson's physical prowess, Brad had to carry Jan down the street only once, while Hudson apparently carried Day through twenty takes.

28. Cynthia Fuchs, for instance, sees the comic presentation of these ideas as recuperative.

29. Moreover, as Shelley herself makes clear, that question itself presupposes an untenable faith in those categories, since Frankenstein's Monster may be less monstrous than his master. The problem becomes more that of locating the monster without or within, a problem to which I will return in chapter 5.

30. My thinking about the status of the human has been deeply influenced by the work of Donna Haraway.

31. See, for instance, Michèle Martin (148). Lana Rakow is quick to point out that, in furthering the separation of public and private spheres "the telephone may have been implicated in creating the very conditions from which it was praised for having rescued women" (209).

32. This problem has been addressed more recently in Public Enemy's famous rap song "911's a joke," which represents the phone as a failed promise of equal technological security. *The Matrix*, on the other hand, is a throwback in the way it represents the phone as the link to safety, though the specifically gendered resonance of telephonic rescue has dropped out.

33. Sade does eventually make the only successful phone call of the film from an upstairs phone, calling a fence to let him know about the loot and save her from the younger gang. While this call does inadvertently save Mrs. Hilliard's life, it remains a purely selfish act and cannot qualify as female networking.

34. For the human, the "thinking, feeling creature," the cage is of course more than the stuck elevator. It is also her house, her assumptions, and especially, with her broken hip, her body.

35. Humans are also the animals that make tools, and it is this more practical activity that occupies Mrs. Hilliard when she is not fruitlessly using language to

rhapsodize about the decline of civilization or to appeal to her tormentors. Her first effort is to turn her cane into a true "extension of man" (McLuhan's phrase), tying it to a bar from the elevator and stretching out to knock the phone off the hook. But *Lady in the Cage* certainly has no time for the triumph of human ingenuity. She waits an agonizingly long time for the phone to ring, and when it does her plan fails. The limitation of her tool is that, like most crude technologies, it loses much in extension. She cannot dial the phone, or even hang it up, with a cane, and must finally watch in frustration as the cane slips out and clatters to the floor. Her second effort, announced by the battle cry "stone age here I come," involves removing parts of the elevator to serve as little knife-like weapons. When first tried, these weapons prove painfully inadequate (another dashed hope and mortification of the heroine). By the end she does finally use them to jab Randall in the eyes and get away from him, but this delayed success hardly does credit to her capacities as a tool-maker.

36. Indeed the rapid spiral of feminism into "post-feminism" may have no more to do with internal difficulties on the Left—reconciling the many strands of identity politics, accommodating the other groups struggling for the rights and dignity of the human—than with the ascendancy of evolutionary narratives that leave the human behind. Whether it is the animal (in the form of genes) or the machine (in the form of digital technology) that would now drive history, it may be that the slow death of humanism, so crudely represented in *Lady in a Cage*, leaves still crueler mythologies in its wake.

37. For an account of the rise of Momism during the Cold War, see Michael Rogin.

38. The film's oedipal thematics are reinforced by a motif of blindness: first the drunk thinks he has gone blind when the gang put a sack over his head, then Randall is in fact blinded by Mrs. Hilliard during their struggle.

39. Despite cultural fantasies of telephonic mastery, Jake's vulnerability seems more accurately to reflect our historical submission to the telephone—in Adrian Martin's words, we are "always open to attack, merely by having one." (134). Jan Olsson has informed me in conversation that, as a rule, characters in early films answer the phone unless physically unable. Later films suggest the persistence of the ringing phone's commanding power: at one point in *The Maltese Falcon* (1941) the police conclude without hesitation that Sam Spade was not at home because they called and he didn't answer, while the eccentricity of Bogart's character in *In a Lonely Place* is neatly figured by his refusal to answer his phone. More famously, the entire plot of *Dial M for Murder* (1954) presupposes that Grace Kelly will get out of bed to answer the phone.

40. Derrida (Law 55–57).

41. John Belton argues similarly that Gittes "remains more intent on satisfying his own curiosity than on fulfilling his professional obligations to his clients" and that the "desire for knowledge which characterizes the detective genre as a whole is translated by Polanski into virtually pornographic interest in sexual misconduct" (942).

42. The director plays a thug who slashes Gittes's nose with a knife. The detective appears subsequently in the film with a ridiculous bandage on his nose.

43. See, for instance, John Belton (944) and Deborah Linderman ("Oedipus" 194).

44. In a marvelous comic piece on Sherlock Holmes and the telephone, Robert E. Robinson suggests that Holmes avoids the phone because he fears it is controlled by his nemesis, the archcriminal Professor James Moriarty. Holmes nonethe-

less made full use of long-distance communication systems in the form of the telegraph, as Siegert notes, citing in particular "The Five Orange Pips" (143–44). We might say that the detective's independence from the telephone was as short-lived as the telegraph's, which according to Siegert was technologically subsumed in 1915 when the invention of the "wave filter" allowed telegrams to be sent over telephone lines (189).

Chapter 4

1. Stephen Farber has suggested that her fate is deserved: "We feel she almost deserves the brutal murder that [her husband] plots for her at the end of the film. It is her own ruthless possessiveness that leads to her violent death" (10). Mary Celeste Kearney claims that, once phones become common in homes, "women's use of private lines for social purposes no longer interfered with commercial telephone calls, and thus failed to inspire much attention or attempts at containment during the remainder of the twentieth century" (581). My contention is that this containment, however unwarranted, continues and even intensifies throughout the century. The hated woman on the phone is nowhere more forcefully depicted than in Maggie Greenwald's film *The Kill-Off* (1990), in which another female invalid rules a small town via the telephone by her bed. Possessed of a mysterious and possibly telepathic access to the secrets of others, she wields this knowledge as a ruthless blackmailer and gossip. The whole town wants her dead, and much of the suspense of the plot turns on who will actually be the one to kill her.

2. See Stephen Farber.

3. In *Detour* the *femme fatale* dies literally tangled up in a phone cord. But in other respects this film keeps its telephonic nightmare further below the surface—the hero, a would-be Phillip Marlowe, always seems carefully in control of his phone conversations.

4. J. P. Telotte makes the compelling observation that, given the general paranoia that characterizes *film noir*, "one never really reaches any 'wrong numbers' in the *noir* world" (87). We might contrast this claim with one made by Nicholas Royle in a discussion of Raymond Chandler's *The Little Sister*, in which the telephone gives us "always the wrong voice; the telephone is always contaminated with otherness" (*Telepathy* 178). Perhaps these insights are not inevitably in opposition. To say that the telephone is contaminated with otherness is another way of stating the telephone's openness to coincidence; the phone is thus always "wrong" in that it cannot sustain the narcissistic feedback loop of what I am calling an ideal phone. At the same time, to the paranoid *noir* subject, there are never any wrong numbers for this very same reason, because the phone always delivers coincidence (to which the paranoiac always replies "I think not").

5. The telegram is from Henry, and the choice is significant, for the archaic form precludes her talking back to him.

6. Such notable films as *Gentleman's Agreement* (1947), *Crossfire* (1947), *Pinky* (1949), and *No Way Out* (1950) appeared at this time.

7. Kaja Silverman (*Acoustic* 78–79).

8. Amy Lawrence (137). Lawrence does not push this insight as far as she might. Her conclusion that the film, in staying true to the conventions of *film noir*, must punish the dominating woman makes sense only if we take the flashbacks at

face value, for Leona does not control Henry in the film's present—indeed, she does not speak with him until the final scene. But the strength of Lawrence's analysis of *Sorry, Wrong Number* comes in the context of her larger argument about the "problem of the speaking woman" and the relationship between sound and image. See in particular her excellent first chapter, which recasts the prehistory of cinema in terms of sound technology.

9. Rick Altman argues that matching sound represents an essential sleight-of-hand or "ventriloquism" in the function of narrative film: "Using the ideology of the visible as a front, the sound track remains free to carry on its own business" (76). In these terms, we might say that *Sorry, Wrong Number* exposes the soundtrack so that its business becomes available to criticism.

10. Reading *Sorry, Wrong Number* as an example of "paranoid textuality," David Crane has made a similar point: "Paranoia becomes a dynamic element in textual and, especially narrative discourse—in the narrating voice" (72).

11. Avital Ronell argues that "technology in some way is always implicated in the feminine. It is young; it is thingly. Thus every instrument of war is given a feminine name" (207).

12. *The Slender Thread* (1965) turns this model of phone use on its head. Having taken an overdose of pills, Anne Bancroft calls a suicide hotline, where Sidney Poitier is working. In this emergency the business of his call *is* sympathy. Clearly the sin here would be to talk too little, since Poitier must keep Bancroft on the line until he can convince her to reveal her location.

13. To be sure, Leona confronts a classic problem: Sally, her main female contact, also happens to be her rival. When Sally calls Leona with partial clues about the mystery, she is thinking about saving Henry, not her. But in light of Sally's considerable resourcefulness as a spy on official male business, her impasse with Leona carries a strong sense of what might have been and therefore contributes to the female network that the film would forge with viewers.

14. Amy Lawrence discusses the cost of identification with Leona in the final scene: "If we identify with Leona, our listener/surrogate, we identify with the victim. The establishment of an alternative identification with the camera allows us to escape at the cost of rejecting Leona and the auditory identification in favor of classical cinema and the primacy of the image" (144).

15. For an account of the historical emergence of telepathy as a concept in the late nineteenth century, see Pamela Thurschwell, who aligns it not only with "new communication technologies" but also with "new psychological theories such as crowd theory, the hypnosis debates of the 1880s and 1890s, and psychoanalysis" in terms of "wider reconceptualizations of the borders of individual consciousness" (2). In another extensive account of telepathy's emergence, Roger Luckhurst confirms that "the conceptualization of telepathy was inevitably theorized in relation to the coincident emergence of tele-technologies" (135). See Jeffrey Sconce for an analysis of how telepathy later gets tangled up in radio.

16. Daniel Frampton has recently argued against the idea of first-person narration in film, claiming that "when [a film] decides to provide a sense of a character's thinking it is only ever producing an inflection of the character's way of understanding. It can say this character is thinking like this, is seeing this scene like this. (It does not 'show' human thought. It does not make human thought visible)" (86). His point is compelling, and indeed all of my examples are transparently representations, rather than replications, of thought.

17. See Pier Paolo Pasolini (547). His analysis does not take up the question of telepathy, because he remains interested in the director's personal expression rather than the viewer's fantasies.

18. Quoted from unpublished work in David Thomson ("Telephones" 30). It has been brought to my attention that this quotation may be apocryphal. Regardless of whether the thought was Marker's or Thomson's, what interests me is the idea and not the attribution.

19. In *The Uncanny* Nicholas Royle proposes that telepathy be taken as an improvement on the idea of omniscient narration, and this notion has been further developed by Jonathan Culler.

20. Sharon Cameron has argued in a discussion of James that consciousness occurs *between* people, and indeed between people and texts (77).

21. Nicholas Royle also quotes this passage (12) and notes that "the history of the term 'telepathy' is intimately related to that of the concept of sympathy" (4).

22. To avoid confusion, I will consistently refer to the uncle as "Uncle Charlie" and the niece as "Charlie."

23. Discussions of incest can be found in Robin Wood ("Ideology"). The most extensive discussions of the double are those of Barbara M. Bannon, Leo Braudy (*World*), and Patrick Crogan.

24. Our own knowledge as viewers of course exceeds Charlie's. In addition to the bare fact of both Charlies wanting Charles to come to Santa Rosa, we see, as is often noted, other correspondences, such as their similar postures in bed as we meet them. Like Charlie, if we choose to credit this coincidence with occult significance, we should not do so without recognizing that of course the doublings exist only through the relays of film technology.

25. In the names Charlotte, Emma, and Anne we might detect an echo of a female literary tradition—of the Brontë sisters as well as very prominent characters from the history of the British novel.

26. *Dracula* is of course also a novel about female telepathy. As the band of Englishmen track Count Dracula from Mina's visions, the question remains whether her telepathy is contained as an instrument of male knowledge or if it remains an unassimilable effect of her desire for the vampire.

27. See James McLaughlin for a full discussion of Uncle Charlie's vampiric qualities.

28. Telepathy is in fact the subject of detective fiction's inaugural episode, when Dupin reads the narrator's mind at the beginning of Poe's first detective story, "The Murders in the Rue Morgue."

29. Paul Gordon and Robin Wood ("Ideology") both ventured such readings.

30. Donald Spoto reports that Uncle Charlie's accident was "exactly modeled" on one in Hitchcock's own childhood (273).

31. Stephen Kern places most of the decisive changes in the bicycle industry at around 1890 and documents anxieties about bicycles well into the twentieth century.

32. Of course it is again the telephone that serves as a justification of this filmic fantasy, producing the ultimate experience of simultaneous location with the split screen. We might say that telepathy and bi-locality are on the opposite ends of the telephonic spectrum: telepathy is radically disembodied telephony, whereas bi-locality places the caller in an imagined state of total rematerialization.

33. Earhart completed the first round trip coast-to-coast flight in 1928.

34. Charlie's mobility is threatened in the garage at another time as well, as it is here that Jack confesses his love for her, bringing marriage into the picture.

35. Of course *A Room of One's Own* is itself very much about the relationship between movement and thought. Charlie's encounter with a library door may well remind us of the famous snub at "Oxbridge" that Woolf describes.

36. James McLaughlin and William Rothman have both made this claim. Paul Gordon has quite rightly challenged this idea, though not from a feminist perspective. Indeed, his view that Emma is "happy" is to my mind as distorted as the view that Charlie is guilty (273–74). Leo Braudy has more interestingly read the possibility of Charlie's guilt as an allegory of American war guilt.

Chapter 5

1. We see this idea taken to its logical conclusion in the recent Jodie Foster film *Panic Room*. Female characters who prefer mobility to shelter, like Moll Flanders, tend to be notably unsocialized.

2. This notion is consistent with Joan Copjec's argument that a locked room must be understood as a product of description and that it can therefore never constitute a closed space, because the detective "represents the always open possibility of one signifier more" (177). I have trouble agreeing, however, with the idea that any final signifier, any "non-empirical object which closes the field," "if it existed, would be the signifier for woman," since this formulation ignores the way the genre founds itself on empirical violence to women (176, 177).

3. Thomas Bailey Aldrich's novel *Out of His Head* (1862) features another early example of a locked room mystery, which again turns on the brutal murder of a woman. As the subgenre takes hold in the twentieth century through the work of masters such as John Dickson Carr, the demographic distribution of victims becomes a bit more balanced. Still, Carr brings his own gothic misogyny to a locked room murder in "Terror's Dark Tower," in which a family devised an undetectable—and grotesquely violent—scheme for punishing its female members who would marry without family approval.

4. D. S. L. Cardwell explains that "What the early railway system was to the telegraph, ships were to wireless. It will be recalled that the first instance of the use of wireless to catch the attention of the general public was the arrest of Dr. Crippen when his ship docked in Canada (1910). Two years later wireless played a vital role in the rescue of the survivors of the *Titanic* disaster" (187n).

5. As far as I've been able to tell, the first movie to locate the killer on a phone inside the house was in fact the lesser-known Canadian film *Black Christmas* (1975).

6. The story of the nightmare of Mount Everest is most famously chronicled in Jon Krakauer's best-selling book *Into Thin Air*.

7. Jerome Christensen has in fact demonstrated that *You've Got Mail* was quite an effective commercial for AOL ("Taking It"). I wish not to mitigate the force of such a critique but merely to suggest that it should not distract us from noting how ambitious the film is in other respects as well, or indeed the remarkable machinations through which these ambitions are pursued.

8. The phone has long been imagined as a link between worlds, in particular between the living and the dead as in Bunuel's *The Phantom of Liberty,* in which

a man gets a phone call from his dead sister; an episode of *The Twilight Zone* called "Long Distance Call," in which a young boy's grandmother calls him to join her beyond the grave; and *Waking the Dead*, in which a young man speaks on the phone with the ex-girlfriend whom he thought was dead and whose status remains a mystery of the film. This theme also appears in recent East Asian horror films such as *Ringu*, *Phone*, and *One Missed Call*. Other fantastic phone connections can be seen in *The Matrix*, *12 Monkeys*, *Lost Highway*, and episodes of *Dr. Who*.

9. Northrop Frye has commented on the close relationship of comedy and danger in *Anatomy of Criticism*, noting that however strongly comedy invokes disaster, it always averts it, even if improbably, and at the last minute (178–79). Thus comic closure works to expel danger, putting it back in its proper, faraway place.

10. And yet when compared with Ernst Lubitsch's *The Shop Around the Corner* (1940), the source for Ephron's script (and the name of Kathleen's store), it becomes clear that much epistolary richness is lost in *You've Got Mail*. Lubitsch's film features not only a kinky epistolary rhetoric, as when Jimmy Stewart tells Margaret Sullavan to "Take your key and open post office box 237 and take me out of my envelope and kiss me," but reminds us of how much the pleasures of mail are not only anticipatory but reflective, since correspondents tend to reread their letters.

11. By contrast, Joe's tiny identity crisis, as expressed in one of his e-mails to shopgirl, moves along a telling trajectory:

> "Do you ever feel you've become the worst version of yourself? That a Pandora's Box of all the secret, hateful parts—your arrogance, your spite, your condescension—has sprung open? Someone provokes you, and instead of just smiling and moving on, you zing them. Hello, it's Mr. Nasty."

Joe's evil twin is not named, say, "Fox III" (the name of his boat) but "Mr. Nasty," a cartoonish villain whose tragic flaw is not greed or corruption but rudeness. Thus the dynamic of this passage, routing questions of character through manners, works greatly to his advantage. Manners can be polished, but money can only be laundered.

12. The film's other main cultural point of reference is of course *Pride and Prejudice*, a novel that Kathleen has read some 200 times and which she inflicts on a reluctant Joe. It is part of *You've Got Mail's* bad faith that it tolerates Joe's impatience with a text that takes the connection between manners and morals far more seriously.

13. One exception is an essay by William J. Rapaport: "However, read literally and conservatively, if the computer is supposed to do this by playing the role of the man, then it appears that the computer has a more complex task, namely, to behave like a man who is trying to convince the interrogator that he is a woman!" But he backs away from this observation: "So it appears that Turing was not overly concerned with the complication discussed in the previous paragraph (although he apparently thought it important that the human in this human-computer contest be represented by a man, not a woman) (468).

14. Timothy Clark raises the problem of racism more broadly, as one of the cultural "equivocations of notions of personhood" that determine the test's "scene of interpretation" (24–25).

15. In fact, Douglas Hofstadter claims to have read a book in which the Turing's essay is reprinted with the section on telepathy omitted (*Gödel* 599). Some readers have suggested that the reference to telepathy is probably a joke, but such an easy dismissal is hardly acceptable from a cultural standpoint, since the appeal of such a joke can only refer us back to anxieties about the borders of science. Turing's biographer, moreover, claims that "He was certainly impressed at the time by J. B. Rhine's claims to have experimental proof of extra-sensory perception. (Hodges 416).

16. I want to thank Lindsay Holmgren for making this point and for calling my attention in general to the importance of telepathy in thinking about *The Conversation*.

17. We might say that what Harry fails to realize is that he has wandered into *Total Recall* and that the bug's true location is in his head.

18. Douglas Hofstadter tells the story of participating in a supposed Turing Test, in which it turned out he was conversing with three college students (*Metamagical*, 513–22). Richard Powers tells of similar tricks being played on the "resident humanist" in his novel *Galatea 2.2*.

19. See, for instance, page 190 of Jeanne Cortiel's essay. This analysis is not a blanket condemnation of the film, however, as Cortiel stresses that "Violet and Corky's triumphantly successful sexual relationship provides a plot template whose impact for lesbian culture cannot be overestimated" (193).

20. For a fuller feminist critique of the idea of the end of history, see Rita Felski (*Doing* 137–53).

Chapter 6

1. I am happy at least to report that polls from October 2003 indicate that charges of sexual harassment did indeed have a negative effect on Schwarzenegger's popularity (Murphy and LeDuff). I am less than confident, though, that this momentary and inconsequential sense of shame exonerates the political unconscious of the California electorate.

2. This image is in fact made literal in one of the film's most terrifying recurring images: the Terminator's red-filtered point-of-view shot, complete with digital readout. And we might think about the implications of this curious conceit that the Terminator would need to represent information to himself visually, clinging to the mediation of the screen. Clearly a cinematic supplement, it provides a ride-along to inform our own bloody gaze. And as harrowing as the view is, the film is careful to help us assimilate this prosthetic. The Terminator-cam does not in fact represent the cyborg's first point-of-view shot; there are several recognizably human (i.e., familiarly cinematic) shots to help us see the world through his eyes. And once we've been exposed to the alien version of his gaze, the film gradually domesticates it with its famous humor—in a minor encounter in a hotel, we watch the Terminator select from a menu on his screen the most aggressive response: "Fuck you, asshole!"

3. In 1990s romantic comedy, answering machines often serve the narrative purpose of exposing female networking that would otherwise remain behind the scenes. Both *Singles* (1992) and *Walking and Talking* (1996) have moments in which prospective boyfriends overhear a discussion of themselves on a woman's answering machine, thereby disrupting female networks in their age-old function of

regulating the marriage market. Such minor exposures take a harrowing turn in *Denise Calls Up* (1995) when the matchmaking busybody (Emma Woodhouse minus the charm) is fatally impaled by her own phone in a car crash. As if the mere idea of this accident is not a sadistic enough revenge against the speaking woman, the horror is doubled when we discover that this humiliating and grotesque death has been recorded on her friend's answering machine. It is a painfully literal example of Kittler's maxim that recording technologies constitute an "expansion of the realms of the dead," infusing our reach across time with a heightened sense of loss (*Gramophone* 125).

4. Banham's other three ecologies are "Surfurbia," "Foothills," and "Autopia." It seems that these have their own movies as well: *Point Break, Mulholland Drive*, and *Speed*.

5. For a discussion of the grandmother paradox see Gallagher, "Undoing."

6. As Jesse Molesworth has reminded me, the egoism of this fantasy also puts Sarah's promotion into perspective as Family Romance, the brutal logic of parental substitution disguised by the fact that Sarah's transformation into a worthy mother can be said to have occurred in advance of John's fantasy life.

7. We might say that the film gets away with this first by playing on the widespread belief, particularly prevalent in 1984, that apocalypse is inevitable (this is a year after the notorious TV movie *The Day After* attempted to dramatize life after a nuclear holocaust). In such a climate perhaps any future seems better than no future at all.

8. The definitive reading of *Klute* remains Christine Gledhill's in *Women and Film Noir*. I consider my account an extension of her work, particularly of her insight into Cable and Klute's essential similarity, and her description of Klute's city tour, which she describes memorably as "a descent into the underside of city life, reminiscent of Bunyan's *Vanity Fair* where each door that is opened displays a tableau representing one further aspect of the city's decadence and corruption" (105).

9. I want to thank Kai Mah for reminding me of the link between tape recorders and ethnography in this context. Indeed ethnography is linked to audio recording via the phonograph at its roots. For an account of this connection see Jonathan Sterne's *The Audible Past*. Jane Campion's *In the Cut* revises *Klute* along these lines. Placing Meg Ryan's character explicitly in the position of the urban ethnographer, the film represents her science as inextricable from her desire.

10. Further signs of an uncanny Klute: when Bree at one point slashes him desperately with a pair of scissors, *he does not bleed*. In light of *The Terminator*, the rational explanation that she cut only his clothes does little to dispel the feeling that Klute may be some sort of automaton, or that he anticipates Donald Sutherland's most uncanny star turn of the 1970s as the pod person in the chilling final scene of *Invasion of the Body Snatchers* (1978).

11. It is in the middle of this period that stalking establishes its ongoing grip on the cultural imagination, as the following list of prominent films would suggest: *Taxi Driver* (1976), *Looking for Mr. Goodbar* (1977), *Halloween* (1978), *Eyes of Laura Mars* (1978), and *Dressed to Kill* (1980). It was moreover during the media coverage of Son of Sam in this period that the term "stalking" began to refer to the obsessive violence of urban predators.

12. Compounding the dubiousness of this identification is a certain fact from the film's production history: "The Zhora we see in the hard copy Deckard prints

out at the end of his session with the Esper is not Joanna Cassidy, the actress who plays the character, but rather a stand-in" (Shetley and Ferguson 70). Pauline Kael observes the problem of the forgotten police photograph and many other plot holes in *Blade Runner*, such as why Tyrell is left unguarded.

13. See for instance Nazare (385) or Rickman (205).
14. See for instance Fitting, who argues that the "hero's distaste for his job of killing escaped androids is contradicted by the film's sensuous and prolonged fascination with those killings" (346).
15. On the critical usefulness of a distinction between shame and guilt, see Newsom's "The Hero's Shame." Felski draws an interesting link between shame and mobility: "The opportunities for experiencing shame increase dramatically with geographic and social mobility, which provide an infinite array of chances for failure, for betraying by word or gesture that one does not belong in one's new environment" (*Doing Time* 43).
16. *Bound's* equation of lesbianism with humanity is still beyond the horizon, as here the question is strictly either/or.
17. As this reading should make clear, if forced to choose I prefer the notion that Deckard is a replicant, as underscored in the director's cut, to the notion that he is human, because I think any humanity constructed on the stalker's terms needs to be unmade before it can be redeemed. More important, though, I would suggest we try to resist the tendency to turn the film itself into a giant Voigt-Kampff Test, with the viewer deciding confidently who is and isn't human.
18. Truffaut (244).
19. Deborah Linderman also notes this anomaly, though she underplays it in her analysis ("Mise-en-Abîme" 55).
20. Charles Barr reports that this scenario was in fact the "official explanation, as spelled out in the intermediate script documentation," but agrees that "as with so much of the first part of the film, an uncanny element lingers on repeated viewings" (46).
21. My understanding of such spaces has been deeply influenced by the work of my colleague Derek Nystrom.
22. Also useful here is the way Freedman situates *Vertigo* with respect to the late Freud in terms of its waning faith in therapeutic progress.
23. One of the more notable flights of fancy this conclusion has prompted is from Leland Poague: "The only evidence we have that Judy fell is her scream. . . . I have no doubt that Judy, of course, is dead to Scottie, dead in his world. My fantasy is that she hovers in space, between his world and our world, like the hovering face of *Vertigo's* credit sequence, a pulsing membrane, a film" (277). I was with him up until the membrane.
24. For an extensive discussion of verticality in *Vertigo* see Pomerance, whose work has brought new attention to the pervasiveness and subtlety of class issues in Hitchcock. An important earlier discussion of class in *Vertigo* is Wexman's.

Epilogue

1. See *Narrative* and "Circulatory," respectively.
2. For theoretical discussions of anachronism see Jay Clayton, Steven Connor, and especially Jerome Christensen's *Romanticism at the End of History*.

3. I should point out that another auditory dimension of Victorian literature is the widespread practice of reading aloud. But this more domestic and communal practice should not deafen us to the wilder side of Eliot's auditory imagination. Indeed, the practice of reading aloud in no way speaks to the aspects of *Middlemarch* I feel compelled to amplify, for this is a novel whose female networks resonate across gaps of space and time, gaps not present in the parlors of shared oral readings. For a broader study of Victorian literature's auditory imagination, see John Picker.

4. McLuhan claims that "All technological extensions of ourselves must be numb and subliminal, else we could not endure the leverage exerted upon us by such extension" (302).

5. Kerry McSweeney has offered a critique of the second sentence: "The sentence about 'the other side of silence' is followed by a gratuitous bellow" (72). While the charge of redundancy is quickly apparent, what strikes me about McSweeney's point is the way it confronts Eliot with her own auditory logic, the term "bellow" insisting that our sympathetic interest requires a certain quietness.

6. Gillian Beer, "Myth." See also Sandra Gilbert and Susan Gubar 475.

7. I am in agreement with Kerry McSweeney's notion that "Perhaps we should call the transformation effected by Dorothea a creative, even a poetic act," particularly because, unlike Ladislaw, McSweeney allows Dorothea to be a poet instead of a poem (112).

8. Here I would echo Kay Young: "Eliot's realism . . . is her acknowledgment of skepticism. However, her yearning to discover how we might know another and be known, and how she might make such a discovery transparent, reveals Eliot's longing for a form of transcendence—an answer to the problem of other minds" (225).

9. This reading challenges Gillian Beer's notion that Dorothea is no more than a "transmissive presence" ("Circulatory" 60).

Bibliography

Abbott, Megan E. "'Nothing You Can't Fix'. Screening Marlowe's Masculinity," *Studies in the Novel* 35:3 (Fall 2003): 305–324.

Altman, Janet. *Epistolarity: Approaches to a Form*. Columbus: Ohio State UP, 1982.

Altman, Rick. "Cinema as Ventriloquism." *Yale French Studies* 60 (1980): 67–79.

Anderson, Earl. R. "Footnotes More Pedestrian than Sublime: A Historical Background for the Footraces in *Evelina* and *Humphrey Clinker*." *Eighteenth-Century Studies* 14 (1980): 56–68.

Arnheim, Rudolph. *Radio*. Salem, N.H.: Ayer, 1986.

Austen, Jane. *Emma*. Oxford: Oxford UP, 2003.

———. *Northanger Abbey*. Oxford: Oxford UP, 1990.

———. *Persuasion*. London: Penguin, 1985.

Banham, Reyner. *Los Angeles: The Architecture of Four Ecologies*. Berkeley: U of California P, 1971.

Bannon, Barbara M. "Double, Double: Toil and Trouble." *Literature/Film Quarterly* 13:1 (1985): 56–65.

Barr, Charles. *Vertigo*. London: BFI, 2002.

Barthes, Roland. *The Pleasure of the Text*, trans. Richard Miller. New York: Hill and Wang, 1975.

———. *S/Z*, trans. Richard Miller. New York: Hill and Wang, 1974.

Beer, Gillian. "Circulatory Systems: Money and Gossip in *Middlemarch*." *Cahiers Victoriens & Edouardiens* 26 (1987): 47–62.

———. "Myth and the Single Consciousness: *Middlemarch* and *The Lifted Veil*." In *This Particular Web*, ed. Ian Adam, 91–116. Toronto: U of Toronto P, 1975.

Bellour, Raymond. "The Obvious and the Code." *Screen* 15:4 (1974): 7–17.

Belton, John. "Language, Oedipus, and *Chinatown*." *MLN* 106 (1991): 933–950.

Bersani, Leo. *A Future for Astyanax*. New York: Columbia UP, 1984.

Boettinger, Henry M. "Our Sixth-and-a-Half Sense." In *The Social Impact of the Telephone*, ed. Ithiel de Sola Pool, 200–207. Cambridge, Mass.: MIT Press, 1977.

Booth, Wayne. *The Rhetoric of Fiction*. Chicago: U of Chicago P, 1961.

Bowers, Toni. *The Politics of Mothering*. Cambridge: Cambridge UP, 1996.

Braudy, Leo. "Penetration and Impenetrability." In *New Approaches to Eighteenth Century Literature: Selected Papers from the English Institute*, ed. Philip Hareh, 177–206. New York: Columbia UP, 1974.

———. *The World in a Frame: What We See in Films*. Chicago: U of Chicago P, 1976.

Bronfen, Elisabeth. *Over Her Dead Body*. Manchester: Manchester UP, 1992.

———. "Risky Resemblances: On Repetition, Mourning, and Representation." In *Death and Representation*, ed. Sarah Webster Goodwin and Elisabeth Bronfen, 103–127. Baltimore: Johns Hopkins UP, 1993.

Brooks, John. "The First and Only Century of Telephone Literature." In *The Social Impact of the Telephone*, ed. Ithiel de Sola Pool, 208–224. Cambridge, Mass: MIT Press, 1977.

Brooks, Peter. *The Melodramatic Imagination*. New Haven, Conn.: Yale UP, 1976.

Brown, Martha. "Fanny Burney's 'Feminism': Gender or Genre?" In *Fetter'd or Free: British Women Novelists, 1670–1815*, ed. Mary Anne Schofield and Cecilia Macheski, 29–39. Athens: Ohio UP, 1986.

Burney, Frances. *Evelina*. Oxford: Oxford UP, 1982.

Butler, Judith. *Bodies that Matter: On the Discursive Limits of "Sex."* New York: Routledge, 1993.

Cameron, Sharon. *Thinking in Henry James*. Chicago: U of Chicago P, 1989.

Cardwell, D. S. L. *Turning Points in Western Technology*. New York: Science History Publications, 1972.

Carroll, David, ed. *George Eliot: The Critical Heritage*, 417–433. New York: Barnes & Noble, 1971.

Carter, Angela. *The Sadeain Woman: An Exercise in Cultural History*. London: Virago, 1979.

Castle, Terry. *Clarissa's Ciphers*. Ithaca, N.Y.: Cornell UP, 1982.

———. *The Female Thermometer*. New York: Oxford UP, 1995.

Cawelti, John. "*Chinatown* and Generic Transformation in Recent American Films." In *Film Theory and Criticism*, 2nd ed., ed. Gerald Mast and Marshall Cohen, 559–579. New York: Oxford UP, 1979. Rpt. in *Film Genre Reader*, ed. Barry Keith Grant, 183–201. Austin: U of Texas P, 1986.

Chandler, Raymond. *The Simple Art of Murder*. New York: Vintage, 1988.

Chevrier, Yves. "*Blade Runner*; or, The Sociology of Anticipation," trans. Will Straw. *Science-Fiction Studies* 11 (1984): 50–59.

Chion, Michel. *The Voice in Cinema*, ed. and trans. Claudia Gorbman. New York: Columbia UP, 1982.

Chodorow, Nancy. *The Reproduction of Mothering: Psychoanalysis and the Sociology of Gender*. Berkeley: U of California P, 1978.

Choi, Samuel. "Signing Evelina: Female Self-Inscription in the Discourse of Letters." *Studies in the Novel* 31:3 (Fall 1999): 259–278.

Christensen, Jerome. *Romanticism at the End of History*. Baltimore: Johns Hopkins UP, 2000.

———. "Taking It to the Next Level: *You've Got Mail*, Havholm and Sandifer." *Critical Inquiry* 30:1 (Fall 2003): 198–215.

Christie, Agatha. *The Mirror Crack'd from Side to Side*. New York: HarperPaperbacks, 1962.

Clark, Timothy. "The Turing Test as a Novel Form of Hermeutics." *International Studies in Philosophy* 24:1 (1992): 17–31.

Clayton, Jay. *Charles Dickens in Cyberspace: The Afterlife of the Nineteenth Century in Postmodern Culture*. Oxford: Oxford UP, 2003.

Clover, Carol. *Men, Women, and Chainsaws: Gender and the Modern Horror Film*. Princeton, N.J.: Princeton UP, 1992.

Cohan, Steven. *Masked Men: Masculinity and the Movies in the Fifties*. Bloomington: Indiana UP, 1997.

Cohen, William. *Sex Scandal*. Durham, N.C.: Duke UP, 1996.

Collins, Wilkie. *The Woman in White*. Oxford: Oxford UP, 1998.

Connor, Steven. *Dumbstruck: A Cultural History of Ventriloquism*. Oxford: Oxford UP, 2000.

Copjec, Joan. "The Phenomenal Nonphenomenal: Private Space in *Film Noir*." In *Shades of Noir*, ed. Joan Copjec, 167–197. London: Verso, 1993.

Corber, Robert J. *In the Name of National Security: Hitchcock, Homophobia, and the Political Construction of Gender in Postwar America*. Durham, N.C.: Duke UP, 1993.

Cortiel, Jeanne. "About Something Queer: Simulated Sexualities in *Bound* and *Showgirls*." In *Simulacrum America*, ed. Elisabeth Kraus and Carolin Auer, 189–201. Rochester, N.Y.: Camden House, 2000.

Crane, David. "Projections and Intersections: Paranoid Textuality in *Sorry, Wrong Number*." *Camera Obscura* 17:3 (2002): 71–114.

Crogan, Patrick. "Between Heads: Thoughts on the Merry Widow Tune in *Shadow of a Doubt*." *Senses of Cinema*. http://www.sensesofcinema.com/contents/00/6/heads.html. April 2000.

Culler, Jonathan. "Omniscience." *Narrative* 12 (January 2004): 22–34.

Curtain, Tyler. "The 'Sinister Fruitiness' of Machines: *Neuromancer*, Internet Sexuality, and the Turing Test." In *Novel Gazing*, ed. Eve Kosofsky Sedgwick, 123–148. Durham, N.C.: Duke UP, 1997.

Defoe, Daniel. *Moll Flanders*. London: Penguin, 1989.

Derrida, Jacques. "The Law of Genre," trans. Avital Ronell. *Critical Inquiry* 7 (Autumn 1980): 55–81.

———. "Telepathy," trans. Nicholas Royle. *Oxford Literary Review* 10 (1988): 3–41.

Doane, Mary Ann. "Film and the Masquerade: Theorising the Female Spectator." In *Feminist Film Theory: A Reader*, ed. Sue Thornham, 131–145. New York: New York UP, 1999.

Doody, Margaret Anne. *Frances Burney: The Life in the Works*. New Brunswick, N.J.: Rutgers UP, 1988.

———. *A Natural Passion: A Study of the Novels of Samuel Richardson*. London: Oxford UP, 1974.

Dyer, Richard. "Rock—The Last Guy You'd Have Figured?" In *You Tarzan: Masculinity, Movies and Men*, ed. Pat Kirkham and Janet Thumim, 27–34. New York: St. Martin's Press, 1993.

Eagleton, Terry. *The Rape of Clarissa*. Minneapolis: U of Minnesota P, 1982.

Eliot, George. *Middlemarch*. London: Penguin, 1994.

———. "Silly Novels by Lady Novelists." *Essays of George Eliot*, ed. Thomas Pinney, 300–324. New York: Columbia UP, 1963.

Epstein, Julia. *The Iron Pen: Frances Burney and the Politics of Women's Writing*. Madison: U of Wisconsin P, 1989.

Ermarth, Elizabeth. *Realism and Consensus in the English Novel*. Princeton, N.J.: Princeton UP, 1983.

Faderman, Lillian. *Surpassing the Love of Men*. New York: William Morrow, 1981.

Farber, Stephen. "Violence and the Bitch Goddess." *Film Comment* 10 (Nov./Dec.1974): 8–11.

Felski, Rita. *Doing Time: Feminist Theory and Postmodern Culture*. New York: NYU Press, 2000.

———. *The Gender of Modernity*. Cambridge, Mass.: Harvard UP, 1995.

Ferguson, Frances. "Rape and the Rise of the Novel." *Representations* 20 (Fall 1987): 88–112.

Fiedler, Leslie. *Love and Death in the American Novel*. New York: Dell, 1960.

Fielding, Henry. *Joseph Andrews and Shamela*. Boston: Houghton Mifflin, 1961.

Finch, Casey, and Peter Bowen. " 'The Tittle-Tattle of Highbury': Gossip and the Free Indirect Style in *Emma*." *Representations* 31 (Summer 1990): 1–18.

Fischer, Claude S. *America Calling*. Berkeley: U of California P, 1992.

Fitting, Peter. "Futurecop: The Neutralization of Revolt in *Blade Runner*." *Science-Fiction Studies* 14 (1987): 340–353.

Frampton, Daniel. *Filmosophy*. London: Wallflower Press, 2006.

Freedman, Jonathan. "From *Spellbound* to *Vertigo*: Alfred Hitchcock and Therapeutic Culture in America." In *Hitchcock's America*, ed. Jonathan Freedman and Richard Millington, 77–98. New York: Oxford UP, 1999.

Friedberg, Anne. *Window Shopping: Cinema and the Postmodern*. Berkeley: U of California P, 1993.

Frye, Northrop. *Anatomy of Criticism*. Princeton, N.J.: Princeton UP, 1957.

Fuchs, Cynthia J. "Split Screens: Framing and Passing in *Pillow Talk*." In *The Other Fifties*, ed. Joel Foreman, 224–251. Urbana: University of Illinois Press, 1997.

Fuss, Diana. *Identification Papers*. New York: Routledge, 1995.

Gallagher, Catherine. "Nobody's Story: Gender, Property and the Rise of the Novel." *Modern Language Quarterly* 53 (September 1992): 266–267.

———. *Nobody's Story: The Vanishing Acts of Women Writers in the Marketplace 1670–1820*. Berkeley: U of California P, 1995.

———. "The Rise of Fictionality." In *The Novel*, ed. Franco Moretti, 336–363. Princeton, N.J.: Princeton UP, 2006.

———. "Undoing." *Time and the Literary*, ed. Karen Newman, Jay Clayton, and Marianne Hirsch, 11–29. New York: Routledge, 2002.

Gilbert, Sandra, and Susan Gubar. *The Madwoman in the Attic*. New Haven, Conn.: Yale University Press, 1979.

Gillis, Christina Marsden. *The Paradox of Privacy*. Gainesville: U of Florida P, 1984.

Girard, René. *Violence and the Sacred*. Baltimore: John Hopkins UP, 1972.

Gledhill, Christine. "*Klute* 2: Feminism and *Klute*." In *Women in Film Noir*, new ed., ed. E. Ann Kaplan, 99–114. London: BFI, 1998.

Gordon, Jan. "A-filiative Families and Subversive Reproduction: Gossip in Jane Austen." *Genre* xxi (Spring 1988): 5–46.

Gordon, Paul. "Sometimes a Cigar Is Not Just a Cigar." *Lit/Film Quarterly* 19:4 (1991): 267–276.

Gunning, Tom. "Fritz Lang Calling: The Telephone and the Circuits of Modernity." In *Allegories of Communication*, ed. John Fullerton and Jan Olsson, 19–27. Rome: John Libbey Publishing, 2004.

————. "Heard Over the Phone: *The Lonely Villa* and the de Lorde Tradition of the Terrors of Technology." *Screen* 32:2 (Summer 1991): 184–196.

Haraway, Donna. *The Haraway Reader*. New York: Routledge, 2004.

Heller, Tamar. *Dead Secrets: Wilkie Collins and the Female Gothic*. New Haven, Conn.: Yale UP, 1992.

Hilliard, Raymond F. "*Clarissa* and Ritual Cannibalism." *PMLA* 105:5 (October 1990) 1083–1097.

Hodges, Andrew. *Alan Turing: the Enigma*. London: Vintage, 1992.

Hofstadter, Douglas R. *Gödel, Escher, Bach: An Eternal Golden Braid*. New York: Vintage, 1980,

————. *Metamagical Themas*. New York: Basic Books, 1985.

Hudson, Nicholas. "Arts of Seduction and the Rhetoric of *Clarissa*." *Modern Language Quarterly* (March 1990): 25–43.

Irwin, John T. "A Clew to a Clue: Locked Rooms and Labyrinths in Poe and Borges." *Raritan* 10:4 (Spring 1991): 40–57.

James, Henry. *The Portrait of a Lady*. Oxford: Oxford UP, 1998.

Jameson, Fredric. "The End of Temporality." *Critical Inquiry* 29:4 (Summer 2003): 695–718.

Johnson, Claudia. *Jane Austen: Women, Politics, and the Novel*. Chicago: U of Chicago P, 1988.

Kael, Pauline. "Baby, the Rain Must Fall." *The New Yorker* (July 12, 1982): 82–85.

Kamir, Orit. *Every Breath You Take: Stalking Narratives and the Law*. Ann Arbor: U of Michigan P, 2001.

Kaplan, Deborah. *Jane Austen Among Women*. Baltimore: Johns Hopkins UP, 1992.

Kauffman, Linda S. *Discourses of Desire: Gender, Genre, and Epistolary Fiction*. Ithaca, N.Y.: Cornell UP, 1986.

Kawin, Bruce. *Mindscreen: Bergman, Godard, and First-Person Film*. Princeton, N.J.: Princeton UP, 1978.

Kearney, Mary Celeste. "Birds on the Wire: Troping Teenage Girlhood through Telephony in Mid-twentieth-century US Media Culture." *Cultural Studies* 19:5 (September 2005), 568–601.

Kern, Stephen. *The Culture of Time and Space: 1880–1918*. Cambridge, Mass: Harvard UP, 1983.

Kettle, Arnold. "Henry James: The Portrait of a Lady." In *The Portrait of a Lady*, ed. Robert D. Bamberg, 671–698. New York: Norton, 1975.

King, Stephen. *On Writing*. New York: Pocket Books, 2000.

Kinkead-Weekes, Mark. *Samuel Richardson: Dramatic Novelist*. Ithaca, N.Y.: Cornell UP, 1973.

Kittler, Friedrich. *Discourse Networks 1800/1900*, trans. Michael Metteer, with Chris Cullens. Stanford, Cal.: Stanford UP, 1990.

————. *Gramophone, Film, Typewriter*, trans. Geoffrey Winthrop-Young and Michael Wutz. Stanford, Cal.: Stanford UP, 1999.

————. *Literature Media: Information Systems*, ed. John Johnston. Amsterdam: OPA, 1997.

Latour, Bruno. *We Have Never Been Modern*, trans. Catherine Porter. Cambridge, Mass.: Harvard UP, 1993.

Lawrence, Amy. *Echo and Narcissus*. Berkeley: U of California P, 1991.

Linderman, Deborah. "The Mise-en-Abîme in Hitchcock's *Vertigo*." *Cinema Journal* 30:4 (Summer 1991): 51–74.

————. "Oedipus in Chinatown." *Enclitic* 5 (Fall 1981): 190–203.

Lipartito, Kenneth. "When Women Were Switches: Technology, Work, and Gender in the Telephone Industry, 1890–1920." *The American Historical Review* 99:4 (October 1994): 1075–1111.

Luckhurst, Roger. *The Invention of Telepathy*. Oxford: Oxford UP, 2002.

Lupton, Ellen. *Mechanical Brides: Women and Machines from Home to Office*. New York: Princeton Architectural Press, 1993.

Lynch, Deidre Shauna. *The Economy of Character*. Chicago: U of Chicago P, 1998.

MacCabe, Colin. "Realism and the Cinema: Notes on Some Brechtian Theses." *Screen* 15:2 (1974): 7–27.

Maddox, Brenda. "Women and the Switchboard." In *The Social Impact of the Telephone*, ed. Ithiel de Sola Pool, 262–280. Cambridge, Mass.: MIT Press, 1977.

Madoff, Mark S. "Inside, Outside, and the Gothic Locked-Room Mystery." In *Gothic Fictions: Prohibition/Transgression*, ed. Kenneth W. Graham, 49–62. New York: AMS Press, 1989.

Marder, Elissa. "*Blade Runner's* Moving Still." *Camera Obscura* 27 (September 1991): 89–107.

Martin, Adrian. *Phantasms*. Ringwood, Australia: McPhee Gribble Publishers, 1994.

Martin, Michèle. *"Hello, Central?"* Montreal: McGill-Queen's UP, 1991.

Marvin, Carolyn. *When Old Technologies Were New*. New York: Oxford UP, 1988.

Mast, Gerald. *Howard Hawks, Storyteller*. Oxford: Oxford UP, 1982.

McCallum, E. L. "Hawthorne and Pynchon on the Line." *Arizona Quarterly* 56:2 (Summer 2000): 65–96.

———. "Mother Talk: Maternal Masquerade and the Problem of the Single Girl." *Camera Obscura* 42 (September 1999): 71–94.

McLaughlin, James B. "All in the Family: Alfred Hitchcock's *Shadow of a Doubt*." *Wide Angle* 4:1 (1980): 12–19.

McLuhan, Marshall. *Understanding Media*. New York: McGraw-Hill, 1964.

McSweeney, Kerry. *Middlemarch*. London: George Allen & Unwin, 1984.

Melville, Stephen. "Taking Clarissa Literally: The Implication of Reading." *Genre* 21 (Summer 1988): 135–156.

Michie, Elsie B. "Unveiling Maternal Desires: Hitchcock and American Domesticity." In *Hitchcock's America*, ed. Jonathan Freedman and Richard Millington, 29–53. New York: Oxford UP, 1999.

Michie, Helena. *Sororophobia*. New York: Oxford UP, 1992.

Miller, D. A. *Narrative and Its Discontents*. Princeton, N.J.: Princeton UP, 1981.

———. *The Novel and the Police*. Berkeley: U of California P, 1988.

Miller, J. Hillis. "What Is a Kiss? Isabel's Moments of Decision" *Critical Inquiry* 31:3 (Spring 2005): 722–746.

Miller, Nancy K. "Emphasis Added: Plots and Plausibilities in Women's Fiction." *PMLA* 96:1 (January 1981): 31–48.

Modleski, Tania. *Loving with a Vengeance: Mass-Produced Fantasies for Women*. New York: Routledge, 1982.

———. *The Women Who Knew Too Much: Hitchcock and Feminist Theory*, 2nd ed. New York: Routledge, 2005.

Moi, Toril. "The Missing Mother: The Oedipal Rivalries of René Girard." *Diacritics* 12 (Summer 1982): 21–32.

Mulvey, Laura. *Death 24 x a Second*. London: Reaktion, 2006.

———. "Visual Pleasure and Narrative Cinema." *Screen* 16:3 (Autumn 1975): 6–18.

Murphy, Dean E., and Charlie LeDuff. "Final Campaign Day for the California Recall Effort Ends 11 Whirlwind Weeks." *The New York Times* (Oct. 7, 2003): A16.

Nazare, Joseph. "Marlowe in Mirroshades: The Cyperbunk (Re-)Vision of Chandler." *Studies in the Novel* 35:3 (Fall 2003).

Newsom, Robert. "The Hero's Shame." *Dickens Studies Annual* 11 (1983): 1–24.

———. *A Likely Story*. New Brunswick, N.J.: Rutgers UP, 1988.

Newton, Judith Lowder. "A Chronicle of Assault." In *Modern Critical Interpretations of Evelina*, ed. Harold Bloom, 72–86. New York: Chelsea House Publishers, 1988.

Ogden, Daryl. *The Language of the Eyes*. Albany: State U of New York P, 2005.

Olsson, Jan. "Framing Silent Calls: Coming to Cinematographic Terms with Telephony." In *Allegories of Communication*, ed. John Fullerton and Jan Olsson, 157–192. Rome: John Libbey Publishing, 2004.

Ostovich, Helen. "'Our *Views* Must Now Be Different': Imprisonment and Friendship in *Clarissa*." *Modern Language Quarterly* 52:2 (June 1991): 153–169.

Pasolini, Pier Paolo. "The Cinema of Poetry," trans. Marianne de Vettimo and Jacques Bontemps. In *Movies and Methods* Vol. 1., ed. Bill Nichols, 542–558. Berkeley: U of California P, 1976.

Penley, Constance. "Time Travel, Primal Scene and the Critical Dystopia." *Camera Obscura* 15 (Fall 1986): 66–85.

Peters, John Durham. *Speaking into the Air*. Chicago: Chicago UP, 1999.

Petro, Patrice. *Aftershocks of the New: Feminism and Film History*. New Brunswick, N.J.: Rutgers UP, 2002.

Picker, John. *Victorian Soundscapes*. Oxford: Oxford UP, 2003.

Poague, Leland. "Engendering *Vertigo*." In *Framing Hitchcock*, ed. Sidney Gottlieb and Christopher Brookhouse, 251–280. Detroit: Wayne State UP, 2002.

Pomerance, Murray. *An Eye for Hitchcock*. New Brunswick, N.J.: Rutgers UP, 2004.

Poovey, Mary. "Fathers and Daughters: The Trauma of Growing Up Female." In *Modern Critical Interpretations of Evelina*, ed. Harold Bloom, 87–98. New York: Chelsea House Publishers, 1988.

Poulet, Georges. "Phenomenology of Reading," *New Literary History* 1:1 (October 1969): 53–68.

Powers, Richard. *Galatea 2.2*. New York: Picador, 1995.

Preston, John. *The Created Self*. New York: Barnes & Noble, 1970.

Rakow, Lana F. "Women and the Telephone: The Gendering of a Communications Technology." In *Technology and Women's Voices: Keeping in Touch*, ed. Cheris Kramarae, 207–228. New York: Routledge & Kegan Paul, 1988.

Rank, Otto. *The Double: A Psychoanalytic Study*, trans. and ed. Harry Tucker, Jr. Chapel Hill: U of North Carolina P, 1971.

Rapaport, William J. "How to Pass a Turing Test." *Journal of Logic, Language, and Information* 9 (2000): 467–490.

Richardson, Leslie. "Leaving Her Father's House: Astell, Locke, and Clarissa's Body Politic." *Studies in Eighteenth-Century Culture* 34 (2005): 151–171.

Richardson, Samuel. *Clarissa*. London: Penguin, 1985.

Rickman, Gregg. "'I Think, Therefore I Am'—Cartesian Motifs in the Filmed Science Fiction of Philip K. Dick." In *The Science Fiction Film Reader*, ed. Gregg Rickman, 287–310. New York: Limelight Editions, 2004.

Robinson, Robert E. "Exit James Moriarty—Enter the Telephone Company." *The Baker Street Journal: An Irregular Quarterly of Sherlockiana* 32:1 (March 1982): 20–24.

Rogin, Michael. "Kiss Me Deadly: Communism, Motherhood, and Cold War Movies." *Representations* 6 (Spring 1984): 1–36.

Ronell, Avital. *The Telephone Book*. Lincoln: U of Nebraska P, 1989.

Rosenberg, Howard. " 'It's a Wonderful Life' Debate, Take 2" *Los Angeles Times* 18 (Dec. 2000): Calendar Live.

———. "A 'Wonderful Life' in Bedford Falls? Bah!" *Los Angeles Times* Dec. 15, 2000: Calendar Live.

Rosmarin, Adena. "Misreading *Emma*: The Powers and Perfidies of Interpretive History." *ELH* 51 (1984): 315–342.

Rothman, William. *Hitchcock—The Murderous Gaze*. Cambridge, Mass: Harvard UP, 1982.

Royle, Nicholas. *Telepathy and Literature: Essays on the Reading Mind*. Cambridge, Mass: Basil Blackwell, 1990.

———. *The Uncanny*. New York: Routledge, 2003.

Russett, Margaret. "Narrative as Enchantment in *The Mysteries of Udolpho*. *ELH*: 65 (1998): 159–186.

Salamensky, Shelly. "Henry James, Oscar Wilde, and '*Fin-de-Siècle* Talk': A Brief Reading." *Henry James Review* 20 (1999): 275–281.

Schellenberg, Betty A. "From Propensity to Profession: Female Authorship and the Early Career of Frances Burney." *Eighteenth-Century Fiction* 14:3–4 (April–July 2002): 345–370.

Schor, Hilary. *Dickens and the Daughter of the House*. Cambridge: Cambridge UP, 1999.

———. "Notes of a Libertine Daughter: *Clarissa*, Feminism, and *The Rise of the Novel*." *Stanford Humanities Review* 8:1 (2000): 94–117.

Sconce, Jeffrey. *Haunted Media*. Durham, N.C.: Duke UP, 2000.

Searle, John R. "Minds, Brains, and Programs." *The Behavioral and Brain Sciences* 3 (1980): 417–424.

Sedgwick, Eve. *Between Men: English Literature and Male Homosocial Desire*. New York: Columbia UP, 1985.

———. *The Coherence of Gothic Conventions*. New York: Methuen, 1986.

———. *Tendencies*. Durham, N.C.: Duke UP, 1993.

Shetley, Vernon, and Alissa Ferguson. "Reflections in a Silver Eye: Lens and Mirror in *Blade Runner*." *Science Fiction Studies* 28 (2001): 66–76.

Siegert, Bernhard. *Relays: Literature as an Epoch of the Postal System*, trans. Kevin Rapp. Stanford, Cal.: Stanford UP, 1999.

Silverman, Kaja. *The Acoustic Mirror*. Bloomington: Indiana UP, 1988.

———. "Back to the Future." *Camera Obscura* 27 (September 1991): 109–132.

Smith-Rosenberg, Carroll. "The Female World of Love and Ritual: Relations between Women in Nineteenth-Century America." *Signs* 1 (1975): 1–30.

Solomon, Melissa. "The Female World of Exorcism and Displacement (Or, Relations Between Women in Henry James's Nineteenth-Century *The Portrait of a Lady*)." *Studies in the Novel* 28 (1996): 395–413.

Spacks, Patricia. *Gossip*. New York: Knopf, 1985.

Spoto, Donald. *The Dark Side of Genius*. New York: Ballantine Books, 1983.

Staves, Susan. "*Evelina*; or Female Difficulties." In *Modern Critical Interpretations of* Evelina, ed. Harold Bloom, 13–30. New York: Chelsea House Publishers, 1988.

Stern, Ellen, and Emily Gwathmey. *Once Upon a Telephone*. New York: Harcourt Brace, 1994.

Sterne, Jonathan. *The Audible Past*. Durham, N.C.: Duke UP, 2003.

Stewart, Garrett. "'Count Me In': *Dracula*, Hypnotic Participation, and the Late Victorian Gothic of Reading." *LIT* 5:1 (1994): 1–18.

Stewart, Susan. *On Longing*. Durham, N.C.: Duke UP, 1993.

Straayer, Chris. "*Femme Fatale* or Lesbian Femme: *Bound* in Sexual *Différance*." In *Women in Film Noir*, new ed., ed. E. Ann Kaplan, 151–163. London: British Film Institute, 1998.

Straub, Kristina. *Divided Fictions: Fanny Burney and Feminine Strategy*. Lexington: UP of Kentucky, 1987.

Studlar, Gaylyn. "Masochism and the Perverse Pleasures of the Cinema." In *Movies and Methods*, Vol. 2, ed. Bill Nichols, 602–621. Berkeley: U of California P, 1985.

Sutherland, John. *Is Heathcliff a Murderer?* Oxford: Oxford UP, 1996.

Tan, Ed S. *Emotion and the Structure of Narrative Film: Film as an Emotion Machine*, trans. Barbara Fasting. Mahwah, N.J.: Erlbaum, 1996.

Telotte, J. P. *Voices in the Dark*. Urbana: U of Illinois P, 1989.

Thomson, David. "At the Acme Bookshop." *Sight and Sound* 50:2 (Spring 1981): 122–125.

———. *The Big Sleep*. London: British Film Institute, 1997.

———. "Telephones." *Film Comment* 20 (1984): 24–32.

Thurschwell, Pamela. *Literature, Technology, and Magical Thinking, 1880–1920*. Cambridge: Cambridge UP, 2001.

Truffaut, François. *Hitchcock*, rev. ed. New York: Simon & Schuster, 1985.

Turing, A. M. "Computing Machinery and Intelligence." *Mind* 59.236 (October 1950): 433–460.

Van Ghent, Dorothy. *The English Novel: Form and Function*. New York: Rinehard, 1953.

Vermeule, Blakey. "Gossip and Literary Narrative." *Philosophy and Literature* 30:1 (April 2006): 102–117.

Vigderman, Patricia. "The Traffic in Men: Female Kinship in Three Novels by George Eliot." *Style* 32:1 (Spring 1998): 18–35.

Virillio, Paul. *The Aesthetics of Disappearance*, trans. Philip Beitchman. New York: Semiotext(e), 1991.

Wallace, Lee. "Continuous Sex: The Editing of Homosexuality in *Bound* and *Rope*." *Screen* 41:4 (Winter 2000): 369–387.

Waldron, Mary. "Men of Sense and Silly Wives: The Confusions of Mr. Knightley." *Studies in the Novel* 28 (Summer 1996): 141–157.

Warner, William. *Reading Clarissa: The Struggles of Interpretation*. New Haven, Conn.: Yale UP, 1979.

———. "Reading Rape: Marxist-Feminist Figurations of the Literal." *Diacritics* (Winter 1983): 12–32.

Watt, Ian. *The Rise of the Novel*. Berkeley: U of California P, 1957.

Weinsheimer, J. "Theory of Character: *Emma*." *Poetics Today* 1 (1979): 185–211.

Wexman, Virginia Wright. "The Critic as Consumer." *Film Quarterly* 39:3 (Spring 1986): 32–41.

White, Howard. "The House of Interest: A Keyword in *The Portrait of a Lady*." *Modern Language Quarterly* 52 (1991): 191–207.

Wilde, Oscar. *The Complete Plays of Oscar Wilde*. London: Methuen, 1993.

Williams, Christopher. "After the Classic, the Classical, and Ideology: the Differences of Realism." In *Reinventing Film Studies*, ed. Christine Gledhill and Linda Williams, 206–220. London: Arnold, 2000.

Williams, Linda. "Melodrama Revised." In *Refiguring American Film Genres*, ed. Nick Browne, 42–88. Berkeley: U of California P, 1998.

Wilson, Edmund. "A Long Talk about Jane Austen." *The New Yorker* 20 (June 1944): 64–70.

Wilt, Judith. "He Could Go No Farther: A Modest Proposal about Lovelace and Clarissa." *PMLA* 92 (1977): 19–32.

———. *Ghosts of the Gothic: Austen, Eliot, & Lawrence*. Princeton, N.J.: Princeton UP, 1980.

Woloch, Alex. *The One vs. the Many: Minor Characters and the Space of the Protagonist in the Novel*. Princeton, N.J.: Princeton UP, 2003.

Wood, Mary McGee. "Signification and Simulation: Barthes's Response to Turing." *Paragraph* 11:3 (Nov. 1988): 210–226.

Wood, Robin. "*Blade Runner*." In *The Science Fiction Film Reader*, ed. Gregg Rickman, 280–286. New York: Limelight Editions, 2004.

———. "Ideology, Genre, Auteur." In *Film Theory and Criticism*, ed. Gerald Mast, Marshall Cohen, and Leo Braudy, 475–485. New York: Oxford UP, 1992.

Young, Kay. "*Middlemarch* and the Problem of Other Minds Heard." *LIT: Literature, Interpretation, Theory* 14:3 (July–Sept. 2003): 223–241.

Index